Incentives and Redistribution in the Welfare State

The Swedish Tax Reform

Jonas Agell
Professor of Economics
Uppsala University

Peter Englund
Professor of Economics
Uppsala University

and

Jan Södersten
Professor of Economics
Uppsala University

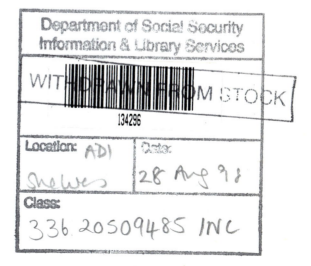

First published in Great Britain 1998 by
MACMILLAN PRESS LTD
Houndmills, Basingstoke, Hampshire RG21 6XS and London
Companies and representatives throughout the world

A catalogue record for this book is available from the British Library.

ISBN 0–333–71201–3

First published in the United States of America 1998 by
ST. MARTIN'S PRESS, INC.,
Scholarly and Reference Division,
175 Fifth Avenue, New York, N.Y. 10010

ISBN 0–312–21072–8

Library of Congress Cataloging-in-Publication Data
Agell, Jonas.
Incentives and redistribution in the welfare state : the Swedish
tax reform / Jonas Agell, Peter Englund, and Jan Södersten.
p. cm.
Revised and translated from Swedish.
Includes bibliographical references and index.
ISBN 0–312–21072–8
1. Taxation—Sweden. 2. Taxation—Law and legislation—Sweden.
3. Saving and investment—Sweden. 4. Labor supply—Sweden.
5. Public welfare—Sweden. I. Englund, Peter, 1950–
II. Södersten, Jan. III. Title.
HJ2835.A65 1998
336.2'05'09485—DC21   97–18337
                                                                CIP

This book is printed on paper suitable for recycling and made from fully managed and
sustained forest sources.

10 9 8 7 6 5 4 3 2 1
07 06 05 04 03 02 01 00 99 98

Printed and bound in Great Britain by
Antony Rowe Ltd, Chippenham, Wiltshire

Contents

Contents

List of Tables

List of Figures

Preface

In June 1990, the Swedish Parliament enacted the most far-reaching tax reform in any industrialized country in recent decades. It was also decided to carry out an evaluation of the economic effects of the reform, a task that was undertaken by us on behalf of the Swedish Economic Council. This book is a revised version of our evaluation report published in Swedish in late 1995.

We are grateful to Daniel Ogden for preparing an English translation of the original text, and to the editor of *National Tax Journal* for permission to reproduce major parts of an article previously published there. We owe a great debt to Eva Holst and Ann-Sofie Wettergren Djerf for secretarial assistance, and to Fredrik Wiklund for handling our data sets. We also wish to thank all colleagues who aided us through commissioned studies of various subfields. Their reports are listed at the end of this book. A selection of these background studies is included in the 1995 Autumn issue of the *Swedish Economic Policy Review*.

We hope the book contains useful lessons both about the scope for comprehensive tax reform in an advanced welfare state, and about the possibilities and problems in evaluating a major reform a few years after its implementation.

Uppsala
October 1997

JONAS AGELL
PETER ENGLUND
JAN SÖDERSTEN

1 Introduction*

Sweden might be best known as the home of film director Ingmar Bergman, and – for better or worse – as the prototype welfare state. What might be less well known is that Sweden recently implemented the most far-reaching tax reform in any western industrialized country. Although Sweden was a latecomer to the bandwagon of worldwide tax reforms of the 1980s, with the US Tax Reform Act of 1986 (TRA86) as a celebrated example, the architects of the Swedish tax reform of 1991 (TR91) applied the strategy of rate cuts *cum* base broadening in an unusually thorough manner. Under the catchy slogan 'tax reform of the century', marginal income taxes were dramatically lowered, and various tax shelters eliminated. According to pre-reform estimates, the rate cuts entailed a revenue loss on the order of six per cent of GDP. Measured in this way, TRA86 stands out as a relatively modest endeavour, with a projected revenue loss of 1–2 per cent of GDP due to rate cuts.

It goes without saying that sharply reduced income tax rates is a sensitive political issue, particularly so in a country where tax policy used to centre on the idea that a steeply progressive income tax is an efficient way of transferring resources from the rich to the poor. To understand why TR91 gathered wide political support, both external and internal considerations are important. The integration of world capital markets during the 1980s implied that it became more difficult to tax capital income at rates that differed very much from those applicable elsewhere. Also, the major changes in the tax structures of a number of other countries provided an impulse. However, it would be wrong to view TR91 as a mechanical response to these developments. After all, Ronald Reagan's tax policy is not a very natural source of inspiration for Sweden's Social Democrats. While many of the arguments of the proponents of TR91 bear a striking resemblance to those put forth in the context of TRA86,[1] their origin should be traced primarily to the domestic debate.

As early as 1978, Nobel Laureate Gunnar Myrdal complained that high marginal tax rates had turned Sweden into a 'nation of wanglers'.

---

* This chapter is a slightly shortened version of the article 'Tax reform of the century – the Swedish experiment', published in *National Tax Journal*, 49 (December 1996), 643–64.

According to Myrdal (1978), the progressive income tax had created such strong incentives for high-income individuals to exploit various tax avoidance schemes (including outright tax fraud), that the Swedish tax system no longer redistributed income. Myrdal's view carried particular weight since he belonged to the political left. Parties more to the right, and quite a few economists, had for long warned that the income tax created large disincentive effects. But Myrdal seemed to suggest that also those in favour of egalitarian outcomes, and concerned less about efficiency, had reason to reconsider the role of progressive income tax. Although Myrdal offered no hard facts to substantiate his claim, the perception that the rich could avoid their fair share of the tax burden was probably instrumental in softening the Social Democrat's traditional resistance to proposals involving lower marginal tax rates.

But there were also other influential arguments. From the late 1970s, when inflation had reached double-digit levels, there had been widespread concern that the tax system promoted the wrong kind of investments. Investments in noncorporate assets, and housing in particular, were given preferential tax treatment. Many Swedish economists argued, echoing their colleagues in other countries, that the uneven playing field created substantial efficiency losses. The nonuniform treatment of the returns on different assets also created considerable scope for a number of straightforward tax arbitrage operations, more often than not involving purchases of low-taxed assets with borrowed money. This spelled bad news for the fisc – for several years households claimed tax deductions to such an extent that net revenue from taxes on personal capital income was negative.

The corporate income tax attracted similar criticism. A variety of tax allowances and a high statutory tax rate were once part of a deliberate strategy of stimulating firms to plough back profits into the business. The idea was that large and expanding firms were good for growth. During the 1980s there was a shift in emphasis. According to the new view, the corporate tax breaks were an obstacle to efficient capital allocation. The high rates of profit retention required to take advantage of the various tax allowances created a capital lock-in effect, which prevented necessary structural readjustments. Finally, towards the mid-1980s, an overheated economy, and concerns about an acute labour shortage, seemed to give added weight to the argument that there was an urgent need to strengthen labour supply incentives.

TR91 was presented as a way of remedying all these problems in one giant stroke. According to its proponents, the reform would avoid the classical goal conflict between efficiency and income distribution. In spite of drastic marginal tax cuts, high-income earners were not supposed to gain relative to other groups. As a result of a generally more efficient economy, all strata in society should gain. Moreover, total tax revenue was not supposed to decrease – the Swedish tax take should remain the highest in the world. The revenue gains from broader tax bases were to make up for the losses from lower tax rates.

What can changes in tax structure accomplish? Did the proverbial free lunch materialize? This book reviews the lessons from a major evaluation effort, commissioned by the Swedish government, and involving a large number of foreign and Swedish researchers. The guiding principle of our presentation is that of Richard Musgrave's classic study, *The Theory of Public Finance* (1959), which has left its mark on many studies of the public sector. In the first part of the book, Chapters 2 to 5, we present our analysis of the effects of TR91 on different markets, and on different economic decisions. The second part, Chapters 6 to 8, focuses on the effects on the main goals of economic policy: stability, distribution and economic efficiency. Since this analysis is based largely on the studies of behaviour found in the previous chapters, the book can be read with benefit from cover to cover. However, to the greatest extent possible, we have tried to format the separate chapters in such a way that they can be read individually without difficulty. Moreover, a self-contained summary of the book is given in the remainder of this introductory chapter.

In addition to analyses of TR91, each chapter contains a broad description of the specific subject area in question. To be sure, the degree of difficulty may vary somewhat between chapters, but we have tried as far as possible to give easily accessible explanations of the basic methods and theories. Our pedagogic ambition has been warranted by the conviction that participants in the often technical and complicated tax debate often talk unnecessarily at cross-purposes. In the chapter on the corporate response to TR91, we explain the difference between taxes on savings and taxes on investments in small, open economies. In the chapter on distribution, we try to give a broad description of the many methodological problems in this field. An important, although subordinate, purpose of our chapter on economic efficiency is to try to explain how economists define and measure the losses in efficiency which arise from taxation. As we shall see, as a rule there is no simple connection between these losses and observable quantities such as employment and growth.

The remainder of this chapter first gives a brief outline of TR91. We proceed by discussing the considerable difficulty in evaluating a tax reform in the midst of a very sharp recession. We review the evidence on behavioural responses, and we seek to identify areas where TR91 mattered the most. We also present an assessment of the overall effects on efficiency and equity. The concluding section draws some lessons for tax reform more generally.

1.1   WHAT TR91 IMPLIED

Pre-reform estimates presented by the Ministry of Finance indicated that the rate cuts for the personal income tax alone, together with additional outlays for housing and child allowances to cushion the distributional effects of the reform, would reduce revenues by an amount equivalent to between 6 and 7 per cent of GDP. Nearly 40 per cent of this loss was to be recouped through a new system of taxing capital income. A broadening of the VAT (of 23 per cent) to include goods and services previously exempted, or granted lower rates, would yield additional revenue on the order of 30 per cent of the budget loss, while almost 15 per cent was to be financed by elimination of loopholes and preferential rules for taxing earned income. Enlarged tax bases due to a generally more efficient economy would offset roughly 5 per cent of the revenue loss. The reform hence brought a major reallocation of the total tax burden away from earned income to consumption and to individual capital income (including the return on housing).

A noteworthy feature of TR91 was the move away from the principle of global income taxation towards a *dual income tax*, by introducing separate tax schedules for earned income and capital income.[2] The new taxation of earned income meant that almost 85 per cent of the income earners would pay only local income tax. In 1991 the countrywide average of the local income tax was 31 per cent. A national income tax of 20 percent was imposed for incomes exceeding 185 000 kronor (equivalent to US $33 500, at the 1991 exchange rate), which meant that the top marginal tax rate on earned income was set at 51 percent. TR91 implied that the marginal rate would be reduced by between 24 and 27 percentage points for large groups of full-time employees.

The new proportional capital income tax was set at 30 per cent, and levied on dividends, interest income, and both long- and short-term realized nominal capital gains. As before, interest on all kinds of debt would be fully deductible. A stated purpose of the separate capital income tax was to reduce the value of interest deductions and to limit the scope for tax avoidance in various forms.

Although the initial ambition of TR91 was to levy a uniform VAT (of an unchanged 23 per cent) on all commercial turnover of goods and services, several areas have remained tax-exempt. These include various cultural and social services, and housing rents. Housing costs have risen as a result of the tax reform, however, partly because VAT was broadened to include real estate maintenance, heating and electricity. Owner-occupiers were further affected by the inclusion of expenditures on housing investment in the new VAT. Before TR91, the rate of tax stood at 13 per cent.

The changes in the corporate income tax were no less dramatic. The statutory tax rate was reduced from 57 to 30 per cent. In order to maintain an unchanged level of revenue from the corporate tax, the rate reduction was combined with substantial broadening of the base. The possibility of undervaluing inventories for tax purposes was eliminated, and the investment funds system, introduced in the mid-1950s as the main tool of a counter-cyclical fiscal policy, was discontinued.

Even a casual comparison reveals obvious similarities between TRA86 and TR91. Both reforms were far-reaching, with the same intent of reducing various behavioural distortions from the tax systems. The approach to tax reform was similar, combining substantial tax cuts with a broadening of the base. TR91 was much larger in scope, both in terms of revenue effects from the rate cuts, and because it covered a wider range of tax instruments. Obviously, these differences partly

Table 1.1 Sources of tax revenue in Sweden and the US

Revenue source	Share of total receipts (per cent)		
	Sweden		US
	1989	*1991*	*1991*
Taxes on personal incomes (including capital gains)	39.3	34.2	34.9
Taxes on corporate incomes	3.8	3.1	7.3
Social security contributions	26.7	28.6	29.8
Payroll taxes	2.5	3.0	—
Property taxes	3.3	4.1	11.2
Taxes on goods and services	24.2	26.9	16.8
Miscellaneous taxes	0.1	0.1	0.0
Total receipts (per cent)	100.0	100.0	100.0
Share of taxes in GDP (per cent)	55.6	52.7	29.5
GDP (Bill. US 1991 dollars)		237	5611

Source: *Revenue Statistics of OECD Member Countries 1965–94* (Paris: OECD, 1995).

reflect the vast difference between Sweden and the US in the financing requirements for the public sector. As a proportion of GDP, the total tax yield was almost 56 per cent in Sweden in 1989, compared to 30 per cent for the US. However, the relative importance of different taxes, summarized in Table 1.1, is broadly similar. In both countries, there is a heavy reliance on receipts from the personal income tax and from social security contributions. Taxes on goods and services are more important in Sweden, whereas corporate and property taxes contribute a larger share of tax revenue in the US. The reallocation of the total tax burden brought by TR91, away from personal income to consumption, is clearly visible.

1.2   A NATURAL EXPERIMENT?

A major reshuffling of the tax structure may seem like that rare opportunity to sharpen the estimates of the behavioural elasticities that would interest a public finance economist. However, TR91 was introduced during the most severe economic downturn since the 1930s. Between 1991 and 1993 GDP fell by more than 5 per cent, open unemployment (that is, excluding those enrolled in various labour market programs) rose from less than 2 per cent to more than 8 per cent, asset prices tumbled, and residential construction activity came to a virtual standstill. At the same time, income inequality increased, and the government deficit reached record heights. In this environment, it is clearly hard to sort out cause and effect with much precision.[3] Macroeconomic time series for the years surrounding TR91 contain very little of the kind of independent information needed to discriminate between alternative hypotheses about behavioural responses. Microeconomic panel data, allowing the analyst to control for individual variation over time, may seem like a safer bet, but there is still an obvious risk that the macroeconomic noise pollutes the microeconometric analysis.

The Swedish tax evaluation effort includes several contributions which try to make do with data sets including pre- and post-reform observations. But the macroeconomic turmoil has led a number of researchers to confine attention to the information that can be gathered from an *ex ante* evaluation of TR91. These evaluations have two ingredients in common. The first is an assessment – based on previous findings reported in the literature, or on new findings based on pre-reform data sets – of the reasonable value of some relevant behavioural parameter. The second ingredient is a careful assessment of the change in the incentive structure implied by TR91. This is a far from trivial exercise, since TR91 contained several provisions with counteracting influences on the relevant incentive margin. Combining these ingredients, the *ex ante* evaluation produces a set of predicted responses, which serve the useful purpose of scrutinizing the political arguments. Do recent research, and refined analysis of the incentive structure, produce the kind of behavioural responses promised by the architects of TR91?

An additional complication stems from the fact that the sharp drop in the activity level cannot be treated as independent of TR91. Towards the end of the 1980s, the Swedish economy showed many signs of overheating.[4] Due to a high demand pressure, wage costs increased substantially, which led to eroded competitiveness in world markets. At the same time, and in the wake of financial deregulation, the indebtedness of households and firms reached very high levels. This left the Swedish economy in a vulnerable position when the international economy slowed down in the early 1990s. While the international recession may explain part of the rise in unemployment, a more important reason for the severity of the recession is probably that macroeconomic policy was firmly devoted to nonaccommodation. As had been the case previously in many other Western European countries, fighting inflation and defending an overvalued exchange rate now became the top priority for Swedish economic policy making. As a result, manufacturing output fell sharply.

These developments, certainly unrelated to TR91, explain a major part of the severe economic recession. But TR91 may help to explain why the slump in the exporting sectors spread to the sheltered parts of the economy. By lowering the value of household interest deductions, TR91 increased real after-tax borrowing costs, and stimulated indebted households to sell off assets. In addition, higher borrowing costs, in conjunction with certain tax hikes aimed specifically at the housing sector, contributed to the collapse of the construction sector. These contractionary impulses amplified the downturn, and contributed to a general weakening of aggregate demand.[5] James Tobin once cautioned that it takes a heap of Harberger triangles to fill an Okun gap. Whatever its long-term merits, it is easy to conclude that the timing of TR91 was unfortunate. While part of this can be blamed on bad luck, TR91 was designed to be implemented in a situation with fair macroeconomic wind. The official inquiry which preceded TR91 contains a wealth of material, but there was hardly any discussion of the macroeconomic aspects.

1.3   BEHAVIOURAL RESPONSES

As suggested by Slemrod (1992), the evidence about the responses to the major US tax reforms of the 1980s can be interpreted as an indication of a behavioural hierarchy. The most responsive decisions, at the top of the hierarchy, are those involving the timing of transactions, followed by a variety of financial, accounting, and evasion responses. The least responsive decisions, at the bottom, concerns the 'real' ones, including labor supply, savings, and investment. Let us review our conclusions discussed at more length in Chapters 2 to 5.

Tax avoidance

A characteristic feature of the pre-TR91 tax system was the nonuniform treatment of income from capital. The returns on different assets were taxed at vastly differing rates, and the tax paid on a given income could vary systematically depending on the identity of the taxpayer, the kind of income concerned, and when it was reported for taxation.

The steeply progressive tax schedule, in combination with the treatment of children as separate taxpayers, meant that the tax burden could be reduced considerably by shifting capital income from parents in high tax brackets to children with little or no earned income. Likewise, differences among corporate firms in availability and possibilities to take advantage of various non-debt tax shields were extensively exploited. On several occasions, schemes to avoid tax were set up as joint ventures between taxpaying private corporations and tax exempt institutions in the public sector, including several Swedish cities (the operations included sale and lease-back of ice-breakers, municipal sewage systems, hospital equipment, etc.).

In Sweden, as elsewhere, the strategy of the tax planners was to claim deductible expenses against fully taxable income, and report income in forms granted preferential tax treatment. The concessions to specific forms of household savings in the late of 1970s and early 1980s provide a simple illustration of this. Savings in special bank accounts were offered a tax-free return plus an initial tax credit, which effectively implied a negative tax. However, nothing prevented households from paying for the contributions to the scheme by borrowed money and deducting the interest against earned income. The special bank account could hence easily be transformed into a *money machine*. Private pension plans which received the equivalent of consumption tax treatment provided similar opportunities for reaping the double benefits of tax exemption and full interest deductibility.

As in other countries, much effort was devoted to transforming corporate source income into low-taxed capital gains. Complicated schemes were set up, often involving the use of new financial instruments, where the tax legislation was either unclear or preliminary in nature. The capital gains tax provided additional opportunities for tax avoidance. Before TR91, short-term gains on shares held for less than two years were fully taxed, while on long-term gains the tax rate was 40 per cent of the income tax rate. The holding-period distinction thus implied that a short-term loss of one krona could be used to offset the tax on a long-term gain, two and a half times as large.

The decades preceding TR91 witnessed a continuing battle between the tax planners and the tax authorities. New and increasingly complicated rules were set up to combat tax avoidance – and yet, to some extent, the added complexity created new and unforeseen opportunities to avoid tax. Rather than continuing along the same path, TR91 cut the Gordian knot by focusing on the circumstances that had opened up for tax planning, that is, the asymmetric tax rules and the high tax rates. Family transactions set up to exploit differences in the marginal tax rates between parents and children were rendered meaningless, since individual capital income was taxed at a proportional rate with no exemption. The uniform tax on capital income also meant that the tax could be levied at source. Transactions among firms driven by differences in taxpaying status were less rewarding because of the lowered statutory tax rate, while the broadening of the tax base reduced the differences in availability of tax shields between companies. The elimination of the holding-period distinction for capital gains meant a further blow to tax planning.

The balance between taxation of labour income and corporate source capital income was much discussed in the tax reform process and during the following years. TR91 retained a difference of some 15 percentage points between the total marginal rate on earned income (including payroll taxes) and the total corporate and personal tax on profits. Hence, for owners of corporate firms active as managers, there remained a clear incentive to reclassify labour income as corporate profits. While a thoroughgoing attack against tax avoidance would seem to require that this incentive be eliminated, the tax legislators do in fact face a difficult dilemma posed by the increased openness of the Swedish economy. Following the deregulation of financial markets and the elimination of currency controls at the end of the 1980s,

Swedish households have both legal and easy access to international portfolio investments. Though taxation of individual income from capital follows the residence principle, Swedish tax authorities in practice have little opportunity to enforce taxes on income earned abroad. The prospect of introducing a functioning reporting system from foreign banks or/and a system of withholding taxes on dividends and interest payments seems bleak indeed. If, on the other hand, the tax legislators would attempt to keep domestic investors at home by more lenient taxation, the difficulties of defending the line of demarcation against labour income would magnify.

Consumption

Private consumption is normally considered to be one of the least volatile of all macroeconomic variables. In Sweden, however, consumption fell by about five percent between 1991 and 1993.[6] Can changes in tax structure explain the consumption bust? TR91 may have had a negative impact on consumption via three channels: (i) intertemporal substitution in response to an increase in the real after-tax interest rate;[7] (ii) a downward revision of expected future labour income; and (iii) wealth effects due to revaluations in asset markets, in particular in the markets for residential real estate. Of these channels, only (iii) seems to offer an explanation of the consumption bust.

With a large intertemporal elasticity of substitution, periods of high expected interest rates should coincide with rapid consumption growth, and periods of low interest rates with stagnant consumption (see, for example, Hall (1988)). However, although there are reasons to be cautious about the information that can be drawn from representative agent models and aggregate data, empirical studies in Sweden and elsewhere suggest that the intertemporal elasticity of substitution is close to zero. Moreover, some basic aspects of the data are hard to reconcile with a story of intertemporal substitution. Between 1986 and 1989, when consumption growth was brisk, the average real after-tax interest rate was negative. Between 1991 and 1993, when consumption growth was negative, the average real after-tax interest rate was exceptionally high. If intertemporal substitution is to characterize the data, consumption growth ought to have followed the opposite pattern.

When households make a downward revision of their forecasts of future labour income, consumption ought to fall. However, while there are good reasons to believe that permanent labour income fell during the Swedish consumption bust,[8] TR91 is not likely to have been an important factor. Indeed, most assessments of the efficiency effects of TR91, discussed below, suggest that it lowered excess burdens due to tax wedges in the labour market. If anything, this effect ought to increase permanent income.

Capitalization effects in asset markets, whether due to TR91 or something else, may certainly affect consumption. The consumption boom of the late 1980s was associated with an increase in real estate prices, and the bust period with decreasing prices. Of course, correlation is not the same as causation. But recent macroeconometric work indicates that variables like real housing prices, and windfalls in the housing market, seem to have power in explaining aggregate Swedish consumption behaviour. Moreover, TR91 led, as discussed below, to a dramatic increase in the rental cost of housing, and contributed to the sharp fall in house prices after 1991. Although these housing market adjustments are unlikely to explain a very large part of the consumption bust, they seem like the most important mechanism for an adverse consumption response to TR91.

Consumption pattern and asset composition

While TR91 may have had a small effect on the aggregate consumption *level*, it mattered more for the *composition* of consumption and savings. The move towards a broader base for the value added tax implied substantial tax hikes for some previously favoured consumption categories. Available data, and a few econometric studies, suggest that there was a strong negative demand response for some of these categories, including hotel and restaurant services, and domestic tourism. These responses serve as a healthy reminder of the fact that one of the guiding principles of TR91 – the purported superiority of a system with uniform tax rates on goods and services – has no obvious connection with the tax structure implied by the 'inverse elasticity rule' of models of optimal commodity taxation.

Our prior was that household asset choice – at the top of the response hierarchy – was an area where TR91 ought to matter. Microeconometric evidence suggested that the old tax system created strong tax clientele effects, in the sense that households tended to specialize in assets according to their marginal tax rate. Macroeconometric evidence suggested that the large shifts from financial to nonfinancial savings outlets (such as consumer durables and housing investment) during the decades preceding TR91 were highly correlated with after-tax returns.

TR91 removed many of the asymmetries on the asset side of households' balance sheets. The 30 per cent tax rate on personal capital income mitigated the tax disadvantage of bank savings, and reduced the tax premium on investments in durables and real estate. There were also important consequences for the treatment of liabilities. In the early 1980s, nominal interest expenses were fully deductible against often quite high marginal income tax rates. This created a strong incentive to inflate balance sheets by purchasing assets with borrowed money. In 1980, an individual with the marginal tax rate of an average blue-collar worker paid a real after-tax interest rate of *minus* 7 percent. In 1991, when nominal interest expenses became deductible at the new flat tax rate of 30 per cent, and inflation was lower, the same individual paid a real after-tax interest rate of *plus* 7 per cent.

On balance, TR91 gave households strong incentives to shift from real to financial savings outlets, and to shrink balance sheets by selling off assets and amortizing debt. Households seem to have adjusted accordingly. In the early 1990s, net investments in tangibles and durables turned negative, and household financial savings increased dramatically. Between 1988 and 1992, net lending as a share of disposable income increased by an astonishing 13 percentage points, while the nonfinancial savings ratio decreased by more than 8 percentage points.[9] Although the rapid fall in inflation and the macroeconomic crisis played a role, calculations reported in Agell, Berg and Edin (1995) indicate that about one-third of the increase in the net lending rate can be attributed to TR91.

Housing

Valuing and taxing the services rendered by owner-occupied housing constitutes a classical difficulty in implementing a comprehensive income tax. In Sweden this has been handled by imputing a measure of the implicit income from an owner-occupied home at 1 to 2 per cent of the market value, and adding this imputed income on top of other taxable income. With nominal interest income being fully taxable and interest payments deductible, this introduced substantial asymmetries in the tax treatment of housing and other sectors of the economy, and within the housing sector itself, especially considering the high inflation and nominal interest rates of the 1970s and 1980s. Owner-occupied housing was tax advantaged relative to other forms of household investment, user costs of owner-occupied housing varied across households according to marginal tax rates, and owner-occupancy had a general tax advantage[10] over rental housing. Apart from the provisions of the income tax code, housing was also favored through government-guaranteed interest-subsidized loans, a lower VAT rate for building and construction, and income-dependent housing allowances. As a reflection of the progressivity of the tax schedule, with widely differing marginal tax rates, after-tax interest payments varied a lot across households. Before TR91, this resulted in rental costs of owner-occupied housing ranging from 2 per cent in the upper marginal tax bracket up to 6 per cent at low marginal tax rates. With the new flat 30 percent tax schedule for all forms of capital income, after-tax interest costs became the same for all households. Owner-occupied housing was no longer cheaper for high-income groups. But TR91 also affected housing costs through increased VAT and reduced interest subsidies. The combined impact of TR91 was to fundamentally transform the price structure in the housing market. Rental costs increased substantially, and became essentially uniform across households.

Based on microsimulations, we predict that these cost changes should lead to an aggregate demand decrease on the order of 15 per cent. Since the stock of housing capital adjusts so sluggishly, the immediate response to the reform should be on prices and new construction. Simulations with a perfect foresight model in the vein of Poterba (1984) suggest a drop in prices of around 10–15 per cent upon announcement of TR91, and a sharp fall in new construction. These predictions of falling prices and a virtual standstill of new construction have been borne out by developments after the implementation of TR91. The reform year of 1991 marks the peak of house prices and of the rate of new construction. Construction virtually ceased after 1992, and nominal house prices fell by a total of 19 per cent from the peak in the third quarter of 1991 to the trough in the first quarter of 1993. The total price fall is well in line with expectations, although here as elsewhere it is hard to isolate the effects of TR91 from those of the severe recession. The timing, however, is somewhat puzzling in view of the fact that the reform could reasonably have been expected by 1989, and was clearly signalled when the reform bill was passed by Parliament in June 1990. The fact that it took two years until this was reflected in house prices casts some doubt on the rationality of pricing in the Swedish housing market.

Once house prices started to fall, however, they did so quite rapidly. In fact, this is the first occasion in modern times to witness falling *nominal* prices, a situation which raises two issues. First, the capital losses of homeowners gave rise to a potentially sizeable redistribution of income both vertically, since the average homeowner is higher up the income distribution than the average renter, and horizontally from homeowner to renter at the same income level. Second, falling house prices dented the net wealth of many homeowners, even to the point of creating negative net equity. This most likely created a temporary lock-in effect, as homeowners short of equity could not provide the down-payment necessary for a new house. Indeed, the transactions volume in the secondary market decreased substantially.

Labour supply

In the public debate surrounding the reform, the potential impact on labour supply played a major role, although many economists cautioned against overly optimistic supply projections. TR91 marks a sharp break of a long-term trend of increasing wedges between the labor costs to the employer and the after-tax remuneration of the employees. Between 1989 and 1991, the wedge decreased from 84 to 71 per cent for an upper-tier white-collar employee and from 69 to 61 per cent for a blue-collar worker. Although such numbers clearly demonstrate the magnitude of the reform, one should not be misled into generalizing to all groups in society. In fact, looking across a representative sample of all individuals it appears that around a quarter saw an *increase* in the tax wedge. The explanation is that a large fraction of Swedish wage-earners work less than full-time at relatively modest marginal-tax rates that were not much affected by the reform, and that many households in this category are entitled to income-dependent housing allowances that were increased as part of the reform. A similar pattern with a mixture of increased and decreased marginal tax rates holds for TRA86; see Hausman and Poterba (1987). In fact, as is emphasized by Auerbach and Slemrod (1996), it lies in the nature of a reform aimed at maintaining the degree of redistribution that it is very difficult to lower marginal taxes for everybody.

Various labour supply studies, conducted before TR91 and as part of the evaluation effort, tend to confirm the 'elasticity pessimism' underlying Slemrod's response hierarchy, with labour supply at the bottom. A representative estimate of the compensated wage elasticity of hours worked among Swedish prime-age males is on the order of magnitude of 0.1, but the estimates are so imprecise that the predicted hours response to the reform of a representative white-collar worker has a typical confidence interval ranging from 1.5 to 15 per cent. Unfortunately, there is a paucity of reliable *ex post* studies of the impact of the reform, but the panel study of Klevmarken (1996) finds that changes in marginal wages between 1985 and 1992 were associated with statistically significant increases of the supply of hours worked, both for men and for women.

Although a very large amount of research has focused on hours worked, it is possible that other margins of labour supply response may prove more important in the longer run. It is noteworthy that TR91 implied a large change in the incentive to undertake investment in education. TR91 lowered tax rates at higher (post-investment) income levels, but left tax rates more or less unchanged at lower (pre-investment) income levels. Edin and Holmlund (1995) calculate internal rates of return to investing in a four-year university program. In the early 1980s, the return was 4 to 5 per cent before tax, and 1 to 3 per cent after tax, implying effective tax rates between 40 and 90 per cent depending on the year chosen as a basis for the calculations. After the reform, the effective tax rate fell to 25 per cent. The impact of this reduction is not confined to formal education, but applies more broadly to the choice between careers with different earnings profiles.

The corporate response

The new corporate tax rules meant a noteworthy departure from the previous long-standing policy of stimulating business investment in fixed capital through a combination of a high statutory tax rate and generous allowances to investing firms. The tax rate was cut almost in half, and to keep the tax payments of the corporate sector roughly constant, the base of the tax was considerable broadened. Many of the innovative incentive provisions that had set the Swedish tax system apart were eliminated, notably the investment funds system.

Though there was a widespread view among policy makers that cutting the statutory tax rate in half would itself greatly improve investment incentives, estimates using conventional methodology indicate that the corporate tax reform had little effect on the cost of capital. The base broadening largely offset the effects of the tax cut. However, TR91 somewhat reduced the previous strong incentives to use debt rather than equity as a source of funds.

An important complication in evaluating the effects of the corporate tax reform is that Swedish companies to a large extent both paid corporate income tax and abstained from fully using the generous tax allowances. A recent study indicates that over the period 1979–88, the average rate of utilization of tax allowances (deductions for depreciation, contributions to investment funds and undervaluation of inventories) among tax-paying firms was a mere 72 per cent. Only one out of five firms used the maximum allowed by the tax code. An increase in the rate of utilization from 72 to 76 per cent would have been sufficient to completely eliminate all tax payments. Conventional estimates of the cost of capital or effective tax rates, assuming full utilization of existing tax allowances, may therefore give a misleading picture of the incentive effects of the corporate tax.

Recent research (Kanniainen and Södersten, 1994) has attributed this rather odd tax behaviour to the uniform reporting convention used in Sweden (and several other OECD countries). Firms can distribute cash dividends only to the extent of their after-tax profits, taking account of fiscal depreciation, contributions to investment funds, etc. Hence corporate civil law imposes a dividend constraint on using tax allowances, and in practice, this constraint seems to have been more tight than the upper limits set by the tax code. When tax allowances on existing assets have not been fully used, an additional investment project will not affect total tax payments, that is, at the margin the corporate tax rate is zero. Put differently, the corporate income tax is effectively turned into a tax on distributions or a cash flow tax with no impact on the cost of capital. The mechanism involved here is similar to that analyzed in the literature about dividend taxation. To the extent that paying dividends is the only way to get cash to the shareholders (share repurchases are disallowed in Sweden), the firm is in a 'trapped equity' regime where the corporate tax is capitalized in share prices.

The possibility that large groups of Swedish firms effectively faced a zero marginal corporate tax rate makes it unclear to what extent the old tax system actually did offer an advantage to debt finance. Even the direction of change in the incentives for borrowing brought by TR91 is unclear, as the base broadening would be expected to raise the rate of utilization of the still remaining tax shields.[11] Firms experiencing a switch from being taxed on their cash flows to being subject to a regular income tax would find the value of interest deductions increase at the margin, despite the sharp cut in the statutory tax rate. Moreover, given that the financial markets in Sweden are highly integrated with the international markets for debt and equity, it seems unlikely that the switch to the dual personal income tax with a flat rate 30 per cent tax on personal capital incomes would be of much importance for corporate financial decisions. The after-tax costs of funds of the large Swedish firms are more likely determined by the operations of international portfolio investors, say US pension funds, than by the savings and portfolio decisions of Swedish households.

Auerbach, Hassett and Södersten (1995) focus on the effects on business fixed investment. A model of equipment investment is estimated in order to determine which of several potential regimes best described investment behaviour before the reform. Even though the regression results do not settle the issue, evidence on the use of tax allowances and investment funds generally supports the view that the pre-reform corporate tax system had essentially no effect on investment. The change in the user cost of capital due to the reform is found to be very small, and swamped in recent years by the impact of the rise in real interest rates and decline in profitability. The authors conclude, 'with some confidence', that the effects of TR91 itself (as opposed to contemporaneous macroeconomic factors) on investment are likely to have been minor.

1.4 INCOME DISTRIBUTION

In the political process of selling TR91 to various interest groups and the electorate in general a key element was the claim that the reform would be distributionally neutral. This was interpreted in a bookkeeping sense to mean an unchanged relation between an exogenously given distribution of pre-tax factor income and the distribution of income after taxes and allowances. Against this background it was natural that a mechanical evaluation of the distributional impact along these lines was one element of the evaluation effort, although it was natural for economists to highlight the limitations of such an exercise.

During the 1980s a growing number of critics came to doubt whether the Swedish tax system achieved much in terms of redistribution. There were three ingredients to the critique. First, various loopholes and tax arbitrage activities created a wedge between 'true' income and taxable income. Second, substitution between market labour and leisure and household production created a discrepancy between taxable income (which only derives from market activities) and potential income (which also includes the value of leisure and home production). Third, taxation based on yearly income redistributes income across different phases in an individual's life cycle, that is, from more toward less productive ages, but it is less clear how much redistribution that actually is achieved across households with different lifetime incomes.

The recent study by Björklund, Palme and Svensson (1995), however, gives little support to the critics of the old system. According to this analysis the old Swedish tax system certainly achieved a substantial amount of redistribution of yearly incomes.[12] The amount of redistribution is not much affected by going from actual income to a measure of full income. Also, when the authors follow a panel of individuals over the period 1974–91, and take the sum of discounted income over this period as a measure of lifetime income, the conclusion is that the tax system redistributes almost as much in terms of lifetime income as in terms of yearly income. Of course, this only says something about the tax system as it evolved over this 18-year period, and gives no conclusive evidence on the long-run redistributive properties of the system of the late 1980s. Nevertheless, it leads us to be somewhat skeptical about the popularly-held view that the old tax system was devoid of any redistributive effect.

Björklund *et al.* (1995) also examine differences in pre- and post-tax Gini coefficients under the old and new tax rules. Looking at the aggregate amount of redistribution across all groups of households, the differences appear minuscule – at least in the short term (up to 1992). In sum, TR91 seems to have lived up to the promise of 'neutrality' with respect to the income distribution. This conclusion, however, conceals important differences in the structure of the tax and subsidy system. Broadly speaking, there are three counteracting differences between the old and new tax system. First, the taxation of earned income is clearly less redistributive under TR91. Second, with the new flat tax on capital income, tax payments become more proportional to actual capital income than under the old system, where it was possible to avoid capital taxes altogether through tax arbitrage. Since capital income is concentrated at the top of the income distribution this tends to make the new system more redistributive than the old one. Third, child and housing allowances play a larger role after TR91 than before. Since they largely redistribute income from households without children to families with children, TR91 represents a shift of emphasis towards more redistribution across various phases of the life cycle rather than between households with different lifetime incomes.

By simply comparing Gini coefficients before and after taxes one takes an unduly narrow view on income distribution. In particular, one takes the pre-tax distribution of factor income for granted, thereby glossing over the strong assumptions about tax incidence implicit in such an excercise. Whereas it may be reasonable for a small open economy like the Swedish one to assume that the pre-tax return to capital is determined in international markets and unaffected by Swedish tax policy, the assumptions about the incidence on wages merit more attention than they are commonly given by income distribution analysts. In fact there has been a recent trend in Sweden, as elsewhere, towards more inequality of factor incomes, and one may ask if this development has been induced by tax reform to any extent. This should depend on the relative supply responses of high- and low-skilled workers, and on the degree of complementarity in production between different types of labor. However, given the generally small labor supply responses, it appears unlikely that the changing wage structure has primarily been induced by changes in tax structure. In the longer run the strengthened incentives to invest in human capital should be more important for the wage distribution. It is hard, though, to have a very definite opinion on the implications for the distributional analysis of TR91.[13]

1.5 EFFICIENCY – A DOUBLE DIVIDEND?

A main argument of the proponents of TR91 was that economic efficiency should improve. For many politicians, efficiency was here interpreted as a synonym for various easy-to-observe responses, like increased labour supply, and higher savings. In some quarters, there was also a hope that TR91 should deliver an easily detectable growth bonus. For an economist, however, efficiency is defined in terms of not directly observable areas between compensated demand and supply curves, and there is no simple relation between the implied tax distortions and the magnitude of behavioural responses. Much the same goes for economic growth. According to the standard neoclassical growth model, a badly designed tax system may create important negative level effects, without the long-term rate of growth being affected. As we will see shortly, TR91 even contained provisions which tended to *reduce* registered GDP growth, but to increase consumption opportunities.

From an excess burden perspective, the most important aspect of TR91 is that it implied a shift in the tax burden from highly taxed labour income, to lightly taxed housing capital. As a consequence, the relative prices of leisure and housing consumption increased. Although there is room for disagreement on the exact magnitudes of some key behavioural elasticities, there is little reason to question the soundness of this strategy. Numerical calculations in Chapter 8 (Table 8.2) demonstrate that even small behavioural elasticities matter, if the marginal tax wedge is sufficiently high. The logic behind the marginal welfare cost per krona of tax revenue implies that there is a region of tax wedges at which the efficiency cost starts to increase rapidly. At some marginal tax wedge, an additional tax hike creates additional excess burdens, but no extra tax revenue. One can hardly rule out the possibility that pre-reform tax wedges were close to that level. The point estimates of labour supply elasticities, not to mention the confidence intervals, reported in recent studies are certainly consistent with the view that the pre-TR91 tax system had marked negative incentive effects.

Of course, estimates suggesting high marginal welfare costs of taxation do not necessarily imply that tax cuts are in order. When there is a binding revenue constraint, lower tax wedges on labour income make sense only if other taxes can be raised in a less distortionary way. The remarkable aspect of the Swedish situation was that there was scope for a 'double dividend'. Higher taxes on housing generated a substantial part of the revenue required to finance the tax cut on labour income, but they also reduced intersectoral investment distortions. Due to the generous tax and subsidy rules, discussed above, housing investment was given a considerable advantage over investments in other sectors. Available estimates indicate (for realistic values of the debt–equity mix, inflation, and so on) that new investments in owner-occupied housing could reap a *net* marginal subsidy – the (financial) cost of capital for the prospective homeowner was well below the real rate of interest. TR91 did much to promote a less inefficient allocation of investment resources.

The case of housing illustrates that the short-term response of an aggregate production measure, like GDP, may provide a poor indicator of the welfare effects of tax reform. Before TR91, household savings were channeled into an activity where the marginal productivity of capital was considerably below the opportunity cost, which in an open economy can be approximated by the world real rate of interest. At the same time, the housing sector gave a substantial contribution to Swedish GDP. In any year, housing investment, valued from the production side, added to aggregate investments. TR91 gave households strong incentives to redirect their savings to other uses, including net purchases of foreign assets.[14] During the adjustment phase (when the housing sector shrinks, and the net foreign asset position improves), GDP growth tends to slacken. In spite of this negative production effect, aggregate consumption possibilities tend to increase – every krona's worth of savings transferred from the housing sector to international asset markets implies that Swedish national income increases with the difference between the world real rate of interest and the marginal productivity of housing capital.

Undoubtedly, TR91 has affected economic efficiency along a number of margins in addition to those just discussed. The reduced progressivity of the income tax has enhanced educational incentives. The new corporate income tax brought about a more uniform treatment of investment projects *within* the corporate sector. The broader base for the value added tax implied higher tax wedges on the 'white' consumer service sector, which competes with do-it-yourself activities and services produced in the underground economy. However, in these cases there is scant evidence on the behavioural response.

Finally, an important objective of TR91 was to simplify the tax code, and there is reason to believe that TR91 did much to reduce the transaction complexity of the tax system. TR91 made it much less profitable to invest resources in a variety of tax avoidance activities. Survey evidence indicates that households' time spent on tax compliance declined substantially in the years after TR91. There is also evidence suggesting that the tax authorities got an easier workload.

1.6 CONCLUSIONS

What is the verdict on TR91 five years after its implementation? Have we seen the behavioural responses that the reform architects expected? Did the reform contribute to a more efficient economy? Although we should keep our fingers crossed in view of the severe crisis in the Swedish economy in the early 1990s, we concur with Auerbach and Slemrod (1996), who argued in their survey of TRA86 that there has been a hierarchy of responses. A number of financial activities related to tax planning were rendered meaningless and have been virtually wiped out. We have also seen large and expected effects on portfolio composition in general, with a shrinking of both sides of private-sector balance sheets. Households have been induced to shift out of owner-occupied housing, resulting in falling house prices and a standstill of new construction. In the longer run, this will result in a more efficient allocation of the capital stock.

At the other end of the spectrum, major real activities like labour supply and savings appear quite insensitive, at least as far as can be inferred from short-run behaviour. Since real activities can be expected to be more important from a welfare perspective, it might be conjectured that the reform only has made a small contribution to increase the efficiency of the Swedish economy, like Auerbach and Slemrod (1996) conclude for TRA86. While such a conclusion may be warranted at US tax rates, it is hardly correct when starting out from marginal tax rates of 70 per cent and more. Further, at such levels – close to the top of the Laffer curve – the marginal excess burden is highly non-linear in tax rates, implying that accounting for heterogeneity and uncertainty about the correct elasticity values is very important; the expected aggregate excess burden is much larger than the marginal excess burden for the average taxpayer evaluated at point estimates of elasticities.

Although a standard efficiency calculation – comparing hypothetical equilibria before and after the reform – unambiguously shows that TR91 was efficiency improving, these benefits were not without costs. In fact, the reform may be viewed as an investment with quite visible short-run costs that have to be weighed against less visible, and perhaps also less certain, long-run benefits. The short-run costs of TR91 were primarily of two types. First, by shifting savings out of real assets like housing and consumer durables into financial assets the reform implied a reduction of effective demand. Since the reform was implemented in a recession when output was arguably demand determined, we conclude that it led to a further deepening of the recession with accompanying short-term production losses. Second, the rapid implementation of the reform led to sizeable capital losses in the housing sector, with an ensuing arbitrary horizontal redistribution across households. These observations serve as a reminder of the point emphasized, for example, by Feldstein (1976), that one has to distinguish between tax reform and *de novo* tax design. While a comparison of the pre- and post-91 tax systems comes out in favour of the post-91 system, an evaluation of the reform has to weigh the long-run benefits against the short-term costs.

The costs of the reform were not unavoidable. The government took a rather careless attitude to the transition problem. A more gradual phase-in of the reform certainly would have dampened the short-run costs considerably without giving up any of the long-run benefits. While this would be a rather obvious recommendation to a benevolent dictator, things are more complex in a parliamentary democracy where one cannot tie the hands of future governments. Indeed, bringing about political consensus about a reform as far-reaching as TR91 involved a rather delicate balance of the gains and losses of different interest groups in society. If parts of the reform would have been implemented gradually or with a lag, they would also have been more susceptible to future political pressures.

Even a 'tax reform of the century' implemented with such force as TR91 did not stay unaffected for very long. In 1994, only three years after its implementation, one could make a list of some 75 tax changes involving minor and major deviations from the original reform. Such a count of changes obviously is a cheap argument; after all, the world changes continuously, and one would hope that the tax law adapts. Nevertheless, some of the changes represent reversals of the guiding principles of TR91. One example is the numerous changes in different VAT rates. Another is the increase of the top marginal tax rate on earned income from 50 to 55 per cent. The latter change was presented as a temporary measure and part of a package to cut the growing budget deficits after 1992. While these deficits are largely attributable to the recession, they partly reflect an underfinancing of the reform by 2 to 3 per cent of GDP. It is not surprising that it was easier to sell an underfunded reform package, where all groups could be portrayed as winners, than a fully financed reform where some groups would appear as losers, at least in a short-run accounting sense.

In what direction should we expect the Swedish tax system to evolve in the future? The 1980s was a decade of tax reforms aimed at a more uniform tax structure, conspicuously ignoring much of the development in public finance since the 1970s emphasizing the role of differentiated taxation in funding government expenditure. In the 1990s, the pendulum of tax reform discussion has swung in the opposite direction, with a renewed emphasis on differentation – for example, for environmental reasons or as a means of fighting unemployment. When these factors now are being considered in Sweden, future reforms can build on a tax structure that has fewer counterproductive asymmetries than the pre-TR91 system.

The Swedish public sector ranks among the largest in the world. As long as this remains, Swedish tax rates will inevitably be high. Our discussion suggests that, especially with a high aggregate tax rate, the structure of taxation matters. TR91 has reduced the aggregate excess burden. However, the ever-growing integration with international capital and labour markets will undoubtedly put increasing pressure on the Swedish tax system in the future.

2 Tax Planning

It almost goes without saying that the taxation process involves contradictory interests. The state must finance the public-sector activities which are collectively decided on by its citizens; at the same time citizens individually try to pay as little tax as possible within the framework provided by legislation. These circumstances create opportunities as well as problems. Environmental taxation and some of the rules within corporate taxation are examples of how legislative measures try to utilize the desire of companies and individuals to reduce their taxes in order to obtain, in various respects, a change in their behaviour.

However, the striving of companies and households to minimize their taxes is sometimes also associated with actions which go beyond, or conflict directly with, the underlying intentions of tax legislation. Here, we are speaking about tax planning, to use a somewhat inappropriate term, in order to provide a comprehensive description of the arrangements which either entirely or to a great extent do not make sense other than as measures to avoid or reduce taxation. Tax planning received great attention in the debate on economic policy before TR91, and probably was also of decisive importance for the general direction of the reform.

The concept, tax planning, is far from unambiguous. There is a lack of clarity as to when tax planning, which is legal, though undesired by the state, becomes illegal tax evasion. In addition, the distinction between what is fully acceptable tax minimization within the framework of normal economic actions, and what is undesired tax planning is not always entirely clear. A company which postpones its investments in order to take advantage of tax savings when investment funds are released, and households, which increase their saving when special savings programmes offer higher returns, cannot be said to be involved in tax planning. Nor does the fact that interest deductions for loans on single-family homes do not correspond to an equivalent taxation of the implicit return in the form of housing, make the homeowner a tax planner. If, on the other hand, deposits in special savings programmes do not come from new saving, but instead are arranged by a transfer from fully taxed bank accounts, we find ourselves closer to tax planning, and we have definitely crossed the line if the deposits have been financed by loans with deductible interest.

The decisive precondition for all types of tax planning is that the tax system contains asymmetries and other non-neutralities which mean that taxes may vary depending on who declares a given income, in what forms the income is declared or when the declaration of income takes place. Tax planning is based on a systematic utilization of such asymmetries or distortions in order to reduce one's own taxes. A comprehensive criticism of the old tax system dealt with this very lack of symmetry and uniformity, which in combination with high marginal taxes made tax planning a profitable and, as far as can be assessed, a very widespread activity as well.[1]

The new tax system, with lower tax rates and, above all, uniform capital taxation, has made much of the old tax planning meaningless. However, other problems remain. Nowadays, not only companies, but also private individuals, can invest their capital abroad without difficulty due to the international integration of the financial system and the deregulation of the currency markets. The lack of taxation at source and a comprehensive and well-functioning international system of reporting means that the return on capital earned abroad, to a great extent, is beyond the reach of both Swedish and foreign taxation. At the same time as domestic tax planning is made more difficult, the tendency to make use of international loopholes for outright tax evasion will increase. Here, tax policy faces a difficult dilemma: In order to prevent international tax evasion, capital taxation in the future may need to be kept at a considerably lower level than at present. At the same time, however, lower taxes on capital would mean a risk of renewed domestic tax planning, which in turn would add to the difficulties in maintaining an effective taxation of earned income.

2.1 DIFFERENTIAL TAXATION OF INDIVIDUALS

When different individuals are taxed differently, total taxes can be reduced by a shifting of income. The incentive to use this possibility is, of course, especially strong for family members. Under the old tax system, family transactions of various kinds provided easy opportunities for tax planning. Under the rules that applied in the 1980s, spouses were taxed separately for earned income, but were taxed jointly for income from capital and wealth. Children, on the other hand, were taxed separately for income from capital, but taxed jointly with their parents for wealth.

The opportunity for tax planning became available here by income from capital being taxed as income along with wage income in combination with the special treatment of children. The easiest step for restricting the effect of progressivity in income taxation at that time was to let all family members take advantage of the savings deduction of 1600 kronor and the previous basic deduction of 10 000 kronor. By making use of these deductions, each child could declare 11 600 kronor in income from capital without being taxed. The transfer of capital income to children, however, was also profitable for larger amounts as long as the marginal tax rate of the children was lower than that of their parents.

The possible difficulty associated with this procedure was how the transfer of capital income could be arranged from the parents to their children without bringing about taxation of some kind. In the case of smaller sums, the exempted amount that applied for gift taxation could provide sufficient opportunities, while shifting on a larger scale, in general, required more complicated arrangements. What measures could be utilized for family transactions of this and similar kinds changed over time, depending on how legislation and legal interpretations changed, in a constant interaction with the inventiveness of the tax planners.

2.2   DIFFERENTIAL TAXATION OF COMPANIES

In a corresponding manner, the difference in taxation between different legal entities during the 1980s was the starting point for comprehensive tax planning within the company sector. In particular, two kinds of distortions acquired great importance. The first had to do with the fact that the generous writedown and depreciation possibilities of corporate taxation were only worthwhile for companies which had new investments and sufficient profits in order to make use of the existing rules. The second kind received attention in connection with the special investment deduction which was implemented in the beginning of the 1980s and which entailed a possibility for companies to obtain tax credits for new investments against payment of VAT. The purpose behind this arrangement was to extend the investment incentive to companies which were not making a profit and therefore did not have the opportunity to make use of investment deductions offered within the framework of ordinary corporation tax. The only problem was that this new investment deduction was not all-inclusive either; companies which were not part of the VAT system – among these, those in the financial sector – did not come into consideration.

Angelin and Jennegren (1995) show how so-called partner leasing came to be used systematically as an instrument to bring together companies with sufficient profits for tax deductions, but which did not have depreciation objects of their own, with companies which had access to such objects but lacked sufficient profits. The case study presented by the authors has to do with a commercial bank which was going to acquire a mainframe computer at the beginning of the 1980s. The bank found itself handicapped tax-wise in the double sense that for the foreseeable future it had a surplus of tax allowances and that it conducted business which was not subject to VAT. In other words, the bank was not entitled to the investment deduction which was linked to the VAT system.

The lack of profits to make use of the future deduction possibilities which the computer investment entailed could, in principle, be remedied by a leasing agreement under which the lessor stood for the tax depreciation. The tax reduction which the deduction generated could then be divided up between the lessor and the bank by a suitable adjustment in the terms of the leasing agreement. However, to gain access to the VAT reduction as well required a further arrangement. In an attempt to prevent tax planning, legislation had namely stipulated that when there was a leasing agreement issued by a finance company, the VAT reduction could only be used by the end user, if the leasing period was more than three years. Thus, according to the intentions of the legislation, since the end user in the case in question was a bank which did not have to pay VAT, and the intended counterpart of the end user was a finance company, there would be no reduction. The solution was to bring in a partner in the form of a limited partnership which for tax purposes functioned as a non-financial company. This partner could assume ownership of the mainframe from the finance company and gain access to both the investment deduction and the tax depreciation. The deficits which this depreciation in turn generated could in the end be used by the owner of the partner, that is, the limited partnership. The role of the finance company was to be responsible for the financial arrangements and to reclaim the VAT payment on the computer.

The possibilities for tax planning which are illustrated by the case studies of Angelin and Jennergren saw extensive application during the second half of the 1980s in transactions not only between private companies but also between private companies and state-owned companies and company-like institutions. In the latter case, the tax-free status of these bodies became an additional circumstance which could generate tax breaks in different buying and selling arrangements. In addition, the change in corporate taxation – which was actually known several years in advance – created its own profit opportunities. High-profit companies invested in ice-breakers, hospital equipment and even (municipal) sewage systems. The point was that depreciation for tax purposes, to a great extent, could be claimed against the high tax rate of the old system, while the rental incomes from the end user were taxed at the new tax rate of 30 per cent.

The tax planning of companies during the high-profit years at the end of the 1980s also had international dimensions. In several cases, which are discussed by Angelin and Jennergren, big Swedish companies invested in depreciation objects in the form of passenger aircraft, bought and financed abroad for immediate rental to foreign end users. The temptation to postpone tax in anticipation of TR91 was once again one of the propelling forces, but there were also possibilities for a so called double-dip: The investment could be depreciated twice, both by the lessor and by the end user.

2.3   DIFFERENTIAL TAXATION OF INCOME

The differences in the effective rates of taxation between different kinds of income was another circumstance which created opportunities for tax planning under the old system. The non-neutralities were most obvious within the area of capital taxation. The main principle was that interest income and dividends of households above a certain threshold were taxed as income in accordance with the progressive schedule which applied to earned income and with fully deductible interest costs, while capital gains were not taxed until realization, and at a lower tax rate. Certain forms of saving, for example, pension insurance and special savings programmes, entitled the holder to a tax-free or low-taxed return.

With an inconsistent tax system, the strategy of tax planning is to shift deductible costs to areas or activities where the principle of full taxation is applied, and income to areas which are favoured by tax law or where there is no taxation. Depending on the circumstances, this basically simple strategy may require anything from simple transfers to extremely complicated arrangements over several stages.

We have already touched upon the obvious and simple opportunities for tax planning which were made available to households through the different schemes which were introduced at the end of the 1970s in order to encourage household saving, and which with varying rules and under different names were kept until TR91.[2] At the time of its implementation, the special tax saving programme yielded a tax-free return for five years on deposits within certain set amounts in addition to a direct tax credit of 20 per cent of the newly deposited funds. Thus the tax saving scheme effectively implied a negative tax. However, nothing prevented households from financing their deposits through loans, which could be done with a minimum of inconvenience by automatic transfers from a wage account with a current account overdraft facility.

With the marginal tax rates which were in force at this time, the state also provided substantial tax breaks on borrowing for people in ordinary income levels. For the sake of argument let us suppose that the value of the interest deduction was 75 per cent. If interest on current account overdrafts was 15 per cent (before tax), and the tax saving account yielded a tax-free return of 10 per cent, each deposited and loan-financed krona yielded a net profit of 54 öre. With the limit for deposits set at 4800 kronor per year and person, this meant a profit of just less than 2600 kronor, without the 'saver' having to do anything in return. In terms of 1995 monetary value this corresponds to just more than 7000 kronor. It ought to be emphasized that with the exception of variations in the rate of interest, this arrangement was entirely risk-free, and moreover could be utilized by all the members of a family. Here, we have an unusually clear example of a *money machine*.

According to the rules which applied before TR91, premiums for pension insurance, within certain limits, could be deducted from income, while pension payments received were taxed as income. Since neither the insurance companies, which administered and invested the premiums, nor the policy holders paid tax on the current yield from the pension capital, pension insurance thus provided a possibility for long-term saving at a tax-free return. Once again, the problem was that the system also encouraged tax planning since the premium payments could just as well be financed with the help of loans with fully deductible interest. Thus, the tax planner could easily combine two different principles of taxation, and as we show in Chapter 3 with the help of numerical examples, the gains could be considerable.

However, it must be emphasized that a pension insurance is not the same kind of *money machine* as the above-mentioned tax savings schemes under the old system, since the required time-horizon of the policies could be long with accompanying risks regarding both returns and permanence in the rules that created the opportunities for gains. Still, it is precisely the opportunities for tax planning which were regarded as an explanation for the growing demand for pension insurance during the 1980s. Another reason advanced for this increased interest was the gains to be made by the new tax reform, which was advertized well in advance. Through the reform, individuals who had saved in pensions under the old system (with or without contributing savings of their own) in many instances obtained considerable windfalls since the pensions payments were taxed at a considerably lower rate than that which had previously applied for the deductible premium payments.

When it came to transforming fully taxable capital income or some other form of income to tax-favoured capital gains, a number of more or less complicated strategies were applied. In some cases, where different taxation principles were combined, the element of tax planning pure and simple was probably of more or less subordinate importance. An example which we have already mentioned – without referring to it as tax planning – is the owner-occupier who, on the one hand, is allowed to deduct mortgage interest, and on the other hand is favoured by low or non-existent capital gains taxation when he sells his house. Another example is the inactive owner of agricultural property who could set off the deficit created by value-enhancing repairs against earned income. Even if, in the same way as for the owner-occupier, these transactions could be seen as part of perfectly normal economic activity, there is a great possibility that there were many instances where acquisition and inactive ownership of agricultural property was guided by this opportunity. In other words, this was a matter of fully taxable current income being converted either into housing consumption or capital gains.

In order to convert income into capital gains on a larger scale, transactions between a controlling shareholder and one or more joint-stock companies were often utilized.[3] Here, the purpose might be to withdraw after-tax profits from a controlled company without the owner having to pay income tax further down the line. This task could be taken care of with the aid of an internal stock transfer. The profitable company in question would be sold for a promissory note, payable to the owner, to another company which was also entirely owned by the person in question and which had been created for this sole purpose; the profit from the old company was then transferred to the new company through dividends, which could be done tax-free under the rules in effect at that time. After the transfer, the profit was used to amortize the promissory note to the owner at a desired speed. As far as the owner was concerned, the operation resulted in taxable capital gains, which was a clear advantage compared with the high, progressive taxes on dividends. He could moreover continue his old profitable business activity in the newly created company.

Different *profit company transactions* involving a company with substantial untaxed reserves provided opportunities for partially or entirely avoiding corporation tax. One technique which was used was to let a company sell its assets, which had been dramatically depreciated for tax purposes, to another controlled company. Since the sale took place at market prices, the untaxed reserves were dissolved, which would have brought about taxation if no other steps were taken. Therefore, the next step was to sell the company, and now with the payment from the sale as the only asset. Potential buyers were companies with deductible losses or other tax allowances without any corresponding profits of their own. In the form this arrangement is described here, it was a matter of dividing the deferred corporation tax between the seller and the external buyer; the original owner/tax planner paid the capital gains tax instead of income tax and could moreover maintain control of the real assets from the original company.

Much of the tax planning of the 1980s was aimed at eliminating or postponing the taxation of capital gains. Not infrequently, the arrangement included several successive steps which took advantage of different innovations in the form of new financial instruments on the fast-expanding financial markets. One of these innovations was warrant financing ('option loans'), combining a regular bond (with deductable interest) with an entitlement, an option, for the holder to purchase shares in the company on predetermined terms. For a long time, the tax treatment of warrant financing was unclear, but after a decision in the Supreme Administrative Court in 1983, it became apparent that warrant financing was not just an instrument for company financing.

The decision of the Supreme Administrative Court meant that the total procurement cost of a so-called unit, consisting of the bond and the option (warrant), for tax purposes should fall entirely on the bond. In other words, as far as taxation was concerned the acquisition cost of the option was zero. Since 'option loans' were regularly issued with a lower coupon interest than that which corresponded to the market rate of interest, the investor could immediately detach and sell the pure bond with a fictive (but useful for tax purposes) capital loss as a result. The option could then be used to buy shares or be sold. According to the rules in effect at that time, only 40 per cent of the profit from sales was taxed after two years; the fictive capital loss on the bond, on the other hand, was 100 per cent deductible. Not surprisingly, the decision of the court was followed by a rapid expansion of the market for 'option loans' with an appended opportunity for tax planning. After a waste of time of a year or so the state responded with special legislation which put an end to this practice.

In keeping with past patterns of behaviour, tax planning continued, focusing now on other techniques. Among these were interest income funds and later dividend funds. Here, the foreseeable fall in market prices after the annual payment of dividends from the funds could be used to generate capital losses to a desirable extent. For people who had taxable capital gains and a deficit of capital income which could be deducted from the dividend income, the matter was settled. For others, who had capital gains but did not have negative capital income, this form of tax planning went an additional step using, among other things, borrowing and accompanying deductible interest payments in order to postpone taxation. Not infrequently these operations were associated with considerable risk-taking on the part of the tax planner, since further investment was required in order to get a return on the loan.

The rules for capital gains taxation also offered possibilities for tax planning. Of decisive importance was the holding-period distinction, which had long been in force. Capital gains on short-term shareholding were fully taxed as income, probably because this was associated with speculation, while profits from longer shareholding, more than two years, were only taxable at 40 per cent. The rules were symmetrical regarding the treatment of profits and losses; short-term losses on shares were accordingly 100 per cent deductible, long-term losses were 40 per cent deductible.

There may be sound economic arguments for symmetrical taxation with the right to set off profits and losses. In combination with the two-year rule, however, the deduction created obvious opportunities to reduce effective taxation. The simple strategy was to realize losses on short-term investments and await the two-year limit when selling shares at a profit. In this manner, a loss on a short-term investment could eliminate the taxation of a gain which was two-and-a-half times as big. Apart from the transaction costs, there was nothing to prevent the investor from immediately repurchasing the loss shares if their future prospects were deemed to be good.

2.4 THE EFFECTS OF TAX PLANNING

It is entirely self-evident that the old tax system provided considerable opportunities to reduce taxation through systematic tax planning. The preconditions for tax planning were created by the non-neutralities of various kinds in the tax rules which meant that taxes varied depending on *who* declared a given income, in what *forms* the income was declared and *when* the declaration was made. We have presented a few, and by no means exhaustive, examples of tax planning which were based on non-neutralities of this very kind.

The question now is what significance this tax planning had for tax revenues and for the tax burden on different categories of tax subjects. Malmer and Persson's (1994) study of income statistics for certain years since 1980 confirms that total income tax in different groups was often strongly below the estimated tax on earned income and on business activity. In other words, in general, the taxation of other activities than employment and business has generated negative tax revenues. It is obvious that tax planning is one of the explanations for these findings and probably the dominating explanation for most of the cases of filing nil-returns. But, in general, we cannot distinguish what is a result of tax planning in the restricted sense we have used this term – arrangements which make no sense other than as steps to reduce taxes – from the consequences of taxpayers having pursued normal economic activities which were favoured by the tax laws.

A more direct indication that tax planning may have had great quantitative importance is presented in a study by the National Tax Board from 1987. The study covered some 70 new introductions to the Stockholm Stock Exchange which were accompanied by sales from the previous major owners. The sales gave rise to capital gains of a little more than one billion kronor. In accordance with the rules in effect at that time, this corresponded to taxable capital gains of just over 300 million kronor. However, the old owners could limit the sum that was actually to be paid in taxes to 15 million kronor, which corresponded to less than 2 per cent of the original profit on the sales.

Despite the difficulties of quantifying the effects, one can plausibly argue that tax planning has had great importance for the accuracy of taxation in terms of redistribution policies. The calculations of Malmer and Persson do not contradict the common view that tax planning was utilized mainly by persons with substantial (economic) resources. It is also obvious that tax planning was widely considered to be a growing threat to the general tax morals and social solidarity of the country. The knowledge that certain groups in society, by more or less advanced tax planning, could avoid paying taxes to an extent which did not correspond to the intentions of the tax code, might be thought liable to lessen the moral inhibitions against outright tax evasion among other social groups.

Tax planning also affects economic efficiency, both directly and indirectly. The direct efficiency cost has to do with the fact that tax planning requires the use of considerable resources. It encroaches on the time taxpayers have for productive activity, and it maintains an overdimensioned corps of tax lawyers and others who are needed to provide the necessary expertise. The indirect efficiency problem is created by the need for the state to compensate the loss of tax revenues that tax planning brings about. The more extensive tax planning is, the greater demands are placed on other parts of the tax system being able to generate sufficient tax revenues. This extra taxation, in turn, may entail economic adaptations which reduce efficiency.

However, not all forms of tax planning necessarily reduce efficiency. Above, we described how tax planning within the company sector has been developed in order to exploit the differences between companies regarding availability of tax allowances. By doing so, tax planning – here, given a positive interpretation – may have made it possible for companies to make investment decisions based on similar conditions. However, corresponding arrangements have also meant that investment incentives have been extended to include companies which have been explicitly excluded by the state. Belonging to the latter category are those foreign companies – which, in a few cases, attracted considerable attention at the end of the 1980s – which were able to take advantage, through various leasing arrangements, of the favourable depreciation rules in Sweden.

2.5   THE TAX REFORM

During the past decades, the struggle against tax planning has been carried out in a continual interaction with the pursuit of the tax planners after new ways to avoid paying taxes. New loopholes have been discovered, have been used for a while, and then done away by special legislation. This process has partially thrived by itself due to the fact that the gradual, growing complexity of the tax rules created new, unforeseen possibilities for tax planning. The 1991 tax reform represents a new form of attack on tax planning by hitting directly at two of the crucial conditions for tax planning, namely the non-neutralities of the tax system and the high marginal taxes.

The new, flat-rate and separate tax on capital did away with the rationality of making the various kinds of family transactions which were used to exploit the differences in taxation between individuals. Since all family members pay 30 per cent in tax on capital income without exemption, taxation remains the same regardless of how income is divided. Since the new, uniform system of taxation permits a preliminary taxation at source of interest and dividends, the possibilities for outright tax evasion are also reduced.

We can also count on there being less interest in the type of tax planning which makes use of the differences in availability of tax allowances between different companies. With the corporation tax rate having been reduced by half, leasing agreements and other arrangements yield less in the form of reduced taxes. At the same time the tax situation of companies has become more similar, since consolidation opportunities have been limited. In addition, with the new tax rules, it becomes pointless to convert current capital income to capital gains since the tax rate is the same. Most of the gains from the systematic set-off of losses on short-term shareholdings against the profits of long-term shareholdings will not materialize, since the tax rules no longer distinguish between 'younger' and 'older' shares. Restrictions on set-off possibilities for non-quoted shares as well as the right to deduct interest exceeding 100 000 kronor have further reduced previous opportunities for profitable tax planning.

However, several important exceptions from uniform capital taxation remained even after the reform, and in recent years new exceptions have come and gone. For example, pension savings and investments via other kinds of institutional intermediaries were granted a special status even after 1991. Thus, the person who is willing to accept the various kinds of risks which are associated with long-term commitments can still make considerable profits by financing pension insurance policies through loans (see Agell, Berg and Edin, 1995).

An important problem which was discussed prior to the 1991 reform and which received renewed importance in connection with subsequent changes in the tax laws, has to do with the possibilities of utilizing, for tax purposes, the differences in taxation between income from employment and income from capital. An expressed goal of the 1991 reform was to achieve a uniform taxation by a consistently implemented double taxation of both employment and capital income. Despite this, however, it is obvious that a considerable difference still remains even after the reform. Total taxes on earned income for 1991 in the highest income bracket was around 65 per cent through the combination of social insurance contributions, payroll taxation and income taxation. For joint-stock companies, total effective taxation was slightly over 50 per cent, in the form of corporation tax and personal capital tax of 30 per cent each.

Thus, the gap in taxation between capital income and earned income was around 25 percentage units for the highest tax bracket after the 1991 reform. This difference increased, however, to twice as much after the decision to eliminate double taxation of corporate profits as of 1 January 1994, to be reduced once again to around 20 per cent in 1995 after an increase in income taxation, new social insurance contributions and renewed tax on share dividends. Thus, for example, a person who is in the consultancy business still has an obvious incentive even after TR91 to transfer activity to a controlled corporation and limit withdrawing a salary at least to the bracket where only local taxes are levied and the tax component of social insurance contributions is less.

In order to prevent behaviour of this kind, however, complicated rules have been included in tax legislation. Expressed simply, these rules stipulate that share dividends and capital gains for close companies over a certain level are to be taxed as income from employment instead of income from capital. However, whether these rules are sufficiently restrictive is a controversial question. For example, just prior to the decision in 1993 to abolish the taxation of share dividends to households the Council on Legislation stated that eliminating double taxation would lead to undesired tax planning if the lines of demarcation between the different forms of income were not clear. In the view of the Council on Legislation, it 'could be questioned whether the legislation fulfilled these requirements'.[4] Other experienced Swedish tax lawyers go further and are more explicit in their criticism; the new rules are hardly seen, in practice, as constituting an effective obstacle to converting earned income to capital income for tax purposes.

However, various international restrictions must also be taken into account in order to assess to what extent flat-rate capital taxation and an equivalent taxation of capital and labour may function as instruments to combat tax planning.[5] A problem which immediately achieved prominence as a result of TR91 had to do with the possibilities to implement and maintain a taxation of private insurance savings in an international environment where tax exemption dominates. In order to stop an obvious possibility to avoid the Swedish tax, a tax of 15 per cent was levied on the premiums of foreign insurance policies, in case the recipient country did not apply a corresponding tax. This tax, however, seems to have largely been a failure. While the annual outflow of insurance premiums abroad, according to the estimates of the Swedish insurance companies, were to have amounted to 4 billion kronor, or more, the amount collected from the tax on premiums was ca. 10 million during 1994, which corresponded to foreign premium payments of barely 70 million kronor. This great discrepancy probably derives from an extensive underreporting as well as from taking advantage of loopholes in the legislation which made possible the purchase of second hand contracts of capital insurance without a tax on the premium.

The international integration of the financial system and the dismantling of currency regulation have made it both simple and legal today for individuals to move capital abroad. The number of applications for permission to open accounts in foreign banks, however, has been extremely limited, and only in a few cases do foreign banks provide the necessary information for a Swedish taxation of foreign capital income. Nor are the possibilities especially great for the Swedish tax authorities to obtain information about income from dividends or other forms of return on capital. In any event, capital investors can avoid countries that provide reports to countries which offer sufficient protection against foreign tax authorities. As Mutén (1995) points out, seen in an international context, the disadvantage which the Swedish tax authorities seem to face *vis-à-vis* capital investors who want to evade Swedish taxes is by no means unique.

There are rather small prospects, within the near future, of bringing about an international, comprehensive and workable taxation at source for capital returns as a substitute for residence taxation of the owners of capital. Regarding this matter, it is enough to refer to the discouraging results from various German attempts to introduce taxation at source for interest income. These attempts quickly brought about a flight of capital abroad of such magnitude that the legislation had to be repealed. The German experience also contributed to a continued deadlock in the work within the European Union to bring about a coordinated taxation at source.[6]

International restrictions hence seem to confront legislatures with a difficult dilemma which will certainly become more problematic in the future. The desire to check domestic tax planning as well as generate sufficient tax revenues, on the one hand, argues in favour of a uniform taxation of income from employment and capital. However, the more effectively domestic tax planning is combated, the greater are the risks of international tax avoidance and evasion. If, on the one hand, capital is induced to stay within the country by considerably lower taxation – which can also reduce the propensity to hide foreign income from capital – the risks of domestic tax planning increase, with increasing difficulties in maintaining demarcation between the taxation of income from capital and the taxation of income from employment.

3 Savings and Consumption

TR91 removed the taxation of household capital income from the ordinary taxation of earned income and instituted a completely new flat-rate capital income tax of 30 per cent. At the same time, various deductions were removed or reduced, and the value of interest deductions for households was set at 30 per cent. Apart from the explicit objective of stimulating saving and decrease indebtedness, the new capital income tax was intended to provide an important contribution to the financing of the reform. It was also to help make TR91 distributionally neutral, since the lowered marginal tax rate on the earned income of high-income individuals would be counteracted by higher taxes on their capital income. Fiscal aspects were also an important reason for the overhaul of indirect taxation, which was carried out as an integral part of TR91. Before TR91, at most 60 per cent of private consumption was affected by VAT. TR91 broadened the tax base, and increased various other commodity taxes.

In this chapter, we will discuss how households have adapted to the new tax on capital income and the changes in indirect taxation. The first important question is to what extent TR91 has affected *household savings*; that is, the choice between consuming today or tomorrow. Since TR91 implied higher real after-tax interest rates, households were given strong incentives to increase savings and pay back their debts. The exceptional increase in recent years of the household savings ratio indicates that TR91 may have led to sizeable adjustments. However, the conventional definition of the savings ratio is a very imperfect measure of intertemporal consumption patterns, since it only includes a fairly narrow set of assets. Using an expanded definition of savings, which includes purchases of consumer durables and savings in contractual pension insurance schemes, savings emerge as more stable over time, and the recent development as less dramatic. Indeed, the increase in household savings in recent years only means that the savings ratio has returned to the levels prevailing towards the end of the 1970s. Nor, as we shall soon see, is there any clear evidence that TR91 is an important explanation for the consumption bust of the early 1990s. To the extent that TR91 had an impact, the main channel seems to be wealth effects stemming from tax-induced capitalization effects in the market for owner-occupied housing.

TR91 also changed the relative tax treatment of different forms of savings, and our second question concerns the response of *household asset composition*. Here, we find a clearer connection. The strong increase in household aggregate financial savings in recent years and the concurrent decrease in savings in real assets (owner-occupied housing, consumer durables, and so on) are highly correlated with changes in taxes and relative returns. These portfolio shifts have both short- and long-term implications (to which we devote a fuller discussion in a later chapter). Before TR91, the effective tax rate on financial savings was much higher than the effective tax rate on investments in real assets. The fact that the new, more uniform, taxation of capital no longer favours investments in real assets creates conditions for a more efficient long-run allocation of household savings. For the short run, the picture is different. A common opinion, which we share, is that the exceptional recession of the early 1990s has been brought about by a dramatic fall in aggregate demand – a shortfall which can be linked to the changed pattern of household savings. As a result, TR91 has probably deepened the recession, something which we analyze more closely in Chapter 6.

Our third question concerns how the change in indirect taxation has affected *consumption patterns*. Given the assumption that increased indirect taxes are passed on to consumers, it is easy to calculate how the tax reform has affected the relative prices of various goods. Many of the goods which were entirely or partially exempted from VAT – like housing consumption, restaurant and hotel services, and personal transport – became much more expensive. A complicating circumstance, which well illustrates the thesis that no tax reform is forever, is that indirect taxation has been changed many times over since 1991. For example, TR91 implied that the so-called tourist VAT, which includes commercial personal transport and hotel services, was set at 25 per cent. In 1992, the tax rate was lowered to 18 per cent; in January 1993 it was raised to 21 per cent, only to be lowered half a year later to 12 per cent.

One of the markets which has been the subject of intensive political attention through the years is the housing market. As already indicated, housing was affected in many different ways by TR91. The change in indirect taxation meant increased operating and maintenance costs for the entire housing stock. The reduced value of interest deductions implied higher capital costs for owner-occupiers and tenant-owners. And to maintain cost parity between different forms of tenure, interest subsidies for newly constructed rental flats were cut.

In all, the cost of housing increased considerably, and our fourth question is how this influenced the *demand for housing*.

3.1 SAVINGS INCENTIVES BEFORE AND AFTER TR91

TR91 implied far-reaching changes in the taxation of capital income. Tax bases were broadened, and marginal tax rates on personal and corporate income were cut. Before TR91 the progressive income tax schedule applied to all sources of personal income; that is, the tax system adhered to the principle of *global* income taxation; cf. Sørensen (1994). After the reform Sweden adheres to the principle of *dual* income taxation. Although a progressive rate schedule still applies to labour income, all kinds of personal capital income are now taxed at a flat rate of 30 per cent.

Before TR91, most observers agreed that the taxation of capital income had two major shortcomings. First, as the tax system treated the returns on different assets in a nonuniform manner, especially in times of inflation, it was feared that savings were channelled to the wrong kind of investments. Second, the old system permitted a number of straightforward tax arbitrage operations, which undermined the tax base and stimulated borrowing. Let us discuss each issue in turn.

Table 3.1 shows the required real rate of return before tax on a marginal investment in four assets if a household investor is to receive a real rate of return of two per cent after all taxes. We assume that all investments are fully equity financed; that is, we disregard leverage effects. In the pre-reform case we assume that the marginal tax rate,

Table 3.1 Real required rate of return before tax (in per cent) when the real return after tax is two per cent

	Old tax system Inflation (in per cent)			New tax system Inflation (in per cent)		
	0	*5*	*10*	*0*	*5*	*10*
Corporate shares	4.1	9.8	15.0	2.9	4.8	6.8
Own homes	3.7	3.7	4.3	2.9	3.4	3.4
Bank savings	5.0	12.5	20.0	2.9	5.0	7.1
Consumer durables	2.0	2.0	2.0	2.0	2.0	2.0

Source: For a documentation of the underlying cost of capital models, see Södersten (1993).

applying to both labour and capital income, of our household investor is 60 per cent. In the post-reform calculations, we set the marginal tax rate, which now only applies to capital income, to 30 per cent.

The first row, columns 1–3, gives the cost of capital in the *corporate sector* under the old tax system. The figures are based on a conventional cost-of-capital calculation, under the assumptions that the source of finance is 50 per cent new issues and 50 per cent retained earnings, and that the investment is a 'sandwich' of machinery, buildings and inventories. As we consider an household owner, the tax wedge depends on the interaction between the corporate profits tax and the personal tax on dividends and capital gains. At the corporate level, the effective tax rate hinges in a complicated manner on various tax allowances, including accelerated depreciation and allocations to the investment fund system.

Under the old tax system the marginal tax wedge on investments in *owner-occupied housing* depended on the tax on imputed housing income (two per cent of the tax-assessed value of the house was added to the income tax base of the owner), and on the property tax (introduced in 1985), which amounted to 1.4 per cent of one-third of the tax assessed value. Also, real capital gains on housing were taxed upon realization, subject to some minor restrictions on the extent of indexation of the acquisition cost. Households' income from *interest bearing assets* ('bank savings') was added without modification to the tax base. At zero per cent inflation, the real pre-tax interest rate required to yield a 2 per cent real rate of return after tax is then 5 per cent, implying a tax wedge of 3 percentage points.

The inter-asset tax distortions created under the old system seem fairly modest when the inflation rate is low. However, since both the personal and corporate tax codes almost exclusively relied on nominal income concepts, higher inflation radically changes the picture. At an inflation rate of ten per cent, the dispersion of tax wedges is very large. The combination of two digit inflation and nominal interest taxation implies that the required real rate of return on bank savings is 20 per cent, that is, the tax wedge increases to 18 percentage points. The increase in the cost of capital in the corporate sector, which is almost as dramatic, reflects the combination of historic cost depreciation, first-in-first-out inventory valution, and taxation of nominal capital gains. The inflation sensitivity of the marginal tax wedge on owner-occupied housing, due to the incomplete indexation of housing capital gains, is much less pronounced.

In short, the old tax system was extremely sensitive to inflation. As the average inflation rate in the 1980s was eight per cent (as measured by the GDP deflator), there was at least in theory a strong motive for shifting savings from corporate assets and interest-bearing assets to durables and housing. In the Swedish policy debate during the 1980s this possibility caused much concern, and it was feared that the discrimination of household financial savings led to too little corporate investment, and too much investment in housing and durables.[1]

Turning to the new tax system, two main features stand out: lower statutory tax rates, and a broadening of the tax base, particularly on the corporate side. As is seen from the table, TR91 did imply a large step in the direction of levelling the playing field. The inflation sensitivity of the tax system was much reduced, and the difference in the tax treatment of investments in corporate assets and housing seems minor. We may also note that this development occurred in spite of the fact that the new tax system, unlike the old one, is based exclusively on nominal income concepts. Thus, while inflation still distorts the measurement of taxable capital income, the reduced statutory tax rates cushion the marginal incentive effect from higher inflation. The new tax system, in conjunction with the fact that it coincided with a rapid fall in inflation, suggests that households were given a strong incentive to shift from real to financial savings outlets. As we will see below, households seem to have adjusted accordingly.

A second major impetus for tax reform was the multitude of tax avoidance operations available under the old system. While often quite complicated in appearance, many of these operations rested on the simple idea of generating a net taxable income loss by purchasing low-taxed assets with borrowed money, and deducting the interest expenses. The main obstacle in implementing this scheme was the fact that a preferential tax treatment of assets in inelastic supply is capitalized in asset prices. In equilibrium the gain from tax arbitrage tends to be driven to zero. However, art and downtown flats were not the only tax shelters available in the 1980s. Let us consider the case of private pension savings in some detail.

Since the early 1950s Swedish tax law has classified private life insurance policy either as private pension (annuities) plans, or capital insurance (endowment) plans. For our purpose, the former category is the most interesting one, as savings in a private pension plan certainly qualify as a low-taxed asset in quite elastic supply. Contributions to a plan were deductible against the personal income tax up to a certain ceiling, and the resulting pensions were, and still are, taxed as earned income when paid out. Thus, a consumption tax treatment applied. Before TR91 the yearly return on private pension plans was untaxed. After the reform, insurance companies pay a return tax of 15 per cent (that is, a rate well below the 30 per cent rate on personal capital income).

Let us see how savings in a private pension plan interact with private borrowing. At time zero a household investor borrows one krona, and allocates the proceeds to a pension plan. Due to the tax deductibility of pension savings, there is an immediate gain corresponding to m, the marginal tax rate of the investor. We assume that time is continuous. To highlight the scope for tax arbitrage, we disregard risk and assume that the nominal borrowing rate r is the same as the instantaneous nominal return on the pension plan. The tax rate, if any, on the latter return is f. The investor finances all interest costs during the holding period by incurring new debt at the instantaneous rate $r(1 - \tau)$, where τ is the constant tax rate at which interest costs are deductible. At time T our individual receives her pension as a one-shot lump-sum, $e^{r(1-f)T}$, taxable at rate m, and pays back accumulated debt, $e^{r(1-\tau)T}$. After discounting back to time zero at the nominal rate $r(1 - \tau)$, the net present value of this asset *cum* borrowing strategy becomes

$$NPV = (1 - m)\{e^{(\tau - f)rT} - 1\} \tag{3.1}$$

where we assume that m is constant over the investment horizon. In the absence of taxes, it follows readily that the net present value is zero. Thus, tax asymmetries are the only reason for a positive *NPV*. Note also that the size of *NPV* depends crucially on the accumulated net return factor $(\tau - f)rT$; for a given m, *NPV* increases with the difference between τ and f, and with the product of r and the holding period T.

Using equation (3.1) it is easy to provide some illustrative calculations on the size of the tax arbitrage gain before and after TR91. With the tax rules applying in the early 1980s, the return tax on insurance companies was zero ($f = 0$), and interest expenses were deductible at the same rate as the marginal tax rate on earned income ($m = \tau$). As a consequence, individuals with a high marginal tax rate could create a considerable leverage effect. With an interest rate of ten per cent, a holding period of 30 years (which suggests that our hypothetical investor is in her early thirties), and a marginal tax rate of 75 per cent, *NPV* becomes 2.12; that is, the net present value is more than twice as large as the original investment outlay! With a holding period of 15 years, *NPV* becomes 0.52.

After TR91, the top marginal tax rate is 50 per cent, which applies for most white collar workers who work full time. As the uniform rate of tax on personal capital income is 30 per cent ($\tau = 0.3$), the leverage gains are correspondingly reduced. In conjunction with the new tax on private pension funds ($f = 0.15$), this implies that the accumulated net return factor gets much smaller, as do the gains from tax arbitrage. At an interest rate of ten per cent, and a holding period of 30 years, an investor with a 50 per cent marginal tax rate will now make a present value gain of 28 per cent of the investment outlay. When the holding period is 15 years, *NPV* is 0.13.

The narrowing of loopholes in the tax system was, as discussed in greater detail in the previous chapter, not confined to private pension savings. On balance, there is every reason to believe that TR91 did much to reduce the arbitrage sensitivity of the tax system, and to reduce the incentive to inflate balance sheets by purchasing assets with borrowed money. On the behavioural side, we thus expect to see an overall shrinking of households' balance sheets, with smaller stocks of assets and debts.

3.2 THE AGGREGATE CONSUMPTION RESPONSE

As shown in Figure 3.1 the 1980s and early 1990s witnessed dramatic changes in the conventionally measured savings ratio of Swedish households. According to the National Accounts (NA) of Statistics Sweden, the savings rate was fairly stable during the 1970s, hovering around 3 per cent. During the second half of the 1980s, savings decreased substantially, reaching an historical low of minus five per cent in 1988–89. This trend was completely reversed during the early 1990s. Between 1989 and 1992 the savings ratio increased by almost 13 percentage points. Indeed, to find a savings ratio as high as the current one has to go back to the early 1950s!

The dramatic development of the NA savings ratio has led to much speculation in the popular debate. However, before jumping to rash conclusions about the likely causes, we should note that the conventional definition of household savings is incomplete. While it includes direct household financial savings and net investments in owner-occupied housing and holiday homes, it ignores net investments in consumer durables, as well as the contributions to a vast array of retirement plans, administered by the government and various labour market organizations. Figure 3.1 also describes an alternative savings

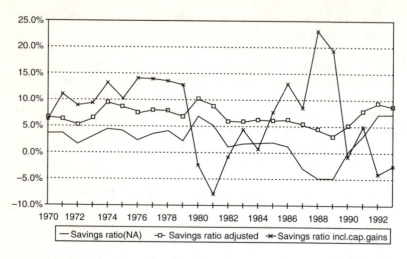

Figure 3.1 The household savings ratio according to three definitions, 1970–93
Source: Agell, Berg and Edin (1995).

series ('adjusted household savings'), where we have added net investments in consumer durables and contributions to retirement plans (supplementary pension schemes) administered by the trade unions and the employers' federations. Clearly, our more broadly defined savings ratio exhibits much less volatility over time. Although the trend reversal in the late 1980s and early 1990s still stands out, the magnitudes involved are much more modest: our extended savings ratio increased by six percentage points between 1989 and 1992.

According to the well-known definition of Haig and Simons, both economic income (the consumption level that is consistent with unchanged real wealth) and savings (the change in real wealth) are measured inclusive of real capital gains on non-human wealth. The third savings rate in the figure ('adjusted household savings including capital gains') is a very close relative of the Haig–Simons savings ratio; basically, we have added accrued real capital gains on owner-occupied housing and shares to both the numerator and denominator of 'adjusted household savings'. The resulting savings ratio obviously has very little in common with our other, more conventional, savings definitions – the simple correlation between the official savings ratio and the one adjusted for capital gains is −0.59.

A basic lesson from this simple definitional exercise is that there are many conceptual problems involved in measuring household savings.

As a consequence, it is not very meaningful to select some arbitrary savings series to examine an issue like the 'interest sensitivity of savings', as the result will depend crucially on the choice of savings concept. To explore how tax incentives affect aggregate behaviour we need a more robust measure of intertemporal adjustment. As we will see, it makes more sense to study household consumption.

Figure 3.2 shows two measures of the development of percentage growth in per capita consumption. The first series is the growth in consumption expenditures, including purchases of consumer durables, and the second is the growth in 'pure' consumption, which is measured as the sum of purchases of non-durables and the imputed consumption value from the stock of durables and owner-occupied housing. Irrespective of the preferred definition, two features stand out. First, the consumption bust in the early 1990s is quite extreme, having no counterpart in the previous postwar period. Second, the consumption bust was preceded by a consumption boom that started in the mid-1980s. The boom to bust cycle is particularly evident for consumption expenditures; the peak in 1986–87 is to a large extent driven by strong growth in purchases of durables.

How can we explain this? A basic observation is that the Swedish experience is far from unique. As discussed by Berg (1994a), consumption has gone through the same cycle in all the Nordic countries

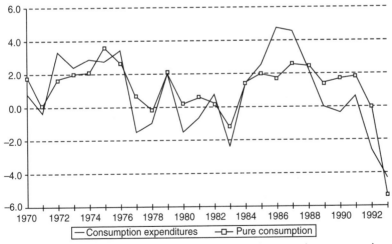

Figure 3.2 Percentage growth in two measures of per capita consumption, 1970–93
Source: Agell, Berg and Edin (1995).

(Denmark, Finland, Norway, Sweden), with a consumption boom of the mid to late 1980s followed by a sharp spending reversal. For those willing to assign a prominent role to tax incentives, a case in point is that the bust period coincides with tax reforms in all four countries. Denmark introduced limits on the deductibility of interest expenses in 1987. The Norwegian tax reform in the same year lowered marginal tax rates, and hence the value of interest deductions. In 1989 Finland also took a moderate step in the direction of reducing various asymmetries in the taxation of capital income.

But invoking tax factors is not the only way of explaining the Nordic experience. Let us briefly review some of the main stylized macroeconomic facts. The strong consumption growth and negative figures for net financial savings during the boom years coincide with the deregulation of financial markets. As noted by many observers, a loosening of borrowing constraints may explain why consumption went up and net financial savings were in the red. It may also help to explain why the trend reversal became so dramatic in the second time period, when adverse macroeconomic shocks hit the Nordic countries (and Finland and Sweden in particular). In an economy with a heavily regulated credit market, consumption can be expected to track disposable income rather closely. However, in a deregulated environment consumers are more likely to respond to changes in expected future income, interest rates, and taxes, implying a more pronounced macroeconomic propagation mechanism.

According to the life cycle/permanent income model of consumption, capitalization effects in asset markets, whether due to deregulation or something else, ought to affect consumption. And the boom years were indeed associated with an increase in house prices in all the Nordic countries, and the bust period with decreasing prices. However, correlation is not the same as causation. In a structural macromodel we would expect asset prices to be determined jointly with consumption. In an attempt to deal with this endogeneity problem, Koskela and Virén (1992) examined the cross-correlation between savings and house prices in the Nordic countries, and found some evidence that house prices led rather than lagged the household savings ratio. As house prices can be expected to depend on real after-tax interest rates, this suggests that tax changes can affect consumption via revaluations in asset markets.

Capital gains on housing are not the only volatile time series in recent years. In all Nordic countries, the consumption bust was accompanied by a dramatic increase in unemployment. The mirror images of this increase are large budget deficits of the central governments (except in Norway). If we temporarily disregard the possibility of reverse causation, we may ask how unemployment and deficits can affect consumption.

A first possibility focuses on the effects on the expected growth of future income. Higher unemployment may induce consumers to make a downward revision of their forecasts of future labour income. A similar effect occurs if consumers expect that the government will deal with a deficit primarily by raising future and potentially very distortionary taxes, rather than cutting spending.[2] In either case, permanent income, and hence consumption, will decrease. Incidentally, a permanent income argument may also go some way towards explaining the consumption boom of the 1980s. If, in the mid-1980s, Swedish households increased their expectations of future income (perhaps because of falling unemployment and a rapid consolidation of the government's balance sheet), a consumption 'boom' accompanied by increased borrowing would be the natural outcome. Thus, pointing to the effects of financial deregulation is not the only way of interpreting aggregate consumption data.[3]

The second possibility, which has been much emphasized in Swedish policy debate, is that unemployment and deficits may slow consumption growth by inducing more precautionary savings. In the case of unemployment, it is not very hard to argue that a sharp increase in aggregate joblessness may increase the uncertainty about future income prospects. In the case of deficits, the key observation is that the Swedish welfare state provides social insurance against a great number of human capital related risks. In a situation where the budget deficit follows a seemingly unsustainable path, consumers may come to the conclusion that the government will be less able to provide income protection in the future. As households respond by building up their own savings buffer, consumption growth decreases, or becomes negative.

Sorting out these alternative explanations of consumption behaviour is bound to be hard. Figure 3.3 plots the development of consumption growth along with housing capital gains, unemployment and net government lending. Most of the correlation stems from observations made since the early 1980s. In the 1970–81 subperiod the correlation between consumption growth and unemployment is −0.08; in the 1982–93 period the same correlation is −0.71! Our correlations also suggest that some of our prospective explanatory variables are subject to a rather severe multicollinearity problem. In the most recent

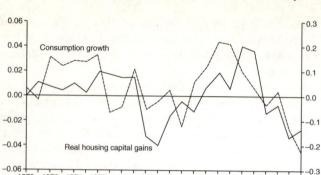

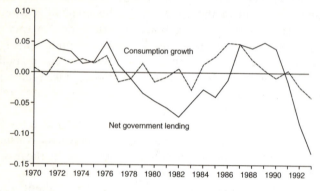

Figure 3.3   Consumption growth, real capital gains on housing, unemployment, and government net lending to GDP, 1970–93

Note: Consumption growth is the per capita growth in consumption expenditures. Real
capital gains on housing is the inflation adjusted kronor-value of accrued capital gains as
a fraction of disposable income. Unemployment is the official measure of open unemployment. Government net lending includes the consolidated public sector.
Source: Agell, Berg and Edin (1995).

subperiod the correlation between government net lending and unemployment is −0.86, while the correlation between government net lending and housing capital gains is 0.98! In short, the macroeconomic instability in recent years implies that it is hard to find much independent variation in many of the variables that may explain consumption.

While it might be exceedingly hard to sort out cause and effect during the Swedish consumption bust, our conclusion is nevertheless that TR91 most likely played a minor role. TR91 may have had a negative impact on consumption via three channels: (i) intertemporal substitution in response to an increase in the real after-tax interest rate; (ii) a downward revision of expected labour income; and (iii) wealth effects due to capital losses in asset markets, in particular in the market for own homes. Of these channels, only (iii) seems to hold some promise.

With a large intertemporal elasticity of substitution, periods of high expected interest rates should coincide with rapid consumption growth, and periods of low interest rates with stagnant consumption. However, although there are reasons to be cautious about the information that can be drawn from representative agent models and aggregate data, empirical studies in Sweden and elsewhere suggest that the intertemporal elasticity of substitution is close to zero.[4] Moreover, some basic aspects of the data are hard to reconcile with a story of intertemporal substitution. Between 1986–89, when consumption growth was brisk, the average real after-tax interest rate was negative. Between 1991–93, when consumption growth was negative, the average real after-tax interest rate was exceptionally high. If intertemporal substitution is to characterize the data, consumption growth ought to have followed the opposite pattern.[5]

When households make a downward revision of their forecasts of labour income, consumption ought to fall. However, while there are good reasons to believe that permanent labour income fell during the Swedish consumption bust, TR91 is most likely a less important factor.[6] Indeed, most assessments of the efficiency effects of TR91 – discussed in Chapter 8 – suggest that it lowered excess burdens due to tax wedges in the labour market. If anything, this effect ought to increase permanent income and consumption.

Capitalization effects in asset markets, whether due to TR91 or some other factor, may certainly affect consumption. The consumption boom of the late 1980s was associated with an increase in real estate prices, and the bust period with decreasing prices. Of course, correlation is not the same as causation. But recent macroeconometric work indicates that variables like house prices and windfalls in the housing market seem to have potency in explaining aggregate Swedish consumption behaviour; see Agell, Berg and Edin (1995), and Berg and Bergström (1995). Moreover, TR91 led to a dramatic increase in the rental cost of housing, and contributed to the sharp fall in house prices after 1991. Although these housing market adjustments are unlikely to explain a very large part of the consumption bust, they seem like the most important mechanism for an adverse consumption response to TR91.

What can explain the sharp decline in private consumption? There are indications that the nature of the Swedish macroeconomic consumption function has changed in the 1990s. Consumption functions estimated on data up until the end of the 1980s are unable to track the changes of recent years – in particular, there are large negative residuals for 1992–93; see further Agell, Berg and Edin (1995) and Giavazzi and Pagano (1996). The findings of Barot (1995) are well in line with the idea that the dramatic rise in unemployment is a potentially very important factor.[7] On the other hand, when they control for reverse causation Agell *et al.* find no clear evidence for an independent influence from unemployment and the fiscal position of the government.

Should the negative residuals be blamed on TR91? As already indicated, we believe that the answer is no. The regressions discussed above do account for some of the more plausible links between tax structure and consumption, including the real interest rate after tax and windfalls in the housing market. We are left with the conclusion that there is something else going on. Either there is some important omitted variable, or consumption behaviour has changed in a more profound way during the economic depression of the 1990s.

3.3   THE PORTFOLIO RESPONSE

One lesson from the previous section is that it is hard to make the case that TR91 has been a very important factor behind the Swedish consumption bust. Matters look different when we turn to household savings composition. Figure 3.4 shows the development since 1970 of two components of the adjusted savings ratio of Figure 3.1, net lending and the sum of new investments in homes and consumer durables. During the 1970s the main part of savings was invested in non-financial assets like housing and durables. In the beginning of the 1990s the situation was quite the opposite, as households shifted from non-financial to financial assets.

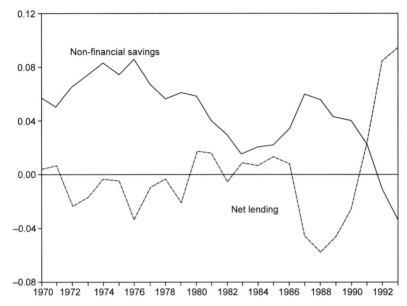

Figure 3.4   Savings ratios for net lending and non-financial savings, 1970–93
Source: Agell, Berg and Edin (1995).

According to our discussion in section 3.1 TR91 implied a large change in the relative tax treatment of financial and non-financial savings, primarily because of a reduction in the effective tax rates on financial savings. But TR91 also had important consequences for the treatment of negative financial savings, that is, borrowing. In Sweden net interest expenses remained fully deductible against the marginal tax rate until 1982. As the tax system was highly progressive with a top marginal tax of around 80 per cent, the tax authorities in effect paid the greater part of the nominal interest cost for many households. The tax reform of 1983–85 reduced the maximum value of interest deductions to 50 per cent, and a further change in 1989 lowered the cap to 47 per cent. TR91 brought the cap in line with the new flat tax rate of 30 per cent on capital income. The consequences for real borrowing costs in times of inflation are well known, and Table 3.2 presents some simple calculations on the real after-tax borrowing rate for three separate years – 1980, 1989 and 1991. The nominal borrowing rates are the actual averages for the three years, the inflation rates are the actual ones over the coming year, and the marginal tax rates are 62, 47 and 30 per cent, respectively. The result is astounding! The real cost of borrowing increased by almost 15 percentage points between 1980 and 1991.

Table 3.2   Real interest rate, after tax for selected years

	1980	1989	1991
1. Interest rate	14.0	14.0	14.0
2. Tax effect	8.7	6.6	4.2
3. Interest rate after tax $(1 - 2)$	5.3	7.4	9.8
4. Inflation rate for coming year	12.3	10.2	2.6
5. Real rate of interest, after tax $(3 - 4)$	−7.0	−2.8	7.2

If households ever respond to economic incentives, we would certainly expect to see some time-series correlation between the net lending ratio and measures of relative returns and tax treatment. The amount of Swedish empirical research on the relation between relative returns and the composition of aggregate savings is relatively modest. Palmer (1984) estimated an asset demand system using annual data for the 1970–82 period. His results suggest that relative returns are important, but the estimated effects are small throughout. For our purposes, Berg (1988) is of greater relevance. Berg used time-series data for the 1954–86 period, and he disaggregated household wealth into one financial and two real (property, consumer durables) entries. After controlling for income growth and a variable designed to capture the influence of credit availability, Berg found that relative after-tax returns had a marked effect on household asset composition. A simulation of the estimated model shows how an increase in the relative return on financial assets along the lines of TR91 can lead to a considerable shift from real to financial savings, even though it may take a long time.

The observations added since 1986 do not seem to warrant a revision of this conclusion. Agell, Berg and Edin (1995) estimate a portfolio model for the household net lending ratio for the 1950–93 period. The relative return measure used in this study is the difference between the real after-tax lending rate and a proxy variable for the expected real price increase on own homes. This test of a simple model gives a strong indication of the existence of an aggregate portfolio response to changes in relative returns. The greater part of the observed increase in the financial savings ratio between 1986 and 1993 can be explained – in a statistical sense – by a higher relative return on financial savings. Another observation is that there is no sign of instability in the estimated equations during the turbulent early years of the 1990s, which was not true for the consumption functions referred to in the previous section.

Although we believe that TR91 has contributed to the observed shifts between important portfolio aggregates, it is difficult to be more precise about the magnitudes. Much of the shift from real to financial assets would have taken place even in the absence of TR91. The macroeconomic conditions during the early 1990s served to increase the relative return on financial savings. These conditions include generally high real interest rates (up until November 1992 as a direct result of the attempt by the Riksbank to defend the fixed exchange rate) and a rapid reduction in the inflation rate after 1991. TR91 contributed to the increase in the return on financial savings, but it also implied a lower return on real savings (including net investments in housing). When we take these effects into account, the results of Agell *et al.* suggest that between three and four percentage points of the increase in the household net lending ratio can be attributed to TR91. Since the net lending ratio increased by slightly more than 13 percentage points between 1989 and 1992, this suggests that between one-quarter and one-third of the increase in the net lending ratio can be attributed to TR91.

The new savings pattern has both short- and long-term ramifications. In the long run, there are better prospects for an efficient allocation of capital, since the preferential tax treatment of investments in durables and housing has been reduced to a considerable extent. In the short run, there is a different story. Each krona which the household sector shifts from real investments in housing and consumer durables to financial saving means that household expenditures will be reduced to a corresponding extent. In normal times, this need not affect aggregate demand – the household sector reduces its purchases, but since at the same time it increases its lending, investment spending can increase in other sectors. In a deep recession, however, with low capacity utilization in all sectors, the picture is a different one. An extra krona saved in the household sector need not logically lead to a compensatory increase in demand elsewhere. Instead, as is discussed in Chapter 6, there will be a net fall in demand which deepens the recession.

Our analysis would not be complete without an account of the development at the micro-level. Previous work suggested that the old tax system created strong tax clientele effects, since individuals tended to specialize in assets according to their marginal income tax rate; see Agell and Edin (1989, 1990).[8] As TR91 implied that all taxpayers now face the same flat tax rate on capital income, the tax clientele effects ought to disappear in the post-reform years. In the process of

eliminating various tax shelters, one would also expect to see dispro-
portionate portfolio adjustments of individuals with high marginal tax
rates under the old system.

However, the new results reported in Agell, Berg and Edin (1995)
do not support these conjectures. After comparing a succession of
cross-sections on the asset holdings of individual households, their
conclusion is that much of the tax clientele effects gradually dissolved
during the late 1980s; that is, well *before* TR91. A potential explanation
is that the connection between the marginal tax rate, which is the
explanatory variable in the microeconometric studies, and the effective
tax rate on asset income had become weaker as the result of tax reform
efforts preceding TR91. A good example of this is the limitation on
interest deductions referred to above. The cap on interest deductions
introduced in 1985, and sharpened in 1989, reduced the differences
among households in the cost of borrowing, and thereby the scope for
tax clientele effects in debt.

If these new results are true, TR91 should in fact affect the portfolio
choice of different households in a fairly uniform manner. In particular, the adjustments of households with high pre-reform marginal tax
rates should not be significantly different from the adjustments of
households with low pre-reform marginal tax rates. And, in fact, this
pattern is exactly what can be seen in the data. The panel estimates
reported in Agell *et al.* – results that derive from a panel of taxpayers
observed immediately before and after TR91 – suggest that households which received a large reduction in their marginal tax rates did
not change their portfolios in a way that was very different from
households which were less affected. In terms of portfolio allocation,
TR91 seems to have the interpretation of a general change in the
macroeconomic environment, rather than a specific shock affecting
particular households.

3.4   CONSUMPTION PATTERNS

Increased indirect taxation was intended to provide an important
contribution to the financing of TR91. Previously, just over 40 per
cent of total household consumption was entirely or partially exempted
from VAT. Although TR91 broadened the tax base, important exceptions still remained, such as health and dental care, child care, education, rents, financial services and consumption of various 'cultural
services'. But TR91 also included a few 'green' elements, and some

Table 3.3   Theoretical relative price increase due to TR91 for previously tax-exempt goods and services

Commodity group	Share of household consumption in 1989 (in per cent)	Price increase (in per cent)
Housing consumption	23.7	9.7
Operating costs, vehicles	3.9	26.0
Hairdresser, beauty care	0.6	8.2
Recreational activities	4.1	4.1
Personal transport	2.0	18.0
Postal, telecommunications	1.6	18.3
Hotel, restaurant	4.5	9.4
Total, entirely or partially tax exempt goods	40.4	

Source: Annex 1 to the *National Accounts 1980–1993* (N 10 SM 9401); Flood and Klevmarken (1990).

selective taxes were introduced (or raised) on the environmentally harmful consumption of fuel and energy (petrol tax, sulphur dioxide tax and carbon dioxide tax).

How has the new indirect taxation affected the relative prices of different goods and services, and household consumption patterns? In Table 3.3 we present the theoretically expected price increase, due to changes in indirect taxes in 1990–91, for goods and services which used to be partially or entirely tax exempt. These theoretical price effects are based on the assumption that all indirect taxes are passed on in full to consumers.[9] Also, they include direct as well as indirect effects. The direct effect refers to the price increase for the consumer when VAT is levied on a product. The indirect effect refers to the price effect which arises when VAT is levied on an intermediate input which is used in a certain VAT-exempted area. One example of the latter is the rent increase which took place when VAT was levied on water, sewage and refuse collection.

For certain commodities, TR91 implied considerable price increases. Operating costs for vehicles increased by 26 per cent, mainly due to higher petrol prices. Big price increases also hit consumers of postal and telecommunications services, as well as the consumption of personal transport (bus, train, and so on), and hotel and restaurant services. In 1990, unreduced VAT was levied on hotel and restaurant services, and in 1991 telecommunications services and personal transport paid full VAT. Also, the consumption of housing services (including heating and electricity costs), which is very important in terms of volume, was affected in a number of ways. VAT was levied on water, sewage, refuse collection, and energy in 1990, and in 1991 the same thing happened to property maintenance, district heating and construction.

Figures 3.5 and 3.6 plot the trends for some of the commodity categories in Table 3.3. In Figure 3.5, we show how housing consumption has changed as a share of total household consumption according to the National Accounts. The increase is dramatic – from a consumption share of little more than 24 per cent in 1988 to just over 32 per cent in 1994. This shift in consumption patterns reflects a relative price increase: Housing has become considerably more expensive, but the consumption of housing services cannot be changed very much in the short run. We also see that housing costs have increased continually since 1990. A big part of the increase coincides with TR91, but the increase during the following years – which among other things reflects the effect of a reduction in interest subsidies to the housing sector – is about as big.

Operating costs for vehicles were subject to especially large tax hikes. As is shown in Figure 3.6, the consumption share for this

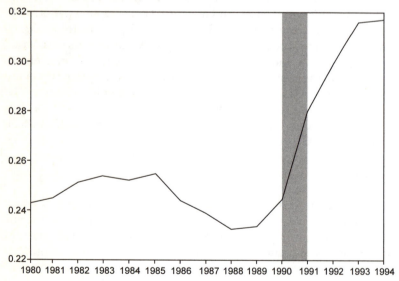

Figure 3.5   Consumption share for housing (including heating and electricity), 1980–94
Source: National Accounts.

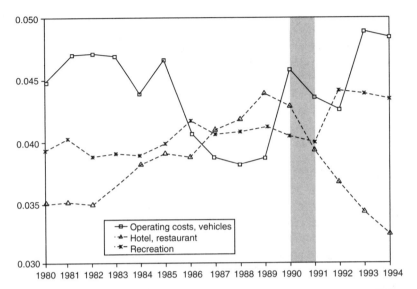

Figure 3.6 Consumption share for some previously tax-exempt commodities
Source: National Accounts.

group increased substantially in 1990 when the tax on petrol was raised, which suggests that demand for this particular good is fairly price inelastic. The volume effects regarding demand for hotel and restaurant services have been far greater. The fall in the share of consumption from 4.5 per cent in 1989 to 3.3 per cent in 1994 reflects a continuing decrease in terms of volume. It is more difficult to distinguish very obvious volume adjustments when it comes to the remaining commodity groups of Table 3.3. One example of this is the demand for various recreational activities (leisure, entertainment and culture). As we can see, the share of consumption for this group increased in 1992 (partly because it became more expensive to go to the cinema), but the volume adjustments were small.

Is it possible to be a bit more precise than this? Important obstacles in assessing how consumers responded to TR91 is the sharp fall in general consumption at the beginning of the 1990s, and the ongoing changes in the tax system, which makes it difficult to isolate the effects of TR91. Consumption patterns have changed a lot in recent years, but so has several other variables.

Hultkrantz (1995) is an interesting attempt to deal with these inference problems. He examines how TR91 has affected domestic and outbound recreational travel. Recreational travel, like other forms of tourism, belong to those commodities which ought to be affected most by a relative price change, since there are close substitutes in the form of home production. If it becomes more expensive to travel or to go to a restaurant, individuals can instead choose to stay at home and watch television, or fix a good dinner in their own kitchen. Hultkrantz uses data from a survey which contains information about the recreational travel patterns of a random sample of 2000 individuals. The database runs from January 1989 to October 1993, a period which contained several tax changes. The econometric analysis of Hultkrantz indicates that TR91 reduced household spending on leisure travel by 15 per cent. However, the reduction was not evenly distributed among different types of travel. Trips abroad and visits to summer cottages increased, while long-distance domestic travel decreased considerably.

All in all, there are commodity groups for which TR91 has created relatively large negative demand effects. This raises two bigger questions. First, the principle of uniform commodity taxation filled an important norm-giving function for the construction of TR91. It also served to make tax arbitrage more difficult. However, from the perspective of optimal taxation, it is easy to imagine situations where certain commodity groups ought to be taxed at a lower rate. An example is the tax on services which are close substitutes for home production. The time a household spends making food, caring for children and making repairs is not taxed. If the household perceives the purchase of corresponding services on the market as a close alternative, efficiency reasons suggest that these market activities should be taxed at a lower rate; see Frederiksen *et al.* (1995) for further discussion.

Second, a large share of the revenue loss from lower marginal tax rates on earned income was to be recovered from increased commodity taxes. With some minor exceptions, however, the revenue projections were based on the assumption that consumption pattern would stay the same. In particular, one assumed that households would continue to consume as much as before of those commodity groups that used to be partially or entirely tax exempt. Since the demand for these commodities has most likely decreased as a result of TR91, the revenue projections tended to exaggerate tax revenue. We will scrutinize the financing of TR91 more closely in Chapter 6.

3.5 HOUSING DEMAND[10]

That TR91 implied increased housing costs should come as no surprise. One of the purposes of TR91 was to reduce both visible and invisible housing subsidies. Examples of visible subsidies are government interest subsidies, and municipal housing allowances. Examples of invisible subsidies are the tax expenditures resulting from the fact that housing consumption and savings in own homes used to be taxed in a more favourably way than other kinds of consumption and saving. These tax expenditures had to do with both direct and indirect taxation of housing.[11]

As we discussed in the previous section, many of the goods and services which are part of housing consumption used to be tax exempt, a tax expenditure which benefited the entire stock of housing. The second tax expenditure was linked to owner-occupancy. A uniform taxation of capital assumes that the returns on different assets are taxed at the same rate. Regarding owner-occupancy, the returns accrue both in the form of a flow of housing services, and in the form of real price appreciation. The tax advantage stemmed from the fact that only a smaller part of this return was taxed, while the nominal interest cost on the debt incurred to finance the house was deductible. In times of rising property prices and high inflation, such as the second half of the 1970s, this meant that in practice many individuals were paid to live in their own homes.

A convenient way of formalizing the impact of taxation is to calculate the user cost; that is, the implicit rent which an owner-occupier must have in order to rent out a unit of his or her property capital on market terms. This rent measures the marginal cost of increasing owner-occupancy by one krona, and it includes both the owner's capital cost, tax payments, and operating and maintenance costs. In formal terms we have a user cost, uc, defined as:

$$uc = r(1 - m) + \tau + \delta + d - \pi \tag{3.2}$$

where r is the nominal interest rate, m is the owner's marginal tax rate, τ is the tax on imputed housing income, δ is the cost of repairs and maintenance required to maintain constant quality, d is the current operating cost for heating, water and sewage, and π is the expected nominal capital gain. In equation (3.2) uc is defined as a share of an investment which is worth one Swedish krona, that is, the investment refers to the product of real house price and invested quantity.[12] If we rather choose to express *uc* as a share of an investment in a *physical housing unit*, the right-hand side must be multiplied by the house price.

TR91 affected the user cost in three different ways. The first term on the right-hand side represents the nominal after-tax cost of capital. If the house is financed by equity, it has the interpretation of an opportunity cost – if the owner had rather invested his capital in a bank he would have received the after-tax return $r(1-m)$. When the house is financed by borrowed capital, $r(1-m)$ is a direct expense, and m is the tax rate against which the household can claim an interest deduction. At the end of the 1970s, the tax system was symmetrical in its treatment of equity and loans. For an owner-occupier with a 70 per cent marginal tax rate, the nominal capital cost was $r(1-0.7)$, regardless of the source of financing. The restriction on the value of interest deductions to a maximum of 50 per cent, implemented in 1983–85, entailed increased costs of borrowing for most households. Households which relied on equity instead were only affected to the extent that they received a lower marginal tax rate on their bank savings. TR91 restored symmetry to the tax treatment of equity and loans. Regardless of the choice of financing, the nominal capital cost was $r(1-0.3)$. With a nominal interest rate of ten per cent, and for an individual with a marginal tax rate of 70 per cent in 1979, the nominal capital cost increased from 3 to 7 per cent – that is, an increase of no less than 133 per cent!

The second tax effect, reflected in the parameter τ, stems from the fact that owner-occupiers are taxed for the implicit user value of the home. According to the tax rules of the 1970s and 1980s, a certain fraction of the tax assessed value of the house constituted imputed housing income, taxable at the same progressive rate as earned income. For most properties the imputation rate was two per cent, but properties with a high tax assessed value could have an imputation rate of up to eight per cent. In terms of the notation of equation (3.2), the normal case was that $\tau = 0.02\lambda m$, where λ is the tax assessed value as a share of market value. In theory, the tax-assessed value should correspond to 75 per cent of market value, but calculations in Englund *et al.* (1995) indicate that λ has been closer to 50 per cent since the beginning of the 1980s. TR91 did away with the imputation system, and replaced it with a property tax, set at 1.5 per cent of the tax assessed value. After TR91, we thus have that $\tau = 0.015\lambda$. If we compare the expressions for the old imputation tax and the new property tax, it is easy to see that taxes have increased for all households which used to have a marginal tax rate lower than 75 per cent.

The third tax effect is connected with that part of *uc* which depends on current operating costs, *d*. If we roughly assume that $d = 0.02$ before TR91, and that 90 per cent of current operating cost represents commodities previously exempted from VAT, it is easy to calculate how the changes in indirect taxes affected *uc*. With a VAT rate of 25 per cent, TR91 implied that $d = 0.02(0.1 + 0.9(1 + 0.25))$, that is, $d = 0.0245$.

It is now easy to describe how the tax changes of the most recent decades have affected user costs. In Table 3.4 we present the user cost for owner-occupied housing according to the tax rules which applied on three occasions, 1981, 1985 and 1991. Since user cost depends on the marginal tax rate of the owner-occupier, we present calculations for two types of households: the average senior white-collar worker and the average blue-collar worker. In order to isolate the effects of the tax system, we also assume, somewhat unrealistically, that the nominal interest rate and expected nominal price increase of housing is the same for all three years; we set $r = 0.1$ and $\pi = 0.07$ (the average annual nominal price increase of single family houses during the 1980s was 7.5 per cent). All changes in user costs between these years therefore only reflect changes in the tax treatment of financial capital costs, imputed housing returns and operating costs.

Not surprisingly, we see that for the steeply progressive tax system of 1981 the user cost was considerably *lower* for the senior white-collar worker than for the average blue-collar worker. The restrictions on the deductibility of interest expenses implemented between 1983 and 1985 changed the picture. Since the senior white-collar worker felt the effect of these restrictions, and since he also paid a higher tax on imputed housing income, his user cost in case of borrowing was higher than that

Table 3.4 Real user cost for owner-occupied housing, 1981, 1985 and 1991

	1981	*1985*	*1991*
Senior white-collar worker:			
Loan	0.028	0.060	0.082
Equity	0.028	0.034	0.082
Blue-collar worker:			
Loan	0.045	0.057	0.082
Equity	0.045	0.057	0.082

Notes: We assume throughout that $r = 0.1$, $\delta = 0.05$, $\pi = 0.07$ and that the tax assessed value is 50 per cent of the market value. The marginal tax rates for 1981 and 1985 are taken from Du Rietz (1994).

of the blue-collar worker. The situation was still the opposite for equity-financing, since the alternative return of the white-collar worker was taxed at a higher marginal tax rate. TR91, with its uniform and proportional capital tax, has levelled off the differences in user costs between households and financing alternatives.

All in all, the tax changes since 1981 have meant noticeably higher user costs for owner-occupied housing. Over the entire 1981–91 period, user costs have increased the most for those households which had the highest marginal tax rate at the beginning of the period. For the senior white-collar worker, user cost has tripled; for the blue-collar worker it has almost doubled. If we limit ourselves to the 1985–91 period, and assume that investment in single family homes was financed through borrowing, user costs increased by 37 per cent (from 0.060 to 0.082) for the senior white-collar worker and by 44 per cent for the blue-collar worker (from 0.057 to 0.082).

Previous Swedish studies indicate that the demand for owner-occupied housing is quite responsive to changes in user costs and taxes. Englund and Persson (1982) use a simulation model to study how the increased tax progression during the 1970s affected housing demand and housing prices. Since during this period the marginal tax rate increased for a vast majority of households, the cost of financing an investment in housing went down. Those households who were homeowners initially tended to demand larger living space, and households who lived in rental flats were given incentives to enter the market for one-family homes. According to the simulations, this may explain an increase in the demand for owner-occupied housing of about 30 per cent. In the short run, with a given housing stock, there is a price – rather than volume – adjustment. According to Englund and Persson (1982), the major part of the increase in the real price of owner-occupied housing during the 1970s can be attributed to the sharp rise in tax progression.

There are also some microeconometric studies on Swedish housing demand; see Brownstone *et al.* (1985, 1988), and Brownstone and Englund (1991). Of special interest in this context are the results reported by Brownstone *et al.* (1985). The authors use a demand system, estimated on data from 1978–79, to study how tax changes between 1983 and 1985 affected housing demand. As we showed in Table 3.4, these tax changes meant that user costs increased substantially for households with a high marginal tax rate. The econometric results suggest that changes in tax structure may explain a drop in the demand for own homes by around 15 per cent. Another interesting result, which is entirely in line with our calculations in Table 3.4, is that the fall in demand appeared to be especially pronounced for larger single-family dwellings, which were owned mainly by households with large incomes and high marginal taxes. The demand for large single-family houses was estimated to decrease by more than 50 per cent, at the same time as the demand for small houses actually increased. Another, somewhat surprising, conclusion is that the share of home-owners was estimated to have increased, the reason being that lower marginal tax rates created positive income effects for many households who lived in rental flats initially.

What, then, can we say about the effects of TR91? A first observation is that, unlike the case of the 1983–85 tax reform, there is no reason to believe that there is any great difference in the way user costs have changed for different types of households. Housing costs have increased in a similar manner for households in most income deciles (see Englund *et al.* (1995) for a systematic treatment). As a result of tax changes between 1989 and 1991, user costs increased by between two and three percentage points for most owner-occupiers who chose to finance their homes by borrowing. According to calculations in Englund *et al.* (1995), the average increase in user cost among homeowners was 24 per cent. Since such figures cannot claim to be very exact, it seems reasonable to calculate on an interval of 20–30 per cent.

To translate this percentage increase into a corresponding percentage demand effect, we need information about the price elasticity of the demand for owner-occupied housing. If the (uncompensated) demand elasticity was unitary, the demand for own homes would decrease just as much as user costs increased; that is, TR91 should lead to a 20 to 30 per cent drop in demand. There are two reasons why we feel that this prediction is an exaggerated one. First, it ignores the fact that the tax hikes on housing made possible a reduction of other taxes. Given the assumption that TR91 was fully financed (which, as we shall see in Chapter 6, is a qualified truth), the average homeowner received as much in tax reductions from other places. These positive income effects tend to soften the drop in demand. If we make a rough adjustment of our prediction, our conclusion is that the decrease in demand should be closer to 20 than 30 per cent.

Second, TR91 affected housing demand on two margins, the discrete and the conditional one. The discrete margin has to do with how TR91 affected the choice between living in a house of one's own and a rental flat. The conditional margin has to do with the effects on housing demand, given the assumption that tenure status remains unchanged. Our unitary demand elasticity reflects the net outcome of these decisions. It captures the effect on the demand for own homes (the number of owners of single-family homes multiplied by average demand) due to increased user costs for owner-occupied housing, given unchanged rents in the rental market. Since this is the same as saying that it became relatively cheaper to rent, part of our projected fall in demand is due quite simply to the fact that the number of homeowners decreases: that is, the discrete choice of tenure matters for the total effect.

In reality, however, we know that TR91 also made it more expensive to live in a rental flat. Rental flats were affected by the change in indirect taxation, property taxes on rental property increased and interest subsidies to newly produced rental units decreased. Let us therefore assume that the cost of housing increased just as much for homeowners as for households living in rental flats. Given this assumption, there is no reason to suppose that TR91 had a very important effect on tenure choice. As a first approximation, we ought to study the response of the conditional demand for owner-occupied housing. How was housing demand affected for households who were homeowners both before and after TR91?

Thus, to translate the user-cost effect of TR91 into a corresponding demand effect, we need information about the *conditional* elasticity of housing demand. The microeconometric study of Brownstone *et al.* (1988), which like Brownstone *et al.* (1985) uses data from the late 1970s, suggests that the conditional demand elasticity is close to one, that is, there is a fairly substantial responsiveness. However, the new results presented in Englund *et al.* (1995), based on data from the mid-1980s, indicate that the conditional demand is far from price-sensitive; the conditional demand elasticity falls in an interval between 0.25 and 0.35. Which of these elasticities should we believe in? The econometric studies use different databases, and they are based on observations from different years. On the whole, we still believe that there are grounds for the assumption that conditional demand is relatively price inelastic.

If we, as a compromise, settle for a conditional demand elasticity of 0.5, and make a correction for the income effect, we find that TR91 may have decreased demand for owner-occupied housing by around 10 per cent. When we allow for the fact that TR91 was of no direct consequence for tenure choice, the fall in demand for own homes turns out to be half as large as our initial prediction. But even if

TR91 succeeded in maintaining cost parity between owner-occupied housing and rental housing, the average unit size is smaller in rental dwellings than in single-family houses. Since the higher relative price of housing implies that the average household, regardless of tenure status, will demand a smaller unit than before, and since it is costly to subdivide single-family houses into smaller units, this size effect tends to tilt housing demand towards rental accommodations: Despite the tenure-neutral impact of TR91, the share of homeowners should diminish.

Therefore, our overall conclusion is that TR91 has decreased demand for owner-occupied housing by more than ten per cent. A probable interval for the demand response, when we also account for the size effect, is a fall in the demand for owner-occupied housing of 10–20 per cent, where the former figure is consistent with a constant share of homeowners, and the latter assumes that the share of home-owners decreases by four percentage points.[13]

In the long run, we can translate this decrease in demand into a quantity adjustment of the same order. In the short run, with a given housing stock, it is the real price of owner-occupied homes that adjusts. How much will prices fall? The answer depends crucially on household expectations of future prices. If households have *static expectations*, in the sense that they do not realize that prices have a tendency to revert towards their long-run levels when the housing stock shrinks, the initial fall in prices will be large. To restore instantaneous equilibrium in the market, real house prices must decrease in direct proportion to the increase in user costs. Since user costs have increased by 20–30 per cent, real prices should decrease by just as much.

If households have forward-looking, or *rational*, expectations, they realize that the initially low price level cannot persist. Since the lower price reduces the incentive for new construction, the stock of single-family homes will decrease over time. When the supply of houses has adjusted to the decrease in demand in the long run, the price of single-family homes will return to the level where the construction industry once again finds it profitable to maintain old buildings and produce new ones. The tendency of prices to gradually recover means, therefore, that a rational household will find it profitable to enter the property market if the immediate capitalization effect is too great. The extent of this counteracting effect depends primarily on the speed of the supply response.

The intuition behind this process has been formalized in a widely quoted paper by Poterba (1984), and a corresponding model has been adapted to Swedish conditions by Åsberg and Åsbrink (1994). Under plausible assumptions about the relevant demand and supply elasticities, their simulations seem to suggest – as did those of Poterba – that the immediate capitalization effect when there is perfect foresight is about half as great as that when there are static expectations. If we assume, somewhat boldly, that the market for single-family homes is dominated by rational households who understand the long-term price dynamics, we are led to conclude that the real price of owner-occupied homes should have fallen by 10–15 per cent as a result of TR91.

Up until now, our discussion has been of an *ex ante* nature. We have tried to find out what effects TR91 *ought to have had*, given our knowledge about historical demand patterns and calculations of user costs for owner-occupied housing. On the other hand, we have not tried to evaluate the effects of TR91 in an *ex post* sense. In Figures 3.7 and 3.8, however, we give two indications. In Figure 3.7, we show the development of the real price of single-family homes. Obviously, there is a cyclical pattern, with large price increases during the 1970s and late 1980s, and dramatic price falls during the first half of the 1980s and the beginning of the 1990s. These price trends track the pattern for user costs relatively well. The price increase during

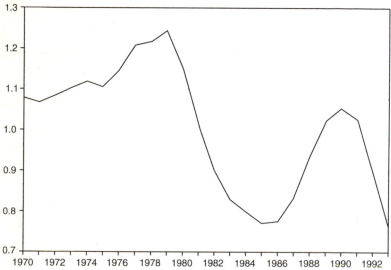

Figure 3.7   Real price of single-family homes, 1970–93 (Index = 1.0, 1981)
Source: Statistics Sweden.

the 1970s coincided with increased tax progression, and the large drop in real prices between 1980 and 1985 coincided with the sharp increase in user costs for households with large incomes and high marginal tax rates. Between 1985 and 1990, when house prices increased, user costs decreased, and the fall in prices after 1991 coincided with TR91, high real interest rates and an announced lowering of government interest subsidies. According to our assessment, TR91 ought to have caused a fall in real house prices of 10–15 per cent. As real prices fell by about 28 per cent between 1990 and 1993, our analysis suggests that about half of the total decline is due to TR91, and that other policy changes and the severe macroeconomic disruptions of the early 1990s are responsible for the other half.

In Figure 3.8 we show the trend for the number of units commenced in single-family homes, that is, a measure of construction activity. We see that the number of units commenced follow the same pattern as that of the real price of single-family homes. During the early 1970s, about 40 000 units were started per year, and during the first half of the 1980s, construction starts were down by more than half. During the second half of the 1980s, a noticeable recovery took place, which however was followed by a more marked decline after 1990. Especially noticeable is the exceptional decrease in the number of units com-

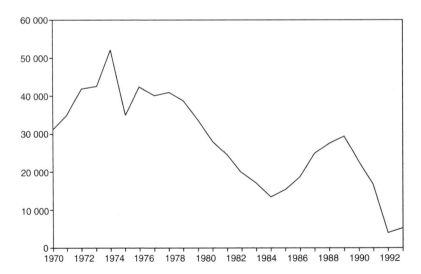

Figure 3.8 Number of units commenced in single-family homes, 1970–94
Source: Statistics Sweden.

menced during 1993 and 1994. During these two years, on average, 3700 units were commenced, which can be compared with the 13 600 units which were begun in 1985 (another year with depressed construction activity). On the whole, there is nothing in the actual development which contradicts our *ex ante* argumentation. The real price of single-family houses has fallen dramatically. The exceptionally weak trend regarding the number of units commenced in small houses imply – given historical demolition patterns and reasonable assumptions about economic depreciation – that the owner-occupied housing sector is going through a comprehensive process of shrinkage.

An economist likes to believe that the market is right, in the sense that asset prices quickly discount new information about changes in taxes and other policy decisions. In the same way, many scholarly observers, including the authors of this book, believed that the housing market would adapt quickly to the information about TR91. The prices of single-family homes should have stagnated or fallen as early as 1989, when the main features of the reform, and its implications for housing costs, became known and attracted media attention. However, this did not happen. In nominal terms, prices continued to increase during 1990 (plus 12 per cent) and 1991 (plus seven per cent), and it was not until 1992, a full year after the implementation of TR91, that prices fell noticeably in both nominal and real terms. As we have seen in Figure 3.8, the same (apparently delayed) adjustment also characterized new construction activity.

Regarding the number of units commenced, one can perhaps argue that the step from planning and projecting to construction is relatively drawn out. The relatively large number of units commenced during 1990 and 1991 to a great extent can reflect investment appraisals which were made before TR91 was made public. This line of reasoning, however, cannot explain the delayed price response. In principle, one can think of two explanations. The first is based on the simple idea that, despite everything, the market quickly absorbed the information about TR91. If TR91 had not taken place, prices of single-family homes would have increased even more during 1990 and 1991. In other words, TR91 slowed down the rapid increase in house prices which began during the second half of the 1980s. Of course, one problem with this line of reasoning is that it is not directly testable: We cannot predict what price trends there would have been if TR91 had not been implemented.

The other possible explanation, which is equally hard to test, is that buyers in the market did not perceive the meaning of TR91 until it was too late. Because of sluggishness in the flow of information, it might have taken time – despite massive media attention – for prospective house buyers to fully understand the importance of the new tax rules. An idea for a deeper study of this question, which we have not had the possibility to follow up, would be to conduct a systematic collection of prospectuses from property agents from, let us say, 1990. To what extent did the calculations of housing costs included in the prospectuses take into account the changes in taxes and subsidies which had been announced, but not yet implemented?

4 The Corporate Response

The postwar tax policies toward companies had two main goals: to stimulate consolidation among companies and to allow the state to actively steer investment activity. Consolidation was pursued by a combination of tax threats in the form of a high statutory tax rate and good possibilities for companies to form untaxed reserves, that is, to avoid paying taxes by keeping profits in the company. In order to affect investment decisions, a number of special rules were implemented, among which the most important and best known was the investment funds system.

The old corporate tax system with its goal of consolidation and stimulating investment was for a long time seen as being favourable to growth. However, in the economic debate of the late 1980s, with its emphasis on the role of the market for a more efficient use of resources, the system was increasingly seen as an obstacle to necessary structural changes within the economy. Criticism of the system was aimed mainly at the combination of a high tax rate and a narrow tax base, which stimulated companies to plough back profits in their enterprises on a large scale. A key concept in the debate was tax-conditioned locking-in effects, with the attendant risk of an inefficient allocation of investment resources between companies and industries. Added to this criticism was a growing scepticism about both the desirability and the possibility of the government steering business investments.

On the whole, the old principles of corporate taxation were abandoned by the 1991 tax reform. As we stated in Chapter 1, the reform meant that the tax rate was generally cut in half, if one takes into account the fact that the special surcharge, known as the profit-sharing tax, was also abolished. The investment funds system was dismantled, the possibility to undervalue inventories was done away with. At the same time, however, a tax equalization reserve (*Skatteutjämnings-reserv*, SURV) was set up which allowed companies a limited possibility to set aside funds free of tax. It is difficult to measure exactly to what extent these changes limited the possibility of forming untaxed reserves, but it is clear that the reform entailed a far-reaching broadening of the tax base. The change in the tax rules was also calibrated with the goal of achieving long-term, unchanged tax revenues.

The new system for the taxation of corporate profits inspired high hopes. The proposals of the Parliamentary Tax Committee on corporate tax reform (URF) (SOU, 1989: 34, p. 301), emphasized especially the importance of the reduced tax rate. Among other things, the Committee stated that:

> At a real interest rate of 3 per cent and a rate of inflation of 4 per cent, today's tax rate of 57 per cent (including the profit-sharing tax) produces a required rate of return of 16.3 per cent on equity financed investments. A lowering of the tax rate to 30 per cent reduces this required rate of return to 10 per cent... the change in taxes that we propose [creates] a considerably improved investment incentive.

In addition to these effects, it was the hope of the Parliamentary Committee and other observers that the new tax system, with fewer locking-in effects, would lead to a better allocation of investment resources. There was also the conviction that the reform had resulted in a simpler and more robust alternative to the old system, which had become increasingly more complicated during the postwar period.

It should immediately be said that an evaluation of the effects of the corporate tax reform is a complicated task. Due to the short period of time that has passed since the reform was initiated and implemented, company adaptation to the new rules is probably still going on. Moreover, the dismantling of the old system of rules extended over several years, during which time new rules were gradually introduced – for example, SURV was abolished as of 1994 and was replaced by tax-free contributions to newly created periodization funds. Further, the possibilities to analyze company reactions to the reform are severely circumscribed by available statistics lagging behind. In addition – and something which is a recurring theme in this book – the first years after the reform were extreme ones in terms of economic performance.

Finally, a special complication is that our knowledge of how the old tax system performed is still incomplete. Postwar Swedish corporate taxation is unique in many ways, which means that its effects are considerably more difficult to evaluate than the rules which are focused on by many of the international studies. This complication has also guided the organization of this chapter, which deals to a great extent with providing a better understanding of the old system. In order to assess the new system, we must be able to understand the old one.

The rest of this chapter is divided into seven sections. In the first of these, section 4.1, a general background and description is given of corporate taxation in recent decades. Among other things, we present information about how the 'effective' amount of taxes paid on real profits has changed over time. The effective tax burden, in general, has been considerably lower than the statutory rate of taxation. This is explained by companies using some of their profits for untaxed consolidation in the form of accelerated depreciation and contributions to inventory reserves and investment funds. In addition, we present new data on how the actual use of the consolidation rules relates to the maximum consolidation permitted by tax legislation. In section 4.2, we analyze the incentive effects of the tax rules; with the aid of hypothetical investment projects, we investigate how both the old and the new systems of corporate taxation affect the cost of capital for new investments. Our interest here also concerns to what extent TR91 has entailed a more uniform treatment of different types of investment projects and of different forms of financing. In section 4.3, we broaden the study of the incentive effects of TR91 to include as well the taxation of a company's financiers – since this was also changed by the reform. In this section, we explain the difference between the taxation of savings and the taxation of investments. This is a distinction which is of great importance in order to assess the effects of the different tax instruments in a small, open economy like the Swedish one. Then, section 4.4 takes up a discussion of the different locking-in effects which have been associated with both the personal taxation of shareholders and corporate taxation. Here, we examine what changes TR91 may have brought about.

Among the hopes linked to the 1991 tax reform was that borrowing would decrease, since reducing the tax rate by half made financing by borrowing more expensive. This question is dealt with in section 4.5, which contains both a general discussion of the importance of taxation for the financing of a company, and an account of certain empirical results from research in the field. Section 4.6 deals with TR91 and investments. However, an assessment of what real importance the new direction has had must be based on the degree of success of the previous tax policy. Therefore, an important question in section 4.6 is, to what extent, in recent decades, the government has really succeeded in affecting the size of investments and their location in time. The section looks especially closely into the effects of the investment funds system.

Section 4.7 concludes the chapter. The information about companies' use of tax allowances which was presented in section 4.1 implies that taxable profits in many cases may have been steered by a desire to pay dividends, or in some other way, by a striving to present after-tax book profits, rather than by the limitations on tax allowances set by the tax rules. A view we develop more fully in section 4.4, is that the old corporate taxation, in all its complexity, on the whole does not seem to have had any negative effects on investment incentives. The change in corporate taxation has probably also lacked importance for the drastic fall in investments after 1991. Nor does corporate taxation seem to have stimulated companies to finance operations through borrowing to the extent that many observers have previously assumed. Thus, when we look at the real economic effects on firms, TR91 seems to have had a rather undramatic impact.

4.1 THE EFFECTIVE TAX BURDEN, 1965–92

During most of the postwar period, Swedish joint-stock companies have paid both a state tax of 40 per cent and (a deductible) municipal income tax. Thus, since the end of the 1950s, the formal corporate tax rate has been gradually raised as the municipal tax has increased. Starting in 1985, however, only a state corporate tax of 52 per cent was charged; a figure which was lowered to 40 per cent in 1989 as part of the phasing-in of the new system with its tax rate of 30 per cent. Between 1984 and 1990, a special profit-sharing tax of 20 per cent was levied in addition to the state corporate tax. After a complicated deduction process this tax added a net 5 percentage points to the formal tax rate.

The development over time of the statutory corporate tax rate can be seen in Figure 4.1. The figure also shows the effective tax rate for manufacturing, calculated as actual taxes paid in relation to 'real' profits, that is, profits net of interest payments and economic depreciation.[1] As can be seen, the effective taxation, with certain very striking exceptions, has been about half as high as the statutory tax rate. The peaks in effective tax rates coincide with the crisis years at the end of the 1970s and the beginning of the 1980s. The recession year of 1981 also displays a high effective tax rate while the opposite applies for the boom year of 1974. The figure also shows a noticeably reversed covariation between profits and effective tax rate. This phenomenon seems to persist even after TR91. However, it is to early to tell whether the 'normal level' for the effective tax rate has been changed by the reform.

There are several explanations as to why the effective tax rate varies inversely to profits. In aggregate data, tax payments from companies

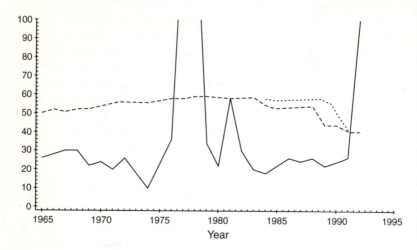

Figure 4.1   Statutory and average effective tax rate for manufacturing, 1965–92
Note: The dotted curve states the statutory tax rate; the upper dotted curve includes the profit-sharing tax for the years 1984–90. The continuous curve is the effective tax rate, according to the definition in the text.
Source: Own calculations.

showing profits are related to the sum of profits and losses from all companies, which automatically results in an inverse variation in the effective tax rate in relation to profits. Business cycle variations in the effective tax rate, however, are also strengthened by the connection that exists in Sweden (and in several other countries, for example, Finland) between accounting and taxation. Among other things, this connection entails a close agreement between the deductions which are claimed when filing tax returns and the deductions which are made in the company's external annual accounts under civil law.[2] The desire for companies to show smooth profit trends for accounting purposes, in order perhaps to be able to finance dividends in the long run with taxed profits, will thus determine the use of the available write down and depreciation opportunities. A decline in profits, which is not accompanied to a corresponding degree by reduced dividends, leads to the space for consolidation measures shrinking. A greater share of real profits must be reported for taxation, that is, the effective tax rate increases.

We can also ascertain from the special studies made by URF and Forsling (1995) that large groups of companies actually refrain from using all available tax allowances and thus pay more in tax than legislation stipulates. According to Forsling, 82 per cent of companies within manufacturing paid tax in the years 1979–88, and on average these companies used 72 per cent of possible deductions,[3] with tangible variations between different years (see Figure 4.2, where the lower curve (A) states actual use, and the upper curve (B) states the utilization rate which reduces taxable profits to zero). A somewhat marginal increase in utilization rate, from 72 to 76 per cent, would have been sufficient in order to completely eliminate tax payments.

Forsling's study also shows, as expected, that utilization varies strongly between individual companies. As can be seen in Figure 4.3, which applies to tax-paying manufacturing companies in 1984, the median company utilized approximately 83 per cent of the available allowances. Only one-fifth of the companies used the rules to the maximum extent, thus unconditionally minimizing their tax payments.

A further observation is that utilization shifts between different kinds of allowances. Utilization is highest for regular tax depreciation, 87 per cent, compared with 69 per cent for creating inventory reserves, and 35 per cent for contributions to investment funds. This difference is probably due to the fact that the measures offer different degrees of flexibility for companies. For each Swedish krona in depreciation of machinery which is not used in a given year, the company can recover only 30 per cent the following year, and 30 per cent of the remainder

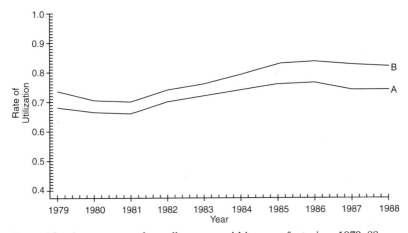

Figure 4.2 Average use of tax allowances within manufacturing, 1979–88
Note: The upper curve (B) states the utilization rate which would eliminate corporate tax payments for the average firm.
Source: Forsling (1995).

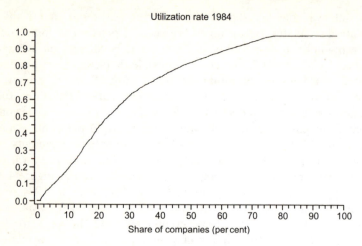

Figure 4.3 Utilization of tax rules in 1984: cumulative distribution of companies across utilization rates

Source: Forsling (1995).

the year after that, etc. Inventory write-down does not have this limitation; whatever is not used a given year can be recovered in its entirety as early as the next year.[4] The fact that contributions to the investment funds (which have now been abolished) appear as the marginal measure is due quite likely to the fact that tax subsidization is above all concentrated to utilization of the funds, which presupposes new investments and may require a shorter or longer waiting period.

The future use of the tax rules is one of the decisive questions for an evaluation of the new tax system. It is difficult to predict use because we do not know with certainty what motivates companies to report profits for taxation to a greater extent than is required by law. However, there are two circumstances which speak in favour of a dramatic increase in use. The first is that the allowances have been restricted, although it is difficult to see with precision by how much. The second is that the reduction in the tax rate, *ceteris paribus*, creates an increased scope for deductions. The reduction in the tax rate from around 57 per cent to 30 per cent means that companies can report before-tax profits which are not quite 40 per cent less, without needing to reduce the reported after-tax profit. All in all, this means that we should be able to count on median companies, at least in normal years, making almost maximum use of the new tax rules. However, what speaks against such an assessment is that companies at the lower corporation tax rate may increase their dividends, since the tax cost for dividends will decrease.

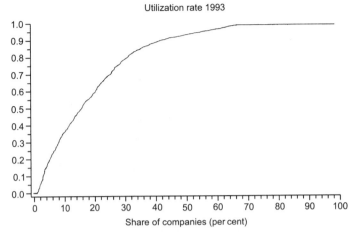

Figure 4.4 Utilization of tax rules in 1993: cumulative distribution of
companies across utilization rates
Source: Forsling (1995).

At higher dividends, the scope for using tax allowances decreases correspondingly.

The data which Forsling has used to study the tax behaviour of joint-stock companies cover the first three years of TR91. During this period, just over 65 per cent of companies paid taxes, and for those that did, the average utilization rate was around 75 per cent, that is, somewhat higher than the average for the 1979–88 period. Figure 4.4 shows the cumulative distribution of companies over different utilization rates for 1993, the year profits began to recover from the extreme crisis years.

In 1993 the median company utilized 93 per cent of available deductions, which is ten percentage points higher than the corresponding figure for 1984. About 30 per cent of the tax- paying companies made maximum use of the tax rules. In conclusion, these figures provide support for the assumption that there is considerably greater use of the tax rules under the new system.

4.2 THE INCENTIVE EFFECTS OF CORPORATE TAXATION

In Figure 4.1 above we showed how large a share of profits had been paid in tax by manufacturing companies. Calculations of this kind shed light on the average tax paid from corporate profits, and as such are of interest when assessing how taxation affects the internal financing of companies.[5] However, in order to ascertain how taxation affects the profitability of new investments, it is not the average but the *marginal* effective tax rate which is important. The problem, however, is that the marginal effective tax rate (that is, that part of profits from marginal investment which must be paid in tax) cannot be observed. However, the marginal tax rate can be calculated using conventional methods of capital budgeting, which also may be used to measure the size of the 'wedge' the tax system drives in between the pre-tax return on marginal investment and the return the company's owners and lenders receive on the savings which are necessary to finance the investment.[6]

In the following pages we will study the impact of TR91 on the marginal tax paid on new investments. We will only consider the effects of corporate taxation; the taxation of the company's owners and lenders will be discussed later in section 4.3. The calculations assume that companies, before as well as after TR91, could and wanted to take advantage of all available tax allowances. As we have just seen, at least for the period prior to TR91, this is hardly a realistic assumption. But it is still of interest to assess what incentive effects were actually built into the tax rules, in the case that these rules were fully taken advantage of in order to minimize tax payments. We will also return in section 4.4 to a more detailed discussion of what a systematic underutilization of the tax rules means for investment incentives.

Tables 4.1 and 4.2 present the pre-tax required rate of return on new investment, that is, the company's (net) capital cost. The estimates assume that the shareholders and lenders require an after-corporate tax rate of return of 4 per cent,[7] corresponding to an internationally determined real market rate of interest. We assume that investments are financed by debt and equity capital to the extent actually used in manufacturing at the end of the 1980s. We also base our analysis on the actual distribution of real investments between machinery, buildings and inventories.[8]

The average capital cost under the old tax system, which is shown in Table 4.1, was only slightly higher than the real market rate of interest – which was set at 4 per cent. Thus, seen as an average, the deviation from a neutrally constructed taxation which does not put a wedge between before- and after-tax returns was small. However, if we look behind this average, we find a different picture. The capital cost of an average debt-financed investment was lower than the market interest rate. The explanation for this is that companies were granted deductions in the form of both accelerated depreciation and nominal interest, which taken together exceeded the present value of the expected

Table 4.1   Real cost of capital for different assets and different sources of funds. Real rate of interest is 4 per cent. Only corporate tax considered, using 1985 rules

| | *Rate of inflation in per cent* | | | |
	0	*4*	*8*	*10*
Assets				
Inventories	4.5	4.9	5.1	5.1
Machinery	4.1	4.0	3.8	3.7
Buildings	4.9	4.7	4.3	4.0
Source of funds				
Debt	3.2	2.1	1.2	0.9
New issues	3.8	3.9	4.0	4.1
Retained earnings	5.4	6.0	6.3	6.3
Average	4.5	4.5	4.3	4.2

Source: Own calculations.

Table 4.2   Real cost of capital for different assets and different sources of funds. Real rate of interest is 4 per cent. Only corporate tax considered, using 1991 rules

| | *Rate of inflation in per cent* | | | |
	0	*4*	*8*	*10*
Assets				
Inventories	4.7	5.5	6.3	6.7
Machinery	3.9	3.8	3.6	3.5
Buildings	4.5	4.4	4.2	4.0
Source of funds				
Debt	3.7	3.1	2.4	2.1
New issues	3.6	3.8	4.0	4.1
Retained earnings	4.8	5.4	6.0	6.2
Average	4.4	4.5	4.6	4.6

Source: Own calculations.

profit from the marginal investment. The so-called Annell deduction had a corresponding effect on the cost of new equity, at moderate rates of inflation. The Annell deduction, which was implemented in the 1960s, gave companies a limited deduction for dividends on new equity capital. Investments financed by retained earnings, on the other hand, carried a higher capital cost.

Capital cost varied to a certain extent also depending on what type of real capital the company invested in. Moreover, it was sensitive to inflation. There are several and partly counteracting reasons for this. The tax depreciations are based on the acquisition cost of assets, and when there is inflation, the real value of these depreciations is reduced. The rules for inventory valuation further build on the FIFO principle. This increases the tax burden during inflation, since companies must pay tax for purely nominal price profits on inventories. However, the fact that companies are entitled to full deductions for nominal interest costs lowers capital costs. Since the increase in the nominal interest rate when there is inflation can be seen as a compensation for the reduction in real debt value this deduction, in practice, means that companies can make deductions for the real loan amortization which was caused by inflation.

Table 4.2 shows the corresponding capital costs under the new tax rules. A noteworthy finding is that TR91 has not entailed any noticeable change in average capital cost, and thus has not appreciably affected the incentive to invest. Nor have the differences in capital costs between different kinds of investments been reduced. Instead, they have increased. Investments in inventories, especially, have been adversely affected by the reform. The new rules still contain a certain sensitivity to inflation, even if the counteracting effects of inflation mainly cancel each other out regarding average capital costs. However, in one respect there has been noticeable improvement. The tax change severely limits the previous subsidization of debt-financed investments, at the same time as the taxation of equity-financed investment projects has been reduced. Thus, the new rules have brought about an equalization in costs between the different sources of financing. This equalization is conditioned by the newly created tax-equalization reserves (SURV), which were tied to equity capital, as well as by the reduction in the value of the interest deduction due to the tax rate being halved.

Several changes in corporate taxation have also been made after the 1991 reform. The change which has attracted the most attention has to do with the implementation of a new technique to mitigate the double taxation of corporation profits. The new rules, which went into effect in 1994, meant that the Annell deduction was done away with; in return, household dividends were made tax-free, and the tax on capital gains on shares was cut in half. The tax equalization reserves were replaced by less advantageous, but administratively simpler *periodization funds*, which gave companies an opportunity to postpone taxation of one-fourth of annual profits for five years. Without the Annell deduction, capital costs for new equity increased to the same level as for retained earnings, when we look at the tax effects of corporate taxation. However, in order to obtain a complete picture of the importance of the reform for capital costs, we must also take into account the already mentioned reliefs in personal taxation. We will return to this topic in the following section.

An additional change after TR91 was the temporary direct deduction of half the cost of investments in buildings which was in force for the period of November 1994–May 1996. The effect of this rule was to reduce the capital cost of investments in buildings to about the same level as that for machinery.

4.3 THE ROLE OF PERSONAL TAXATION

The incentive effects presented in Tables 4.1 and 4.2 only take into account corporate taxation. However, profits which are generated in the company are also taxed in the form of personal taxes on interest, dividends and capital gains. TR91 changed personal capital income taxation in important respects. Among other things, the earlier income taxation of household interest and dividends was replaced by a separate and uniform flat-rate tax of 30 per cent, which also applies to realized capital gains. In this section, we will discuss the importance of these changes for the investment incentives of companies.

In order to obtain a precise starting-point for our line of reasoning, we will first introduce a simple formalized model in order to clarify the mechanisms by which personal taxation can affect capital costs. Afterwards, we will gradually complicate and add to the picture, for example, by taking into account the fact that in many instances company owners are a rather heterogeneous group, nowadays containing a high percentage of foreign institutional investors.

Thus, by way of introduction, let us picture a closed economy where there is no uncertainty about the future and where there is only one category of investor. The tax on interest income is m, and the tax on dividends is m_d; the capital gains on shares are taxed by z. We let ρ be the lowest return after corporation tax, which the company can accept from its investment projects. Our problem here is how to determine ρ, taking into account the fact that the company owners and lenders are taxed for personal capital income. Having determined ρ, we can also – just like in section 4.2 – determine the company's required return before corporate tax, that is, the capital cost.

We further assume that investors price shares so that the investment in shares yields an after-tax return which corresponds to the best available return on alternative investments. With a well-functioning capital market, we can assume that this alternative return corresponds to the after-tax market interest rate, in other words, $i(1 - m)$, where i is the market interest rate. If the return after corporate tax on a marginal investment project – the investment project which is just barely acceptable by the company – according to the above is ρ, and this return is given to the owners in the form of dividends, the net after-tax return remaining in the hands of the owners is $\rho(1 - m_d)$. In order for the owners to be prepared to finance this investment by participating in a new share issue, then the following must apply:

$$\rho(1 - m_d) = i(1 - m) \tag{4.1}$$

that is, the after-tax return on the share investment must (at least) correspond to the alternative after-tax return of the owners. Thus the required return of the company after corporate tax, or the company's discount rate, when there is a new share issue is

$$\rho = \frac{i(1 - m)}{1 - m_d} \tag{4.2}$$

If taxation reduces the alternative return of the owners in the same proportion as it reduces dividend income, that is $m = m_d$, then personal taxation does not affect ρ; nor does it affect the cost of capital. In order to reduce capital cost in the case of new share issues, the tax on dividends must be reduced in relation to the tax on interest income, that is $m_d < m$.

An important difference between new share issues and retained earnings has to do with the amount owners must sacrifice in order to finance a new investment in the company. New share issues are paid with after-tax funds, and an investment of one krona in the company thus costs shareholders just as much. But when financing takes place using the retained earnings of the company, the shareholders only sacrifice the sum $1 - m_d$ per krona invested, in the form of foregone dividends after tax. Therefore, the shareholders can be content with a return after corporate tax, but before personal tax, which is only $1/1 - m_d$ times the corresponding return in the case of new equity financing. In order for the ploughing back of profits to be acceptable in the view of the owners, however, it must result in an increase in value of the company's shares as a sign of expected future increases in dividends. The increase in value is taxed according to the above by the tax rate z. Thus, each krona in after-tax profits from an increase in value corresponds to a before-tax increase in value of $1/1 - z$. This means that the required return after corporate tax must be adjusted upwards by the factor $1/1 - z$, compared with the corresponding required return in the case of new share issues. Thus, we have two effects that counteract each other from the personal taxation of capital. If we combine these, the result will be that the cost of the company for internal financing is $(1 - m_d)/(1 - z)$ times the corresponding cost of new share issues, that is

$$\rho = \frac{i(1 - m)}{1 - z} \qquad [(4.3)]$$

Thus, for retained earnings, it is the relationship between the taxation of capital gains, z, and the tax on the alternative return, m, which is decisive. In most countries, including Sweden, capital gains, at least as far as households are concerned, have been taxed much more favourably than both dividends and interest. This means that, *ceteris paribus*, personal taxation tends to make it cheaper to finance new investments with retained earnings instead of new share issues.

As can be seen, the taxation of dividend income (m_d) lacks significance when investment is financed by retained earnings. The explanation for this is that ploughed-back profits, seen from the viewpoint of shareholders, are untaxed, and remain untaxed as long as the profits are kept within the company as a source of financing. This means that the state participates in the financing of the company's investments by providing an interest-free loan. To be sure, if the tax on dividends is done away with, the after-tax value of the dividend will increase, but at the same time the size of the deferred tax (the interest free loan) diminishes by exactly the same degree. This means that the required rate of return on new investments, ρ, calculated after corporate tax, will be unaffected by the size of the tax on dividends.

Thus, even if the tax on dividends does not have any significance for the company's required rate of return with retained earnings as the source of funds, it is obviously decisive for the wealth position of the company shareholders. The taxation of dividends is capitalized in the company's value on the stock exchange. The higher the tax on dividends is compared with the tax on alternative investments, the lower the market price will be. Therefore, changes in the tax on dividends will give rise to windfall gains or losses for already existing share-holders. On the other hand, for new shareholders, this capitalization effect means that shares can be bought at a reduced price; the size of the discount being a direct reflection of the level of the tax on dividends.

The question now is what this simplified model can tell us about the effects of the 1991 tax reform. Both dividend income and interest were taxed as income prior to the reform. According to equation (4.2), this means that personal capital taxation would not have made new share issues more expensive. The new capital taxation which was implemented in 1991 did not change this equal treatment. The numerical results presented in Tables 4.1 and 4.2 – which considered only corporate taxation – can also be said to show the combined effects of the changes in corporate and personal taxation on the cost of issuing new shares. In the same way, we find that the exemption from taxation of household dividends as of 1 January 1994 – which, however, was short – lived due to a change in government – reduced the cost of new share issues. However, the effect must be weighed against the above-mentioned increase in expense which resulted from the Annell deduction being abolished and SURV being replaced by the less favourable period-ization funds. What the net result of these counteracting effects was for the capital costs of a company depends, as we discuss below, on what importance Swedish households can have for setting the market value of the companies.

The old tax system meant that capital gains were taxed much more favourably than either dividends or interest, and this made it cheaper to finance new investments with retained earnings than with new share issues. TR91 meant that realized capital gains on share investments would be taxed at the same rate as interest and dividends. However, capital gains are still favoured because the tax is not paid until the shares are sold. As is well known, the deferral of tax reduces the real effective tax rate.

Thus, by way of conclusion, taking into account personal taxes in our estimations would *reduce* the cost of using retained earnings, compared with the numbers which are presented in Tables 4.1 and 4.2. But on the other hand, it would not affect capital cost when new shares were issued. However, it is difficult to exactly quantify this affect. As we have already implied, one of the problems is that (domestic) owners are a rather heterogeneous group, and that the composition of the owner group varies between different categories of companies. On the stock exchange (before the reform) we found highly taxed households alongside both taxed and tax-exempt institutions. The question is which category should be seen as being representative for the 'marginal' investor who determines the market values and thus the costs of equity capital. We also have large groups of mainly small companies for which no continuous market assessment is made at all, but where ownership is dominated by natural persons.

If we only include household ownership of company capital, we find that with the old tax rules financing new investments with retained earnings produced a capital cost which was considerably lower than that which is stated in Table 4.1; in other words, despite the Annell deduction, new share issues were a decidedly more expensive source of equity capital. The 1991 tax rules, which both reduced personal capital taxation and limited the favourable treatment of capital gains, entailed an obvious change. Retained earnings actually became a somewhat more expensive form of financing compared with new equity. The 1994 tax rules (which took away the Annell deduction for companies, included tax-free dividends and halved capital gains tax for households) strengthened this difference to the advantage of new equity.

However, a different picture emerges if we also include other financiers who are taxed less heavily. Using three categories of investors, namely, households, tax-free institutions (which include pension funds, see further King and Fullerton (1984)), and insurance companies, weighted in relation to their relative importance as final owners of stock exchange capital, the difference between undistributed profits and new share issues seems to be rather limited under the old system. However, even here there was a certain advantage for ploughing back profits. The 1991 tax rules meant that new equity, just as was the case with sole household ownership, became a somewhat less expensive form of financing than ploughing back profits.

However, our discussion must be further qualified. Adding to the complexity of this picture is the fact that nowadays there is a great degree of international mobility of investment, with a far-reaching international integration of the equity capital markets. After the abolition of various restrictions for the export of shares and the depreciation of the Swedish krona starting in the autumn of 1992, foreign ownership in the Swedish economy has expanded rapidly, and in 1995 a full one-quarter of stock exchange capital was in foreign hands.

The taxation of Swedish shareholders, and especially the taxation of households, cannot reasonably have any independent and decisive effect on the valuation of corporations whose shares are traded freely – and to a great extent – on international markets. Taking into consideration the growing internationalization, which moreover is not limited to the stock exchange, one can actually easily question the relevance of our earlier analysis and argue that the cost of equity capital – ρ in our formalized analysis – is internationally determined. Nor is the internationalization of ownership the only channel through which global return requirements are brought into the Swedish economy. For the greater part of the postwar period, companies in Sweden have, in practice, had unlimited access to direct investments abroad, offering the opportunity to compare rates of return after corporate tax in different countries.

The sum total of this line of reasoning is that in a small, open economy like Sweden, it is corporate taxation rather than personal taxation which is decisive for the effect of the tax system on capital costs. This is due to the two completely different tax principles on which corporate taxation and personal taxation are based. Personal taxation, both in Sweden and internationally, follows mainly the residence principle, which states that all income, regardless of where it originates, is to be taxed at the rates and according to the tax rules which apply in the country where the owner has his place of residence. If the residence principle is applied consistently, it does not matter, from a tax perspective, whether savings are invested at home or abroad, since it is the global income of the investor which is taxed in his native country. This means further that it is possible to base investment on comparisons of returns *before* tax in different countries. In long-term equilibrium, the before-tax return and return requirement in different countries would tend to be levelled out for investment instruments which may be traded freely internationally. Regarding our line of reasoning, this means that the price – the return requirement – of equity capital, calculated after corporate tax, but before personal tax, is not affected by Swedish personal taxation.

Instead, corporate taxation follows the source principle, which means that tax is levied in the country where the income is earned, all in accordance with the rules that apply in that particular country. Since, for the private investor (company), it is the after-tax return that decides how investment resources are to be allocated between alternative uses, an international application of source taxation tends to create differences in before-tax returns between different countries, as a direct reflection of the differences in the taxes levied.

The distinction between residence and source taxation is also a distinction between taxation of savings and taxation of investment. In an open economy, the direct link between savings and investment is broken. This means, among other things, that a tax on the return on savings in the hands of the financier is not equivalent to a tax on corporate earnings. A reduction in personal capital taxation can stimulate saving (see Chapter 3 for a treatment of this subject), but the increased savings need not be invested within the country. Correspondingly, reduced corporate taxation can increase investment, but in a small, open economy the increased investments can also be financed by imported saving.

However, there are also objections to the thesis that personal taxation lacks importance for the capital costs of Swedish companies. For residence taxation of the return on shares to equalize the return before (personal) tax between different countries share instruments must be traded freely on international markets. However, in practice, foreign ownership of Swedish company capital is very unevenly distributed, and to a great extent is concentrated to a few large companies. Smaller and medium-sized companies, for obvious reasons, lack the opportunity to issue new shares on internationalized markets, while information and transaction costs of various kinds in the main exclude foreigners as owners. In the debate on the 1994 technique for mitigating double taxation (with tax-free dividends and halved capital gains taxation), the differences in these respects between different groups of companies were especially emphasized. The government commission which paved the way for the new rules argued that Sweden, in practice, functioned as a closed economy regarding the smaller and medium-sized companies' supply of equity capital. Based on this approach, the reduced taxation of household share income would make it easier for companies to obtain new share capital and lower capital costs.[9]

Obviously, in the final analysis it is an empirical question how capital costs are determined, and to what extent different categories of companies meet other return requirements than those which apply on the internationalized capital markets. It is certainly possible to find companies/owners of capital for whom consumption or interest-bearing assets of different kinds are the only alternative to investments in their own company. For this category of owners, abolishing the tax on dividends would lower capital costs. But if the after-tax yield requirement of the owners is determined based on a broader spectrum of alternative investment possibilities including internationally traded shares, then the conclusion might be a different one. The prices of the shares which are listed internationally are not likely to be affected by the fact that some of the owners – the Swedish ones – receive a lower tax. The after-tax return for the Swedish investors therefore rises, and if these investors act rationally, their required rate of return also increases when they buy shares in companies which are traded only on the domestic market. Thus, the favourable effect on capital costs for smaller and medium-sized companies from doing away with the tax on dividends may be partially or entirely negated.

In other words, there are good theoretical arguments for believing that the international required rate of return also has an effect on companies whose shares are not directly subject to international trading. Even for companies which themselves cannot take advantage of the international markets for their supply of equity capital, capital costs may be internationally determined, to the extent that the *shareholders* set their return requirement taking into account their *own* investment and return possibilities on the internationally open share markets.[10]

A further complication in determining the effects of TR91 on the cost of capital, has to do with the very fact that returns on equity investments are uncertain. The investor can have expectations about what the average return might be, and also how risky the investment is. The investment decision means weighting the expected return and risk together. Depending on differences in risk aversion, this deliberation may differ from investor to investor. An investor with high risk aversion may invest in relatively safe assets with a low return, while an investor with low risk aversion may choose a more risky investment alternative which yields a higher expected return.

It is sometimes argued that household propensity to invest savings in shares would increase if the tax on share investment would be reduced, compared with the tax on returns from safer forms of savings. However, this conclusion is not automatically correct. A tax on returns from a risky investment has namely two effects on the choice of investment which counteract each other. On the one hand, taxation reduces the expected return, which, *ceteris paribus*, reduces demand. On the other hand, taxation also has an important insurance function. The positive outcomes are reduced by taxation, but so are the negative ones – in accordance with the tax rules providing for loss deductions and set off opportunities. In other words, the state assumes part of the risk, and this tends to stimulate demand. Which of these counteracting effects dominates cannot in general be determined based on theoretical considerations. In other words, it is not absolutely certain that having a higher tax on risky investments than on safe bank savings means that risky investments are discriminated.

4.4 LOCKING-IN EFFECTS

A recurring theme in the public debate preceding TR91 was the need to reduce different locking-in effects of the tax system. It was argued that, to a considerable extent, the old tax system made it profitable to retain earnings within the company where they had once been generated even if there were investment alternatives yielding a higher pre-tax rate of return available in other companies.

Both personal and corporate taxation can, at least in principle, bring about a locking-in of profits in existing companies, and thus prevent or delay a reallocation of investment resources. If dividends are taxed heavier than capital gains, then attempts to redistribute profits through increased dividends will mean that there will be an extra taxation compared with the alternative of retaining profits and internally financing further investments. It is this potential extra taxation which creates the locking-in effect. The alternative value of profits *outside* the company decreases, which makes it rational for companies to lower the required rate of return on investments *within* the company. These are the very mechanisms that we have already dealt with in section 4.3, where, among other things, we showed that under certain conditions it is cheaper to finance investments with retained earnings rather than with new share issues.

The new tax rules, which both reduce the dividend tax and limit the favourable treatment of capital gains, should reduce the cost difference between ploughing back profits and issuing new shares. As a result of this, new investments can receive a more equal assessment, regardless of whether they are carried out by companies with a high degree of internal financing, or by newly established and/or fast expanding companies, which to a great extent must rely on new share issues.

However, as our discussion in section 4.3 also showed, one can question what practical importance these locking-in tax mechanisms can have in a small, open economy like the Swedish one. As far as large companies are concerned, the Swedish owner taxation probably has no impact whatsoever on capital costs. The importance of personal taxation of dividends and capital gains lies on another level; it can affect the propensity of households to keep shares in their wealth portfolios, and by doing so it constitutes one of several factors which determine ownership patterns. The fact that the position of households on the Swedish stock exchange has been successively weakened in the last decades may be a reflection of both tax favours given to institutional investors and the previously high income taxation of dividends.

The underutilization of the tax rules by joint-stock companies, which was dealt with in the previous section, is a further, and at least for the medium-sized and larger companies, probably a more important locking-in mechanism. For companies which have been unable to take maximum advantage of the tax rules, attempts to redistribute profits to other parts of the economy through increased dividends would have meant that greater profits would have become subject to taxation, that is, more would have been paid in corporate taxes. It is this potential extra taxation which creates locking-in effects. Since the alternative value of profits outside the company is low, the company can carry out investments which would not have been accepted if the financing had taken place with external equity capital. However, the question is what does this mean for economic efficiency.

As we will discuss in more detail in Chapter 8, an efficient allocation of capital in a small, open economy requires that the before-tax returns on investments are the same as the internationally determined required rate of return, that is the real interest rate in the surrounding world. Therefore, from an efficiency point of view, the effective marginal corporate tax rate should be zero, that is, we should have a neutral corporate tax. There are two main alternatives for constructing such a neutral taxation of profits.[11] The best known of these two alternatives is where taxable profit is calculated after deducting the real costs of funds and allowing for economic depreciation. The other alternative is an expenditure tax which gives companies the right to deduct the acquisition cost of capital assets in the first year. At the same time, the right to deduct interest is done away with. The current value of the tax relief obtained by the company through an immediate deduction of investment costs is exactly the same as that obtained by the administratively more difficult combination of economic depreciations and deductions for real financing costs.

Formally, the Swedish corporate taxation is an income tax. But as we have seen in section 4.1, it seems that for large groups of companies tax payments have been determined by the requirement to pay dividends out of after-tax book profits, rather than by a limited availability of tax allowances. With a certain amount of generalization, we can argue that the corporation income tax, in practice, has functioned as something which can be better compared to a *tax on dividends*. It is easy to show that the effects of a tax on dividends is equivalent to the above-mentioned expenditure tax, and thus – to the extent debt and retained earnings are used as sources of funds – is an alternative model for neutral taxation.[12] [13]

This line of reasoning implies that the locking-in effect which has been associated with the old corporate tax system did not necessarily cause any efficiency problems. The locking-in effect has quite simply offset the tax effect on the cost for using retained earnings; this is exactly what should take place in the case of neutral taxation. However, what may have been problematic is that the looking-in effects varied between different groups of companies according to their ability to take advantage of the consolidation possibilities offered by the tax legislation. Companies which expected to pay taxes on profits from new investments had to require a higher rate of return compared with companies which could escape taxes by increasing the rate of utilization of tax allowances.

In addition to this, the locking-in effect of the corporate tax discriminated against the use of new share issues, which automatically hit newly established companies and other companies in expansive phases of development. The reason for this discrimination is that new share issues are paid for by taxed funds, in other words, funds which are outside the 'corporate tax fence' surrounding internally generated profits in many companies. However, the previously mentioned Annell deduction limited this effect, partially or entirely.[14]

Under the new tax system, the locking-in effects of corporate taxation are probably considerably more limited. The possibilities for tax-free consolidation have been curtailed, and according to the rough estimates we have presented above, companies should take advantage of the remaining tax allowances to a greater extent now that profitability has improved after the crisis years. Thus, differences in how companies make use of the tax rules should diminish, which should be efficiency enhancing. However, as can be seen in Table 4.2, this does not mean that we now have a neutral corporate tax. Considerable distortion effects remain, regarding the selection of investment projects and the choice of financing. In addition, the required rate of return is, on average, somewhat higher than the real market interest rate.

4.5 TR91 AND CORPORATE FINANCING

The discussion in the previous section about the incentive effects of taxation has illustrated the asymmetry which characterized the taxation of corporate profits in the past few decades. Companies have been granted deductions for interest, but in general not for the costs of equity funds. As could be seen in Table 4.1, this means that the tax system has favoured debt financing.

The asymmetry in corporate taxation is not unique to the Swedish tax system. Internationally, we find more or less complicated arrangements to integrate corporate and owner taxation, for example, by granting shareholders a credit for the tax which has already been paid by the company on distributed profits, or by a differentiation in corporate taxation between distributed and retained earnings. The Swedish Annell deduction, which we have already discussed, represents an alternative technique for reducing the tax discrimination of new share issues.

The methods for arranging the taxation of corporate profits, as well as the effect of taxation on companies' choice of financing, has attracted considerable attention in the scholarly literature. However, the extent of the literature is in sharp contrast to the small success research has had up until now when it comes to being able to capture and prove, in empirical studies, tax effects on financing behaviour. A crucial problem is that research is still unclear regarding what determines a company's financial structure in the absence of taxes.

The two Nobel laureates, Franco Modigliani and Merton Miller, in their fundamental contributions to the theoretical literature (Modigliani and Miller, 1958), actually argue that a company's choice of financing, under certain conditions, has no importance for its market value or its capital cost. The analysis of Modigliani and Miller is valid for an idealized economy with perfect capital markets, and in the absence of transaction costs and taxes. Under these stringent conditions, there is no reason for shareholders to put a premium on debt-financed companies. The leverage profits the company can make through debt financing investment projects that yield a return which exceeds the cost of borrowing can be obtained by the shareholders themselves through *homemade leverage*, that is, by investing in debt-free companies and then borrowing on their own share portfolio. In a corresponding manner, Modigliani and Miller also show how the dividend policy – which determines a company's choice between ploughing back profits and new share issues as a source of equity capital – ought to lack importance for the market evaluation of the company. For example, the shareholders themselves can create the liquidity necessary for desired consumption by purchasing or selling shares. The dividend policy of a company need not determine the owners' choice of investment.

The analysis of Modigliani and Miller has been the starting-point and comparative norm for more recent theoretical work which has tried to establish under what conditions the choice of financing is actually relevant for market valuation and capital costs. One approach, which was also discussed in an early study by Modigliani and Miller, has emphasized the importance of the tax factor. The deductability of debt interest for corporate taxation lowers the relative cost of debt compared to equity capital (cf. Tables 4.1 and 4.2). However, this effect is counteracted by the interest on loans being taxable as income for the lenders. At the same time, the return on shares is in general taxed less heavily than interest, due to the favourable treatment of capital gains. In an influential study, Miller (1977) has argued that these tax effects, under certain conditions, can cancel out each other by affecting the market prices of debt and equity instruments, so that for the individual company, the choice of financing is irrelevant, despite taxation.

More recent research has tried to show that even in situations where the counteracting tax effects do not cancel each other out, that is, when the tax system gives a net advantage to debt financing, there can be an optimal financing structure which is characterized by companies using both debt and equity. The idea is that the tax advantages that debt financing offers are outweighed by the direct and indirect costs of different kinds which are closely associated with borrowing.[15] Included in the implicit costs of debt financing are the disruptions in regular operations which as a rule arise if the company is forced into a financial reconstruction due to difficulties of meeting the fixed payment obligations when heavily in debt. The literature also emphasizes the fact that asymmetric information between companies and financiers may warrant costly monitoring or complicated contracts which limit the possibilities of the company management, or the owners, to gain advantages at the expense of the lenders.

In principle, this discussion offers an opportunity to empirically examine the tax effects on the choice of financing. What we need are calculations of the effective marginal tax rate on returns on equity capital and the marginal tax rate for the company's interest on debt. The difference between the two expresses the tax advantage of debt, which, when the company is optimally adjusted, should correspond to the above-mentioned marginal implicit borrowing cost. If we assume – which is reasonable – that the implicit borrowing cost increases with the average degree of indebtedness of the company, we then have a simple, and in principle, testable model for how changes in taxation affect corporate financing.

In the international literature, there are few successful attempts to empirically test the above model for loan financing. One reason for this may be that the tax advantage of debt is difficult to measure. As far as Sweden is concerned, the considerable underutilization of the consolidation rules, before and after TR91, creates uncertainty regarding the relevant effective rate of corporate taxation. In addition, the marginal tax rate of the owners on equity returns is difficult to assess, among other reasons, because shareholders are far from being a homogeneous group. The same applies to the marginal tax rate of lenders on interest income. Added to this is the above-mentioned basic question whether Swedish shareholders and lenders, and their tax situation, have any independent effect on price formation on the international markets, and thus on the cost difference between debt and equity for companies.

The absence of studies which might be able to give evidence of tax effects is probably also connected with the fact that the debt ratio for companies, which is the variable to be explained, actually constitutes the aggregate result of a number of different financing decisions at different points in time. Taking this into account, it is hardly surprising that it is difficult to explain the debt ratio for any given year with the aid of the tax advantage of debt financing.

Instead, a more promising way of tackling the problem, which has been attempted in very recent years, appears to be to use data of individual companies to study the *marginal* financing choice.[16] Given the assumption that a company is in need of external financing, will the choice fall on new share emissions or loans? The hypothesis is that companies with high expected marginal tax rates, for which interest deductions have a high value, are more likely to issue bonds, while new share issues are preferred by companies with low expected marginal tax rates. This approach also helps to solve the above-mentioned measurement problem, since the effective marginal tax rate of companies can be captured with the aid of different proxy variables.

In a study based on data from Swedish companies carried out by Erik Ekman (Ekman, 1995), and which uses this approach, we can find evidence for the Swedish corporate taxation actually having had an effect on the choice of financing. Ekman examines some 300 companies with more than 50 employees which either issued new shares or bonds in the years 1985–87. Ekman finds that the likelihood of a company choosing bonds is significantly greater if in the past the company had accumulated considerable untaxed reserves, than if it had not done so at all. Large untaxed reserves with accompanying future tax payments are interpreted here as an indication of a high expected future marginal tax rate which makes interest deductions valuable. Correspondingly, Ekman finds that the greater the company's potential is for acquiring untaxed reserves in the future – large inventory assets and fast investment growth are assumed to indicate such potential – the less likely it is that the company will choose debt instead of new share issues. In other words, the possibility of keeping tax payments down in the future by acquiring *tax debt* crowds out regular debt financing.[17]

In Ekman's analysis, a company's financing decision is seen as a dynamic process. History, in the form of already accumulated untaxed reserves (tax debt), as well as the future, in the form of potential for further deferring tax payments tax, affect the marginal financing choice. It is not self-evident what implications his results have for assessing the effects of TR91. For those companies which were able to make maximum use of the tax rules under the old system, the reform has probably reduced the incentive for borrowing. Interest deductions have become less valuable due to the considerably lowered statutory tax rate. Paradoxically, for the considerably larger group of companies which underutilized the tax rules before the reform, the incentive to borrow may instead have increased. With unutilized possibilities for untaxed consolidation under the old system, there were no extra tax savings to be had from further borrowing; the marginal interest deductions were worthless. After the reform, when interest deductions were crowded out only to a limited extent by contributions to untaxed reserves, interest deductions instead become worth 30 per cent.

4.6 TR91 AND CORPORATE INVESTMENTS

Swedish corporate taxation in the postwar period has been characterized to a great extent by an attempt to actively promote corporate investments. Throughout this period, legislation added a number of special rules, including those concerning the special investment deductions and the investment funds system. Originally, the purpose was to level out business cycle variations in investments, but with the emergence of balance-of-payments deficits, starting in the middle of the 1960s, the ambitions increased. The additional goal of tax policy at that time then became one of generally increasing the level of investment, mainly in the industrial sector, in order to increase our long-term ability to export and to eradicate the current account deficit.

Investment deductions became more and more generous, and investment funds were released more and more frequently. It can be said that this policy culminated at the time of the Swedish economic crisis which took place in the middle of the 1970s, and which initiated a ten-year period of what was in practice a permanent release of investment funds.

The 1991 tax reform entailed a sharp reversal of the previous policy; the new corporate tax system completely lacks instruments for directly affecting investment behaviour. In order to obtain a perspective on this new direction, in this section we are going to examine the experiences of the last few decades of promoting investment via taxation of profits. We will present some new data in order to shed light on the effects of the investment funds system, and we will give an account of a few empirical studies of taxation and investment demand. Our most important question here is to what extent the government has actually succeeded in influencing the size and timing of investments by actively utilizing the corporation tax. We will also present a study of the importance of TR91 for the drastic fall in investments in the first years of the 1990s.

The investment funds system

Perhaps the best-known instrument for affecting investment was the *investment funds system* (IF), which was designed in the middle of the 1950s. This became something of a Swedish innovation in the field of fiscal policy. It attracted considerable interest and many imitators abroad.[18] The investment funds system stimulated companies to reserve profits in good years, partly in the form of deposits in the Riksbank. Then, in years of recession, companies were allowed to use these funds for investments.

Investments financed by releases of the investment funds received a substantial subsidy, comparable to that obtained by immediate write-off. It is a common belief that the fund releases also brought about a substantial reduction in the capital costs of companies, providing a strong stimulus to increase investments. Such an interpretation of the effects of the IF system requires that the fund releases actually were sufficient to finance all investments, including marginal investment projects. However, Forsling's study (1995), which we have already cited in section 4.1, shows that the releases in the years of 'permanent' releases actually included rather limited shares of investment volumes. IF financing of investments in buildings varied between 15 and 28 per

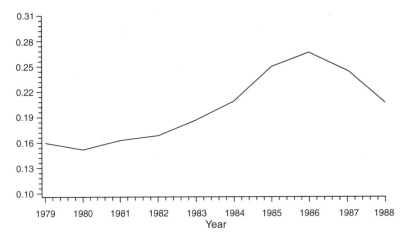

Figure 4.5 Share of manufacturing investments in buildings financed via investment funds, 1979–88

cent (see Figure 4.5) during the years fund contributions were still allowed, that is through 1988. For investments in machinery, for which the use of funds produced a substantially smaller subsidy effect, the shares were even lower.

A reasonable conclusion to be drawn from Forsling's study is that companies, despite continual releases of investment funds, were actually forced to utilize the regular depreciation rules for their marginal investment projects. If that is the case, then the investment funds system had lost most of its effectiveness as a policy instrument, and it has gone from promoting new investments to being a general tax break, constructed as a subsidization of investments which for the most part would have been carried out even without the corresponding subsidies.[19]

However, it should be emphasized that the average numbers in Figure 4.5 also conceal big differences between different groups of companies. Even if the fund releases, on average, have been limited in relation to investment volumes, there are many companies for which the IF system may have really been the marginal source of financing. Forsling's data, which covers the years 1979–88, indicate that, on average 14 per cent of companies each year have been able to finance 90 per cent or more of their construction investments via the system. Certain rough estimations imply that corresponding investment expenditures stood for around one-quarter of the total construction investments in the corporate sector. The peak years in this respect were 1985–87 when the companies which could finance 90 per cent or more of their investments in buildings by the investment funds system stood for 35 per cent of the total investment volume.

A further reservation for an assessment of the investment funds system has to do with its function in the years preceding the permanent fund releases when the funds were mainly used as a tool of a counter-cyclical policy. For two decades, counting from the middle of the 1950s, periods during which companies could build up their investment funds were followed by clearly demarcated periods of time when there was a release of funds. Even though corresponding material is lacking regarding the importance of the release of funds as a source of financing for this period, the way which the funds were handled by the government speaks in favour of the view that efficiency in affecting investments was greater at that time, something which was closer to the original intentions of the system.

Tax policy and investment incentives

In previous sections we have compared the incentive effects of the old and the new corporate taxation by calculating company capital costs. In Figure 4.6 we return to this, but now with a considerably extended time perspective. The figure presents a stylized and comprehensive picture of how the postwar tax policy towards manufacturing has affected capital costs. The 'tax wedge' which is shown in the figure states how much corporate tax would have raised the capital costs if companies had been able to fully utilize available tax allowances. The curve reflects both equity and debt financing and assumes that the required returns of shareholders after corporate tax but before personal tax corresponds to 1.5 times the nominal interest rate on long-term industrial bonds. The tax wedge applies for an average of investments in machinery and buildings.[20]

The figure shows a clear connection between the tax policy and the size of the tax wedge. The abolition of the free depreciations of machinery and inventory (introduced as early as 1938), and the utilization of investment taxes in the 1950s forced up the tax wedge, while noticeable and time-specific reductions in the tax wedge are noted when there was a release of the investment funds to even out business cycles in the 1950s and 1960s. However, as early as the mid-1960s, the corporate tax wedge became negative. The combination of deductions for nominal interest and different forms of accelerated depreciation made it possible for companies to deduct more than the pre-tax income from marginal investments. This meant that the tax system subsidized

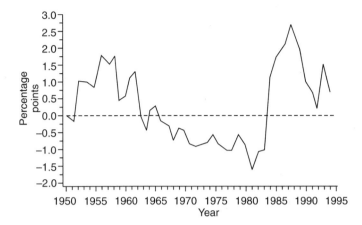

Figure 4.6 Corporate tax wedge, 1950–93 (percentage points)
Note: The corporate tax wedge shows the difference between the pre-tax net cost of capital and the real after-tax required rate of the return, as defined in the text.
Source: Own calculations.

marginal investment projects, a subsidization which was strengthened by increasing inflation, the 'permanent' IF releases from the mid-1970s to the mid-1980s, and the increasingly generous investment deductions. We also note the transition to a less favourable tax policy towards manufacturing investments from the mid-1980s, including the abolition of the special investment deductions and the tightening of the investment funds policy.

Empirical studies

The importance of corporate taxation for the investment decisions of companies has been the subject of a number of empirical studies using a variety of methods. The earliest studies dealt with the release of the investment funds in the 1960s and were based on questionnaires to the companies concerned.[21] The results imply that fund releases have had a noticeable and time-specific effect on industrial investments. Investments in buildings especially increased, and the net effect is calculated at between 15 and 20 per cent.

During the 1970s, several econometric studies of industrial investments were carried out.[22] The tax policy effects were captured with the aid of a capital cost variable, defined in the traditional way and assuming static expectations of tax policy. The fund releases were assumed, without further discussion, to bring about a substantial reduction in the capital costs. A common characteristic of these studies is that the tax policy effect is seen as small compared with other explanatory variables, and that the effect moreover can be described as poorly demarcated in time. An unanswered question, however, is to what extent the results are driven by the very assumption about static expectations. At any rate, such an assumption appears as a questionable starting-point for an analysis of a counter-cyclical tax policy.

The investment funds system has also been analyzed by foreign scholars. A prominent example of this is Taylor's study (1982) from the beginning of the 1980s which covers the years before the 'permanent' releases. Taylor estimates investment functions where the effects of the IF system are captured by a contracyclical cost variable. His conclusion is that the investment funds system – seen as a 'policy rule' by companies – was actually able to even out cyclical swings in investment volumes.

In the past decade, a couple of studies have been carried out which explicitly deal with the question whether capital costs can really be affected by changes in the tax rules. Bergström and Södersten (1984) test several alternative formulations of the capital cost variable regarding tax effects. According to the alternative which provides the best fit, the IF is assumed to function according to the conventional model up until the mid-1970s, to change in recent years into what is mainly a general profit tax relief, in the manner discussed above. Dufwenberg *et al.* (1994) deal with the 1966–90 period using modern methods for time-series analysis. To be sure, the authors find that capital costs have had a considerable effect on the investment behaviour, both short and long term, but they cannot find any notable tax effects. Corporate taxation does not seem to have affected capital costs. However, a potentially important problem concerning these studies is that company expectations about future changes in the tax system are captured in a very rudimentary way.

In a study by Auerbach, Hassett and Södersten (1995), interest is directly focused on assessing the effects of TR91 on the investments in machinery of the corporate sector. The study deals with the 1969–93 period, and thus covers the first three years following TR91.[23] The authors state that an evaluation of the new tax rules is especially complicated since the effects of the old tax system are difficult to interpret. No less than four different tax regimes are distinguished, each having different capital costs, in which companies may have found themselves prior to the reform. Regime one means that companies completely ignored the investment funds system, but otherwise utilized the regular tax deductions. Under regime two, the investment funds system functioned according to the conventional model, that is, the fund releases were sufficient to finance marginal investment projects. The alternative interpretation of the investment funds system as a general subsidy to profits, which we dealt with above, is regime three. Under this regime, the marginal investments are written off using the regular rules for depreciation, despite on-going fund releases. The fourth regime, finally, is the case when companies refrain from fully utilizing the consolidation opportunities of the tax system. In this instance, as we discussed in section 4.4, corporate taxation has no importance for capital costs.

The econometric analysis provides clear grounds to reject only regime two, which represents the conventional interpretation of the investment funds system. The other regimes provide basically the same fit of the estimated investment function. It is true that capital costs differ, but they covary to such an extent – the correlation coefficient is more than 90 per cent – that one cannot point to any of the three remaining regimes as being superior when it comes to explaining investments. The covariation in the time-series for capital costs, in turn, is explained by the fact that the fluctuations in the real interest rate during the observation period in practice have come to dominate the changes in the tax parameters of the different regimes.

Auerbach *et al.* (1995) find that a permanent reduction of capital cost by one percentage point (depending on which regime the company finds itself in, this corresponds to an investment subsidy of between 2 and 3 per cent) results in an increase in the investment ratio, defined as the relationship between investments and capital stock, of between 0.3 and 0.4 percentage points, or just over two per cent of gross investments (at the level for the average investment ratio which applied during 1969–85). The response is comparable to that which was obtained in a corresponding study using the same methodology on American data, see Auerbach and Hassett (1992), and that which was reported in the study by Dufwenberg *et al.* for Sweden.

Between 1985 and 1993, the investment ratio decreased for investments in machinery by more than 40 per cent, and according to the calculations of the authors, approximately one-fourth of this reduction can be attributed to increased capital costs. However, the impact of TR91 appears to be negligible. Nor is TR91 expected to result in any notable changes in long-term investment incentives.[24] To the extent that companies have shifted from regime four to regime one – which is the most likely change judging from Forsling's data – capital costs will remain practically the same. The explanation for this is that the deduction opportunities for marginal investments in machinery which are financed by a combination of debt and equity are sufficient to largely eliminate the effect of corporate taxation.[25]

4.7   CONCLUSION

The basic principle of TR91, that is, lower tax rates and broader tax bases, was applied with great consistency when the new rules for corporate taxation were drawn up. The tax rate was reduced by half, and the investment funds and the deduction for inventories were abolished. The reform meant that the government gave up the idea of actively affecting investments, and toned down the striving to stimulate companies to consolidate. Perhaps the single most important finding of this chapter has to do with the utilization of various consolidation rules. Before TR91, only one-fifth of companies utilized the tax rules to the maximum extent, and by doing so unconditionally minimizing their tax payments. A possible explanation of this phenomenon is that in most cases the tax payments were motivated by the company's dividend policy, or in some other way by a preference for reporting fully taxed book profits, rather than by a limited availability of tax allowances. The old corporate taxation seems, in all its complexity, to have functioned as a tax on dividends. As we discussed in section 4.4, a tax on dividends is an alternative model for a neutral corporate taxation.

The stated underutilization of the consolidation rules is an indication that the effects of TR91 on the choice of financing of companies varies between different groups of companies. For those companies which utilized the old tax rules to the full extent, the reform has probably led to a reduction in the incentive to borrow; the interest deductions have become worth less. For the considerably larger group of companies, which underutilized the tax rules, the marginal interest deductions were worthless before the reform. After the reform, using the tax rules to a full extent, interest deductions are instead worth 30 per cent. Thus, the incentive to borrow has increased, despite the drastic cut in the statutory tax rate.

The study by Auerbach *et al.* implies that TR91 has not had any significance for the drastic fall in investments in machinery in the crisis years. The long-term effect of the reform on the demand for investment is quite likely small. However, for those companies which could finance all, or almost all, of their investments through the investment funds system, investments will become decidedly more expensive. Moreover, the differences between companies regarding different tax effects will decrease, which ought to mean that investment projects will be evaluated in a more uniform and unconditional manner.

5 The Supply of Labour

Between 1989 and 1991, the marginal tax rate was reduced by 14 per cent for an average industrial worker and by 22 per cent for a typical salaried employee. This meant that, in one fell swoop, tax wedges had returned to the levels which existed at the end of the 1960s. With such a substantial reform, it was not unreasonable to expect visible effects on labour supply, even in the short run. This was also the view expressed by the minister of finance in the 1990 bill, but as it turned out no positive short-term effects took place. Instead, the unemployment crisis arrived, and the number of hours worked decreased from the first year of the new tax system, to fall by a total of 9 per cent between 1990 and 1993. The question is whether we can still see any signs, in the middle of this severe crisis, that the tax reform has affected the supply of labour, even if such effects cannot be fully realized in the form of more hours worked until demand has picked up again.

The supply of labour is often seen merely as a matter of number of hours worked. It was thought that TR91 would increase people's willingness to work overtime, or to increase the number of ordinary weekly working hours in the case of part-time employment. But there are other aspects to labour supply, such as choice of education, and the decision whether to participate at all in the labour force. A survey of different aspects of labour supply is given in section 5.1. Section 5.2 discusses how TR91 has affected the marginal return on labour supply. When various income-dependent allowances are included, we find great variation across households. For considerable groups at lower income levels the marginal wage after taxes and allowances hardly increased at all. The effects of the reform on labour supply depend on how incentives have changed as well as on how sensitive labour supply is to economic incentives. A number of econometric studies have analyzed the supply of hours worked using Swedish data. These studies, which are discussed in section 5.3, indicate that the after-tax wage has rather small, but statistically significant effects on the length of working hours. In section 5.4 we ask what effects TR91 could have been expected to have on the number of hours worked. The answer is a modest increase for men, in the neighbourhood of 5 per cent or less, and a very minor effect, on average, for women. In sections 5.5 and 5.6, two special aspects are dealt with, namely, work done at home and the choice of education. In both of the following sections, we evaluate the effects of TR91 on the labour supply after 1991. In section 5.7, we discuss what conclusions can be drawn from interview studies where households themselves are allowed to state how TR91 has affected their labour supply. Finally, in section 5.8 we attempt to interpret the aggregate trends on the labour market after 1991.

5.1 THE DIMENSIONS OF LABOUR SUPPLY

Labour supply is a multifaceted concept. Often, the choice of the individual is seen only as a choice between *leisure* and *work*. But it also involves dividing the time not spent on the market between *pure leisure* and *work done in the home*, a choice which in turn is determined by the conditions for buying domestic services on the market. Labour supply on the market can be divided into different components. First is the question whether or not to *participate* at all in the workforce. Doing so normally entails certain fixed costs, for example, in the form of traveling time to work. At the same time, participation *per se*, irrespective of working hours, entails a number of benefits tied to the social insurance system, for example, the right to parents' allowance and unemployment benefits. Given that a person has chosen gainful employment, it is then a matter of choosing the number of *working hours*. This choice is often associated with certain restrictions. Few forms of employment permit a completely free choice of working hours; agreements may stipulate minimum as well as maximum working hours, and employers can make more or less formal demands regarding overtime, etc. Therefore, the choice of working hours is closely integrated with the choice of *profession, employer* and *form of contract*.

Many of the most important decisions are not made in a static perspective but as a result of more long-term considerations. Decisions about participating in the workforce, retiring and choosing a profession and a career are examples of such decisions since they involve fixed once-and-for-all costs which do not have to be paid anew unless one chooses a new profession or leaves the workforce entirely. An even more obvious example is *education*, which can be seen as an investment decision where the investment cost is unpaid wages during the period of education and the return is in the form of higher wages and better working conditions later on in life.

A progressive tax system, where the marginal tax rate increases with income, can affect the choice of the individual in all of these respects. Decisions about marginal changes in working hours for a person who has already chosen a profession and participates in the workforce is affected by the *marginal tax rate*. Decisions about participating in the workforce are affected by the *average tax over a greater interval*, between zero and normal working hours. Choices about education – or between different careers with different aggregate lifetime salary profiles – are affected above all by *differences in average tax* between the wage which would have been paid during the period of education and the wage which one would have received after completing the education. Thus, one can distinguish at least three different tax wedges relevant to different components of labour supply.

5.2   TAX INCENTIVES

The effect of the tax system on the economic exchange of an extra hour of work can be measured in various ways. One usually uses the *marginal tax rate* of the income tax schedule. However, the income tax is only one of the taxes which drives a wedge between the extra purchasing power an individual receives and the market value of an extra work effort. Firstly, there are income-dependent allowances and taxes on public services to take into account, and we can talk about the aggregate *marginal effect* of the tax and allowance system. Secondly, taxes not only determine how many Swedish kronor an individual receives in his hand, but also, through indirect taxes and employers' contributions which affect the prices of commodities, the purchasing power of these kronor. When indirect taxes and employers' contributions are taken into account, we talk about a *tax wedge*. This measures the relationship between the remuneration the individual is allowed to keep after tax, and what it would have cost him to buy that which he has produced himself, assuming that the price consists of wage costs, employers' contributions and indirect taxes. Expressed differently, it measures the difference between the financial compensation to the individual and the social value of his contribution to production. The tax wedge can be calculated based on either the marginal tax rate or a marginal effect taking allowances into account.

In order to assess labour supply incentives, it can be more pedagogical to state how large a share of an extra krona of income remains after taxes and allowances rather than how much goes to taxes, that is,

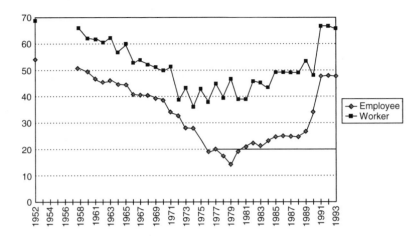

Figure 5.1 Marginal income (per cent) after income tax for a full-time
          employed industrial worker and an upper-level salaried employee
Source: DuRietz (1994), Table 3.1.

one minus the tax wedge. We describe such a measurement as *marginal income*. Figure 5.1 illustrates the development of marginal income after income taxes, and Figure 5.2 shows marginal income taking the full tax wedge into account. During the 1980s the latter was only around 30 per cent of the market wage of an average blue-collar worker and below 20 per cent for a white-collar employee. The increase from 1989 to 1991 was 23 per cent (7 percentage units) for the blue-collar worker and 76 per cent (12 percentage units) for the white-collar employee.

A couple of representative after-tax marginal incomes may suffice to give a first impression of the long-term trend, but the picture is incomplete and possibly biased since the figures only apply to individuals in full-time employment. In fact, only around 90 per cent of employed men, and less than 60 per cent of women, work more than 35 hours per week. For women in the most occupationally active ages, the average work week is not more than 33 hours. This means that marginal incomes at shorter working hours, can be as important for the aggregate labour supply as the marginal incomes for various groups of full-time employed individuals.

In the case of shorter working hours and lower incomes it is especially important to take into account the marginal effects which arise because of various income-dependent allowances; above all the housing allowances, rules for the repayment of student loans and

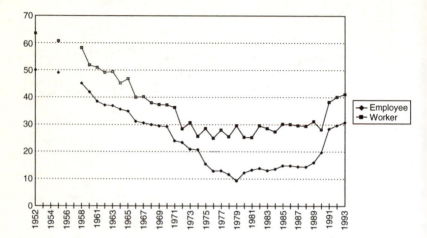

Figure 5.2 Marginal income (per cent) after tax wedge for a full-time employed
industrial worker and an upper-level salaried employee
Source: DuRietz (1994), Table 3.1.

income-dependent day-care fees. The most extensive of these
systems is that of housing allowances, the marginal effect of which in
1991 was 20 per cent for families with children, 10 per cent for households without children and 33 per cent for young people under the
age of 29 without children. Increased housing allowances for
families without children counteracted the lowered marginal tax rates
for this group. Since these allowances are gradually reduced at
relatively low income levels, they may assume the nature of poverty
traps.

An example of how marginal effects are modified when allowances
are included is given in Figure 5.3, which refers to single persons under
the age of 29 without children. Above the regular tax schedule are two
humps associated with housing allowances and the repayment of student loans. These raise the marginal effect from the nominal 30 per
cent of the tax rate to 50–60 per cent over rather wide income intervals.
Corresponding figures can be drawn for other household categories,
where, for example, the construction of day-care fees is very important.
How important are these extra marginal-effect humps in practice? Is it
not true that they only apply to a small number of households with very
special income situations? The answer is given in Table 5.1 which

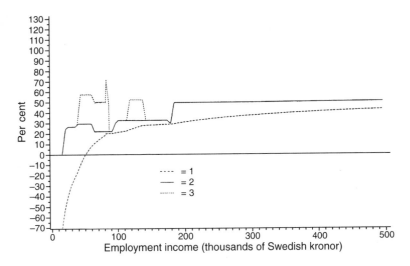

Figure 5.3   Gross income, the marginal tax rate and the marginal effect for single young people under the age of 29 without children, 1991 average tax rate (net after transfers)

1 average tax rate (net after transfers)
2 marginal tax rate
3 marginal effect

Source: Andersson and Gustafsson (1992), Figure 2.

utilizes data from the HINK survey[1] to calculate the total marginal effect for representative households in different income deciles.

As can be seen, a considerable share of households have marginal effects well over 50 per cent, despite the fact that the central government marginal tax rate did not exceed 20 per cent in any segment. Comparisons with the rules which applied at the beginning of the 1980s indicate that the marginal effect was not lowered at all for many households with housing allowances; see further the budget sets for different representative households given in Aronsson and Walker (1995). Note also that the figures in Table 5.1 do not represent the total tax wedges including indirect taxes and employers' contributions. In other words, they should be compared with the marginal tax rate in Figure 5.1 and not the tax wedge in Figure 5.2.

It can of course be discussed if *all* the allowance rules and fees should be accounted for. If the purpose is to assess how the labour supply of individuals is affected, then perhaps it is most reasonable to limit oneself to the system of rules which can be assumed to be so well known and easy to understand that they really affect behaviour.

Table 5.1 Typical marginal effects (per cent) for different types of households and income deciles: the 1991 tax and allowance rules

	Single		Cohabitation			
	Under 29	29–64 years	*no children*	*one child*	*two children*	*three children*
Decile						
1	0	0	35	42	48	49
2	4	22	37(40)	46	52	54
3	27	42	28	40	52(64)	54
4	58	42(63)	33	33	33(78)	54(66)
5	52	42(63)	45	42	46	55(67)
6	33	33	45	42	46	68
7	33(53)	33	45(33)	42	46	68(85)
8	33(44)	33	45(53)	42	46	50
9	33	50	50	42(52)	46(56)	50
10	50	50	50	50	49	50

Note: The figures are based on the 1989 HINK survey. Households are divided into deciles according to employment income. The division into deciles refers to each category of households separately. The figures within parenthesis apply to persons who have a repayable student loan under the older rules.
Source: Andersson and Gustafsson (1992), Table 7 and Table 10.

Among less visible marginal effects are, for example, those due to day-care fees, as well as pension entitlements, parents' allowances and other forms of social insurance which do not go into effect until later in life.[2] Further, the rules for social welfare benefits have become more important in pace with unemployment growing among uninsured individuals and people struck off the rolls. Taking these rules into account would further increase the marginal effects at low income levels. In principle, social welfare benefits can be said to yield 100 per cent marginal effects up to the norm which is applied.[3]

The debate about the incentive effects of the tax system often deals with the marginal exchange of an extra increment of labour. However, marginal effects over large intervals also have an effect on total disposable income. For example, many high-income earners, who were not hit by the decreased value of the interest deductions, received considerably increased total income as a result of the reform. This income increase can in itself have led to a *decreased* labour supply. Therefore, it is important to describe the entire budget restriction and not just the marginal effects. Such calculations have been made for a representative selection of over one thousand households from the HUS panel by Klevmarken *et al.* (1995).[4] The resulting numbers, which state how disposable income after tax and allowances depends on the numbers of hours worked, are given for two years: 1992 and 1985. Account is taken of the new taxation of capital, the broadening of the VAT base and other commodity tax changes and the income-dependency of housing allowances and day-care fees. Real wages and other kinds of income have been assumed unchanged in real terms between the two points in time. Typically, the two budget sets intersect each other; at low working hours, disposable income was higher using the 1985 tax system than using the 1992 system; at working hours over a certain number of hours (depending on the individual's wage and other factors) it was lower. This is obviously a reflection of the reduced marginal effects.

Such budget restrictions have been constructed for every household in the HUS panel.[5] Since households have different wages, capital income and so on, there is a large spread not only in the position of the budget sets, but also in how they have changed as a result of TR91. In addition, it is no trivial task to summarize the information about labour supply incentives which they contain. One way of doing this, which focuses on the difference in marginal effect between the two points in time, is to calculate the difference in disposable income between the 1985 and the 1992 rules for each number of hours and each individual household. This results in a set of distributions over the differences in income across households between the two years, one distribution for each number of hours. Figure 5.4 provides an illustrative example of these distributions for one category of households, namely single women. For each number of working hours, medians and the 25th and 75th percentiles respectively are given of the income differences between the 1985 and the 1992 tax. These values at different working hours are then connected to form three curves. Note that the curves do not necessarily represent one and the same household at different numbers of hours.

The new tax system entails a loss for most of the households at short working hours; the curve for the 75th percentile intersects the axis at around 1200 working hours. At the median number of working hours, 1428 hours, there are about as many winners as losers. The figure only takes into account tax changes. When allowances are included, the picture is changed; most of the households will make a profit at normal working hours.[6] The fact that most households should have gained from the reform may be seen as an indication that it was not fully financed (see further our discussion in Chapter 6). In the next section, we discuss how one should relate to such income effects when analyzing the effects of the reform on labour supply.

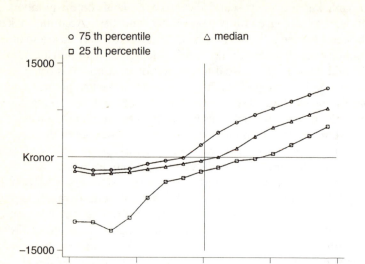

Figure 5.4   Labour supply and change in disposable income as a result of
changes in taxation 1985–92, single women
Source: Klevmarken *et al*. (1995), Figure 2.11.

We can also gather from the figure how marginal effects have
changed. The slope of the curves are namely a measure of the change
of marginal income (with the reservation that the curves do not apply
to identical households).[7] We see that the slope for most households
has barely increased at all at working hours up to the median. On the
other hand, the marginal income for all categories of households has
increased substantially at working hours and wages at, or above, the
median. One can also ask how large the spread is in changed marginal
effects at the actual numbers of hours worked. Table 5.2 shows the
percentage changes in marginal income between 1985 and 1992 at
actual 1985 working hours. For more than a quarter of the households
in each category of the panel marginal income has fallen. It has
increased by 10–25 per cent for median households, and one-fourth
of households have had increases of more than 30–40 per cent.

Another aspect of labour supply, alongside the choice of hours, is
the *decision to work at all*. Here, it is the average tax at the desired
number of working hours that matters. Probably, this choice is primarily relevant for married or cohabiting women. Assume that they

Table 5.2 Percentage change in marginal income per extra working hour after income tax and allowances, 1985–92

	Both spouses working		Couples, one spouse working		Singles	
	Men	*Women*	*Men*	*Women*	*Men*	*Women*
25th percentile	−0.6	−3.1	−8.8	−6.8	−1.1	−3.3
Median	24.2	19.0	15.4	9.7	9.9	10.8
75th percentile	40.0	33.7	43.6	28.4	30.9	31.0

Source: Calculations by Anders Klevmarken for the HUS panel.

contemplate working half-time. The calculations in Klevmarken *et al.* (1995) indicate small changes over the interval 0–1000 hours for this group. Hence, it is unlikely that participation in the workforce has been affected by TR91 to any great extent.

The third aspect of labour supply is the choice of *education* and *career*. Here, it is difficult to gather anything directly from an individual curve in the figures, since incentives for education depend on the relation between taxes at different levels of income at different stages in life. An assessment must be based on expectations about future tax systems and wage structures. Assuming unchanged taxes and wages, one can get a rough picture of the incentives for education by comparing disposable income after tax and allowances for a relatively low-paid full-time worker (opportunity wage during the period of education) with income after tax and allowances for a highly paid full-time worker (after education). It is obvious that the difference in disposable income between different wage levels has increased throughout.[8] See section 5.6 for a more detailed discussion of the incentives for education.

We conclude that the incentives to work an extra hour have increased substantially for most individuals, above all, at working hours around full-time; that the change has been slight, or has even gone in the opposite direction in certain instances at part-time work hours and/or low wage levels; that the incentives to participate in the workforce have been changed insignificantly for those persons (cohabiting women) who primarily can contemplate staying outside the workforce; and that the incentives for education have been strengthened, on the whole, for all groups.

5.3   WHAT DETERMINES THE SUPPLY OF HOURS WORKED?

A number of empirical studies have examined the connection between hours worked and marginal income after tax. Before we get further involved in a discussion about the conclusions that can be drawn from this literature, a matter of principle deserves closer investigation. The empirical studies try to establish the correlation between the individual's labour supply and the marginal wage after taxes and allowances and other explanatory factors. In principle, the wage elasticity can be positive as well as negative. A wage increase has two distinguishable effects. In the first place, the individual gets a higher income for a given number of hours worked. If we consider leisure as a commodity among others, then higher income would be expected to increase the propensity to consume leisure and would thus reduce the supply of labour. This is the *income effect* of a wage increase on the supply of labour which, according to the above line of reasoning, probably is negative. However, it is an empirical question whether this is actually the case; it could be positive. Secondly, the marginal income from an extra hour of work increases. This effect itself, for a given income level, ought to stimulate an increase in labour supply. This is the *substitution effect* of a wage increase. It can be taken for granted to be positive (or at any rate not negative).

It is often pointed out that one cannot be certain in what direction a reduction of the marginal tax rate will affect labour supply, since the income and substitution effects probably counteract each other, and the net effect can either be positive or negative. However, this statement, which in itself is correct, is misleading as a basis for an analysis of a tax reform. It is namely based on the assumption that taxpayers in general will enjoy the full income effect of a tax reduction. But such a reform would normally not be fully financed (except in the rather unlikely instance where the economy had already passed the top of the Laffer curve, so that total tax revenues increased when taxes were lowered).[9] Since, taking a long-term perspective, the state's budget must always balance, it must be assumed that sooner or later taxpayers will have to finance that part of TR91 which is not immediately financed. Normally, it is not possible to know what forms this will take. A rough assumption is that it takes place through taxes which neutralize the income effect, but do not affect incentives (so-called lump-sum taxes). If the income effect is neutralized individual by individual, in this way, the effects of TR91 on labour supply would only be due to substitution effects. In such a pure instance one can say *a priori* that a tax reform with generally reduced taxes should lead to an increase in labour supply.

The conclusion that income effects should be ignored must be modified for three reasons. In the first place, no tax reforms can have an entirely neutral effect on income distribution. Therefore income effects will affect the supply of labour for individual groups, upwards for some and downwards for others. However, this is important for the aggregate supply of labour only if income elasticities differ in a systematic way between different groups. We know little about this, and it is reasonable to assume that the income effects mainly cancel out each other. Secondly, a tax reform which helps increase efficiency – for example, as a result of an increased supply of labour – need not be completely financed, krona for krona. Thirdly, even if one accepts the idea that a tax reform must be financed, there is a difference between the case when it is fully financed by tax increases the same year the reform goes into effect, and the case when it is allowed to give rise to continuing budget deficits (as in the case with the current Swedish reform). Sooner or later, a deficit must be covered by tax increases,[10] which will partly hit today's taxpayers and partly future generations. The question now is how today's taxpayers weigh this future negative income effect, which can be difficult to foresee and partly does not affect them directly, against the tangible positive income effects which are noticed immediately on their wage slips. If it is not believed that these effects will fully balance out each other, there may be cause to take into account the income effects on labour supply of an underfinanced tax reform, if one is interested in the short-term effects on labour supply. To be consistent, one should also take into account the income effect in the opposite direction when the reform is to be financed in the future.

Keeping in mind the great uncertainty about the potential income effects, it may in general be reasonable to look primarily at the substitution effects. However, when assessing the present reform, arguments in favour of accounting for income changes can be made for two reasons. First, TR91 was underfinanced. Second, as we will discuss in Chapter 8, our assessment is that in the long run it will improve the functioning of the economy and increase social efficiency.

There are a number of studies of Swedish households' choice of working hours. These are mostly pure cross-section studies, but there are also examples of panel studies. A basic problem of methodology is that wages after tax, due to the progressive nature of the tax system are endogenous. Modern labour supply studies handle this problem by measuring the marginal tax rate at a standardized number of working hours, or by modeling the entire budget restriction with all its kink points. An early Swedish study which explicitly modeled the entire budget restriction is Blomquist (1983). In recent years, there has been an intensive analysis and discussion surrounding the importance of estimation methods and stochastic model specification in this context; see Flood and MaCurdy (1993), Blomquist (1995, 1996) and articles in *Ekonomisk Debatt*, issues 1 and 3 for 1990 for applications of this discussion on Swedish data. It is still too early to draw any definite conclusions from this research. However, it is worthwhile noting that there does not seem to be any systematic connection between estimation methods and the size of the estimated labour supply elasticities.[11]

The group which has been studied the most is the one which works the most, namely, *married men between 25 and 55 years of age*, a group which accounts for slightly more than 40 per cent of the aggregate number of working hours in the Swedish economy. Their share of total wages and salaries is even greater. Most of these studies are based on data from the beginning of the 1980s or earlier; for example, Blomquist (1983, 1989), Blomquist and Hansson Brusewitz (1990) and Flood and MaCurdy (1993). This, of course, limits their usefulness for drawing conclusions a decade later. However, an advantage can be that the variation in marginal tax rates was greater then, which means that data from these years ought to be especially informative about the effects of marginal tax rates. It can perhaps be argued as well that the tax system was seen to be more stable at that time, than later during the 1980s, when behaviour may have been characterized by expectations about impending tax reforms.

Despite the differences in estimation methods, the different studies arrive at broadly similar results. The estimated elasticities[12] are consistently low. Representative income elasticities are between minus 0.10 and zero. Wage elasticities which keep income constant and thus isolate the substitution effect – so-called compensated elasticities – lie between 0.08 and 0.24[13] with a certain concentration around 0.10. These might seem like small figures, but for high-income earners whose after-tax marginal income has increased by an entire 75 per cent as a result of the reform, they can be translated into an increase of weekly working hours by as much as three hours. However, this group is rather small, and the marginal income for married men has increased, on average, by only around 20 per cent; see Table 5.2.

With an elasticity of 0.10, this would give rise to an increase of labour supply by two per cent.

Women's working hours vary much more than those of men. Participation in the workforce is also still somewhat lower, especially among older women. Both these conditions indicate that one may expect larger elasticities for women than for men. This presumption is confirmed by studies of married women done by Blomquist and Hansson Brusewitz (1990), Aronsson (1991) and Ackum Agell and Apel (1993). However, the variation in estimated elasticities is greater for women than for men. Reported income elasticities vary between −0.03 and −0.24, and compensated wage elasticities vary between plus 0.22 and 1.07. Let us assume that the true wage elasticity is 0.4, a bit below the middle of this interval.[14] We have previously seen that the reduction in marginal effect as a result of TR91 is somewhat lower for women than for men. The figures in Table 5.2 indicate an increase of marginal wages after tax by between 10 and 20 per cent for the median among married women. This translates into an expected increase of labour supply by between four and eight per cent.

The choice of working hours is normally a joint concern for *both spouses*. The studies referred to above take this into account only by treating the other spouse's income as exogenously given. Therefore, variations in the spouse's working hours affect the estimated income elasticity, but it is not possible to identify any cross effects between the wages of the two spouses. A study by Aronsson and Palme (1994) looks at the labour supply of both spouses as a result of a simultaneous decision.[15] Like the previous studies, they find the income elasticities to be very close to zero, weakly negative for women (−0.06) and very weakly positive for men (+0.01). There are now two wage elasticities: one for one's own wage and another for the wage of the spouse. For men, they find about the same result as in the other studies, an elasticity of +0.15 regarding one's own wage and a completely insignificant elasticity (+0.01) for the wife's wage. For women, the own-wage elasticity is once again higher (+0.31) than for men, but the cross elasticity regarding the husband's wage is negative (−0.10). This can be interpreted as the woman assuming more of the housework when the man increases his working hours. It means that the net effect of TR91 on the labour supply of women is probably not as great as suggested by the calculations in the previous paragraph.

Swedish, as well as foreign, studies have concentrated on cohabiting persons, even if these only represent about 45 per cent of all occupationally active Swedish households. In an unpublished work, Tomas Aronsson and Mårten Palme study a sample of single women from the 1981 and 1991 *Level of Living Surveys* (LNU).[16] They find a relatively large compensated wage elasticity of ca. 0.2 which is significantly different from zero, while the income elasticity is numerically small and not significantly different from zero.

Actual working hours consist of contracted hours and overtime. In the short-term perspective, in many occupations contracted hours are fixed by agreements and conventions, and the preferences of the individual are expressed only by his choice of extra work, overtime and leaves of absence. This means that certain individuals can be rationed as to their choice of working hours. According to answers to interview questions in the LNU and HUS panels, 10–20 per cent of all employees find themselves in this category. Among such employees it is somewhat more common to want to reduce working hours than to increase them. Sacklén (1995) has used data from the 1981 LNU panel to study what consequences rationing effects have for the estimated wage elasticities. He compares a standard estimation method with one where he uses information about how individuals would like to adjust their working hours, if they could. According to his results, the compensated wage elasticity is only half as big (0.07) when information about the desired number of working hours is used compared to when this is not the case.[17]

The studies referred to above are basically static cross-section studies and do not use the information in variation in wages and taxes over time. The only Swedish labour supply study that is based on individual data over a long period of time is Ackum Agell and Meghir (1995), which looks at labour supply for a panel of workers in the engineering industry for the years 1970–87, a period with considerable variations in marginal tax rates. They estimate several different models, and like the other studies, they consistently find small wage elasticities. In one model which is directly analogous to a static model, they express the change in labour supply from one year to another as a function of the change in real wages between the years. The estimated elasticities in their two model specifications come very close to what the other studies found, 0.12 and 0.14 respectively.[18] A fundamental methodological problem even with the dynamic study by Ackum Agell and Meghir is that it treats the wage path over life as exogenously given. Therefore, it has nothing to say about what are probably the most important dynamic aspects, namely the choice of education and career. Investing in education means little or no working hours early in life in exchange for a higher wage later on. We will return to the effects on choice of education in section 5.6.[19]

A good understanding of the wage elasticity of labour supply has decisive importance for our assessment of TR91; see the discussion about social efficiency in section 8.3 Despite differences in methodology the literature agrees that the (compensated) wage elasticity is low, between 0.05–0.15 for married prime age men. Most of the studies report estimates around 0.10 with confidence intervals which include the point estimates from other studies. The discussion about econometric methodology of recent years has hardly changed opinions in this respect. Unfortunately, there are only a few studies that deal with other groups than married men. These indicate considerably greater own-wage elasticities for women, perhaps around 0.3. However, for married women, these seem to be counteracted by negative cross-effects with their husbands' wages. An unexplored area is the labour supply of young people. This is largely due to the fact that the conventional static model for labour supply is especially unsatisfactory, and the problems of measurement are especially difficult for this group.

5.4 THE ANTICIPATED EFFECTS OF TR91 ON HOURS WORKED

A rough way to calculate the effects of the reform on labour supply is to multiply the estimated compensated wage elasticity by the percentage change in marginal wage after tax for a representative individual. The simple calculations of this kind presented above imply that the reform could have been expected to increase labour supply by a few percent for men as well as women. Calculations based on separate studies of men and women indicate that the effect would be bigger for women, but calculations based on the household model of Aronsson and Palme (1994) give the opposite result. Reform effects estimated in this way should be considered uncertain for three different reasons. Firstly, they are the result of a small elasticity multiplied by a large percentage change of wage after tax. This means that even if the elasticity is estimated with reasonable precision, the prediction of the effect of the reform will be quite uncertain. An illustrative, if extreme, example can be constructed from a model used by Ackum Agell and Meghir (1995) which has a statistically significant wage elasticity of 0.14 with a 95 per cent confidence interval of 0.01–0.27. Multiplied by a change in marginal income of 76 per cent for a typical upper-level salaried employee (see Figure 5.2) this means that the effect of the reform can be anywhere between 14 and 370 hours per year.

Secondly, we have ignored income effects, which could be important if we believe that households have adapted themselves to an under-financed reform, or if redistribution effects have been of great import-ance. However, since aggregate income changes are rather small and the redistribution effects counteract each other, income elasticities must be rather large for such effects to matter for the aggregate labour supply. Most studies have found elasticities between −0.1 and −0.2, magnitudes that hardly suggest that income effects could be of major importance.

Thirdly, households are heterogeneous, and their behaviour cannot be captured well by a wage elasticity which is the same for all. The problem can be illustrated by a somewhat realistic example. Assume that there are two equally large groups: one group (women) with a large elasticity, and one group (men) whose wage elasticity is zero, and that the men, but not the women, have their marginal tax rate lowered. In this case, the supply of labour would not be changed at all, despite the fact that both the average wage elasticity and the average tax reduction were positive. Therefore, an assessment of the effects of TR91 should be based on separate calculations for different groups of households. The ideal is to use a data base with randomly chosen households which are representative for the entire population.

Only a few studies have presented results based on microsimulations for individual households. One example is Aronsson and Palme's study (1994) of spouses' labour supply. They predict the number of hours worked for the tax systems of 1981, 1989 and 1991, taking into account indirect taxes and children's allowances and housing allowances. They find the average number of working hours for men to be 5 per cent higher under the 1991 tax system than under the 1989 tax system, and an additional 3 per cent higher than under the 1981 rules. For women, the differences in the number of working hours were completely insignificant. In part, the small effects can be explained by the fact that the simulated reform was not fully financed and that the results were affected by income effects. The gender pattern is a result of men receiving a relatively bigger tax reduction as well as the strong negative cross-effect between women's supply of labour and men's wages.

Klevmarken *et al.* (1995) use 1985 data from the HUS survey to carry out microsimulations for a sample representing all household types. However, their study is not based on estimated labour supply functions, but instead characterises household behaviour by using assumed parameters.[20] Since TR91, when increased allowances are taken into account, entails a noticeable increase in income for most households, the simulated labour supply effects will be affected by income effects. As we previously discussed, this presumes that today's households adapt themselves to what they see on their pay slips and tax assessment notices without taking future taxes fully into account. This may be reasonable in the short run, but in order to assess the effects in a longer-term perspective, one ought to consider a fully financed reform. Since the future method of financing is not known today, such an assessment must be based on an assumption. Here, it is assumed that the reform is balanced with the aid of lump-sum taxes which are levied in proportion to the average disposable incomes within broad groups of households. The idea is that there should not be any income effects in the aggregate, but only in the form of redistribution across different households.

Simulation results which refer to differences between the 1985 system (which was about the same as the 1989 system) and two specifications of the 1991 system, consistently show small effects, and for certain groups even negative effects. In the specification which refers to a fully financed reform, labour supply for men increases by 2–5 per cent, while that of women decreases by 0–8 per cent depending on the parameter assumptions. The upper limits in these intervals agree with the figures of Aronsson and Palme for the difference between the 1989 and the 1991 systems.[21] Weighed together for all households, the result is an increased labour supply by 0.4 per cent for the fully financed reform.

In conclusion, it is our view that the reform can be expected to have generated positive supply effects of five per cent or somewhat less among cohabiting men, while the effect on the labour supply of cohabiting women is probably close to zero. For single people, assessments are more uncertain. Keeping in mind the fact that the group 'cohabiting men' has the highest salaries and works the most hours, this group is especially important for aggregate labour supply. Our best guess is that the aggregate labour supply may have increased by around 3 per cent as a result of TR91.

5.5 TAXES AND HOUSEHOLD WORK

Besides sleep, the time which people have at their disposal can be used in roughly three ways: leisure, household work and work on the market. Almost all studies refer to work on the market without making a distinction between alternative ways of using remaining time. However, economic incentives also affect the weighing of pure leisure against household work. Many jobs in the home can be done with the aid of services bought on the market, and in many instances, like painting and other work done by craftsmen, the purchase of a service ought to be a very close substitute to home production. The existence of household work, in itself, does not affect the interpretation of the labour supply elasticities. They are still valid estimates of how the supply of labour on the market is affected by wages after tax. But it means that the taxation of work on the market has distorting effects in addition to those which are associated with the substitution between work and leisure. This entails a social cost, since it prevents utilising the advantages of the division of labour. Less efficient work methods will be used when home maintenance work is done by amateurs instead of professionals.

Swedish data on the use of time by households come primarily from the HUS surveys in 1984 and 1993. Data from the earlier survey have been compared with those of some other countries by Juster and Stafford (1991). It turns out that Swedish men spend more time at home than men in the other countries studied, which is consistent with Sweden having the highest marginal tax rates. The difference in relation to our Nordic neighbours in the beginning of the 1980s was between one and six hours per week.

A comparison of the two HUS surveys shows that the time spent on care, meals and rest has for the most part not changed between 1984 and 1993. The distribution between other activities can be seen in Figure 5.5. Certain changes have taken place in a direction consistent with the decreased marginal effects. The amount of time spent on household work and on repairs and maintenance has decreased by nine and seven per cent respectively; above all, more time is spent watching television today than before. It is tempting to interpret these changes as effects of market work becoming more profitable after tax in relation to household work. However, behind these figures there are substantially altered gender patterns. Men actually set aside around one hour *more* a week for household work in 1993, whereas women had reduced time spent in the home by as much as 3–4 hours. It is also reasonable to assume that these figures reflect more long-term trends and changes in attitude. In the econometric study that Flood (1988) carried out based on the 1984 survey, no support was found for the hypothesis of a connection between market after-tax wages and

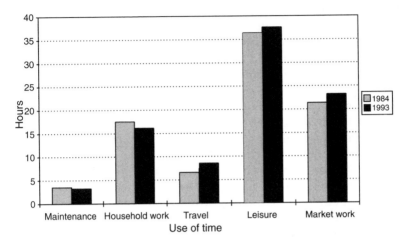

Figure 5.5   The use of time by Swedish households in 1984 and 1993, hours
per week
Source: Flood and Gråsjö (1995).

household work. Unfortunately, we do not know to what extent the decreased amount of household work has been replaced by services purchased on the market. The effect on household work is an important component in assessing the effects of TR91 on social efficiency.[22] Unfortunately, our knowledge about this issue is limited to the studies that have been presented here, and it is not possible to draw any far-reaching conclusions from them.

5.6   EDUCATION INCENTIVES

Even if the effect on the choice of education and career hardly were emphasized in connection with TR91, the step from a strongly progressive to a more proportional tax scale has had great importance for the incentive to refrain from (relatively low) income early in life in favour of future (higher) income. In order to understand how the tax system affects the return on education, one can think of the occupationally active part of one's life as consisting of two periods: a first period when one can choose to work or study, and a second period when everybody works and education leads to a higher wage.

The pecuniary income from getting an education can be measured by the difference in after-tax wages between educated and uneducated labour. The size of this difference depends on how progressive the tax scale is; the more progressive the greater is the difference in average tax between individuals at different levels of education. The most important cost for education is the opportunity wage (after tax) during the period of education. The return on this investment in education can be measured by its internal rate of return, that is, the rate of interest which makes the discounted current value of the higher income after education exactly the same as the income from which one refrained during the period of education. The difference between the internal rate of interest before and after tax at given wages can then be seen as a measure of how the tax system affects the incentive to invest in education. This can be illustrated by a simplified case with two wage levels, one for educated, w_e, and one for uneducated labour, w_u. With corresponding notation for tax rates, the return on an investment in education (the internal rate of interest) can be expressed as

$$\frac{w_e(1 - t_e) - w_u(1 - t_u)}{w_u(1 - t_u)}$$

where t_e and t_u are the average tax rates at normal working hours for educated and uneducated labour. In other words, the return is the after-tax wage differential divided by the cost of education, that is, the after-tax wage for uneducated labour. In the case of a completely proportional tax system both tax rates are the same and can be cancelled out. Thus, a proportional system is neutral, regardless of the tax rate, assuming that there are no other education costs than the wage foregone, or that such costs are deductible.[23] TR91 can be interpreted as a substantial reduction of t_e combined with an insignificant change of t_u and is thus a step in the direction toward a neutral taxation and a noticeable improvement of the incentive for education.

In order to calculate in more detail the importance of the tax system for education incentives, we need figures on the before-tax wage premium tied to a certain education decision. Such calculations have been made by Edin and Holmlund (1993) for a twenty-year-old man with a secondary education who considers pursuing four more years of study. The wage premium is taken from wage equations estimated on cross-section data. The figures can thus be interpreted as *real* internal interest rates calculated on the assumption that today's real wages are expected to remain in the future. The results are summarized in

Table 5.3 The real internal rate of interest before and after tax on a four-year post-secondary education

| | Real internal rate of interest | | |
	Before tax	After tax	Effective tax rate
1968	15.7	11.9	24
1974	6.9	3.6	48
1981	4.3	0.5	88
1984	3.9	1.7	56
1986	5.3	3.3	38
1988	4.7	2.7	43
1991	6.0	4.5	25

Source: Edin and Holmlund (1993), Table 5.

Table 5.3, where the effective tax rate is calculated as the difference in internal interest rate before and after tax divided by the before-tax internal interest rate.

The sequence of reforms in the 1980s with gradually reduced progressive taxes has meant a considerable reduction of the tax on investments in education. We have gone from a system with close to confiscation levels of taxation to a situation where education is taxed about as much as investments in buildings and machinery. However, the figures in the table do not tell the whole story since they do not take into account the fact that the government also subsidizes higher education through student loans. If one also includes student loans in the estimate, the internal rate of interest after tax and student loan increases, and the level of effective taxation decreases. However, since education is only partially financed by student loans, the conclusion remains that effective taxation of investments in education has decreased as a result of TR91.

The next question concerns the effects of tax variations on the propensity to get an education. Fredriksson (1994) has studied the patterns in time series of the number of students registered at universities and university colleges for the 1967–91 period. He found that the share of men under 22 years of age who were newly registered is well explained by economic incentives. The elasticity for the share of first-year university students (relative to all men between the ages of 18 and 22) is as high as 2.9 with respect to the after-tax salary for men with a university degree, and −1.0 with respect to the after-tax salary for men with only secondary school (*gymnasium*).[24] These figures should not be taken too literally because variations in the number of students in higher education reflect the *supply* of the number of university places as well as demand; the economic crisis has created its own incentive for education since the school desk is the only available workplace for many young people. Let us still use these figures as a rough example and characterize TR91 as an increase in the average salary for university graduates by 20 per cent after tax with unchanged pay at lower incomes. In this case Fredriksson's estimates imply that the tax reform entailed an increase in the share of first-year students by as much as 60 per cent, or from ca. 15 per cent to almost 25 per cent of all men under the age of 22.

The empirical studies discussed deal with formal education, but similar incentives also affect other types of investment in human capital, e.g. whether to participate in poorly paid education during working hours and whether to further one's career by working over-time. They might also involve the choice between occupations with different expected lifetime pay trends. Industrial workers, as well as teachers and health care workers with little individual wage setting have a relatively even wage trend over their professional careers, while large groups of salaried employees and many freelance professionals have a more uneven wage trend. A progressive tax system, as opposed to a proportional one, works to the disadvantage of the latter group, and the 1991 reform can generally been seen as entailing an improvement for groups with an uneven wage profile.

5.7   THE OPINIONS OF HOUSEHOLDS

TR91 changed incentives for labour supply in a number of ways. Did households, in fact, adjust to the new rules of the game? We will try to answer this question in two different ways. In this section, we will look at evidence from interview questions, and in the next section, we will study actual trends in the number of hours worked for different groups. We will also discuss the results of an econometric study which tries to isolate the effects of changed marginal taxes on the supply of labour.

The most direct method might seem quite simply to ask people whether TR91 has induced them to change the number of hours they have worked. Economists are often skeptical about interpreting such introspective questions. A common view is that actions speak louder than words. Answers to interview questions might reflect ideologically influenced ideas about how one ought to behave rather than how one actually behaves. It can also be difficult to get interview subjects to distinguish between the partial effect of a tax reform and other factors that have an impact. For example, in a Sweden in a state of economic crisis the tax reform may have contributed to a smaller reduction in hours worked than would otherwise have been the case, even if few would say that they worked more because of the reform. However, these problems of interpretation must of course be weighed against the objections that can be raised against other methods of attacking the problem, where one interprets data using more or less refined statistical methods.

An ambitious interview study was carried out by Halleröd (1993). It is based on supplementary questions to the *Labour Market Survey* (*AKU*) asked immediately after the implementation of TR91 in March and September of 1991. The reform was sufficiently new at that time in order for the interviewees to be able to make a fair comparison with the old system. But it was during 1991 that unemployment began to accelerate, and labour supply was probably already then limited by demand. It can also be argued that households had not had sufficient time to adjust to the new rules of the game so quickly after the reform.

A relatively large share of those interviewed (12 per cent in March and 16 per cent in September) stated that they had increased their number of working hours as a result of the tax reform, but relatively few (6 per cent) stated this on both occasions. Still, these figures indicate that the reform had by no means negligible positive effects on the supply of labour. However, this interpretation is complicated by the fact that among the persons interviewed there was no connection whatsoever between the trend in the actual number of hours worked and answers to the question about the effects of the tax reform. Only 40 per cent of those who stated on both occasions that they had increased their number of working hours as a result of the reform had actually increased their number of working hours. This is the same percentage as for all employees. It is, of course, possible to interpret this relation to mean that there were other factors which affected the labour supply of these specific individuals in a diametrically opposed direction, but this interpretation seems so unlikely that one is led to doubt the credibility of this kind of interview information. Perhaps we can still agree with the concluding remarks of Halleröd (1993, p. 353) that the fact that almost one-quarter of those interviewed stated on at least one occasion that they had begun to work more as a result of TR91 can be seen as a sign of an increased *willingness* to increase the number of working hours, that is, an increase in the *supply* of labour.

Households have also been asked within the framework of the HUS survey about their reactions to TR91 (Klevmarken *et al.*, 1995, Table 5.1). Here, as well, a certain share, ca. 15 per cent, answered that they worked more following the reform, while 4 per cent stated that they worked less. The differences dependent on gender and education are small. In relation to the surveys of 1984 and 1986, an increased propensity to receive compensation for overtime in the form of money instead of compensation leave is also noted. On the whole, and with reservation for all the problems of interpretation, both these interview surveys provide some support for the claim that TR91 has had limited positive effects on the supply of labour.

5.8   AN INTERPRETATION OF TRENDS SINCE 1991

The total number of hours worked in the Swedish economy has decreased by almost ten per cent since 1990; see Figure 5.6. The main driving force behind this trend has most likely been declining aggregate demand. The question is whether it is possible to distinguish any effects from TR91. Can the decline in the number of hours worked

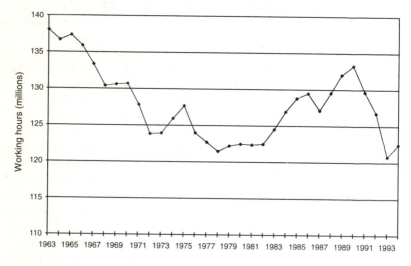

Figure 5.6   Millions of working hours per week, annual average
Source: Labour Market Survey (AKU).

be divided into a negative effect due to declining *demand* and positive *supply* effects due to the tax reform? One way of approaching such a division is to note that the decline in the number of hours worked is composed of three components: substantially increased unemployment, a change in the number of individuals participating in the workforce, and a change in the number of hours worked for those who have work.

It appears natural to attribute the increasing *unemployment* to the decline in demand, even if there may be a connection between the degree of progressivity in the tax system and the unemployment rate. Holmlund and Kolm (1995) analyze how a progressive tax system can have a dampening effect on wage formation, since it makes the wage costs of companies, and thus equilibrium employment, extra sensitive to increased wage demands after tax. Therefore, in bargaining over wages, the final effect would be wage agreements on a lower level, and thus lower unemployment, compared with a less progressive tax system. Another mechanism, which links progression in the tax system and unemployment, is analyzed by Ljungqvist and Sargent (1995). It works through the search behaviour of individuals. A person seeking employment decides on a reservation wage and accepts the first job offer with a wage above the reservation wage. How high this is depends, among other things, on the spread of wages in the economy; the greater the spread, the higher the reservation wage, since the chance of finding a really good wage offer if one waits is greater if this is the case. Since the after-tax wage spread decreases as taxes become more progressive, the conclusion is that an increased after-tax wage spread can be expected to increase search unemployment. Both these mechanisms point to the possibility that TR91 might have contributed to an increased equilibrium unemployment, but they can hardly have been the main explanations for the rapid upswing after 1990.

The trends of *participation in the workforce* and *the number of hours worked* are determined in a more complicated way by a combination of supply and demand factors. It is well known that high unemployment deters those who have an especially small chance of getting work from participating at all in the workforce. Further, we judge that the reform hardly strengthened the incentives to participate for the groups which can consider leaving or entering the workforce. In fact, it is likely that the incentive to participate has decreased for younger people, since it has become more profitable to invest in education. One should therefore unequivocally expect that the years after 1990 would be characterized by decreased participation in the workforce, above all for younger age groups.

The number of *hours worked* for individuals in work is constituted by the contractual number of working hours, which has remained constant during these years, and by overtime and extra work. The demand for overtime normally tends to diminish in times of weak general demand and high unemployment. Employers can then force a shorter work week on certain groups. At the same time, TR91 has meant an increased incentive to work more hours. In other words, supply and demand effects pull in opposite directions. However, the supply effects may be expected to be unevenly distributed. Incentives have increased especially in upper income levels. In addition, the econometric studies indicate that the effects on supply ought to be somewhat greater for men than women. If the effect of demand factors were the same for both groups, one would therefore expect that hours decreased less (increased more) for men and high income earners (higher education) than for women and low income earners (poor education).

How do our hypotheses agree with trends since 1990? Starting with the *participation frequency*, figures from the workforce surveys show that it has gone down by about as much for both sexes. The decline is much greater for younger people than for other groups; see Figure 5.7.

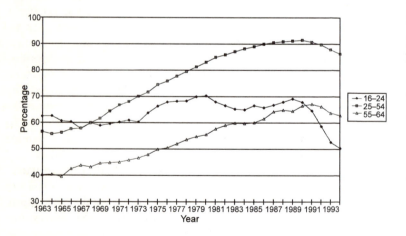

Figure 5.7a   The share of women of working age who participate in the workforce, 1963–94
Source: Labour Market Survey (AKU).

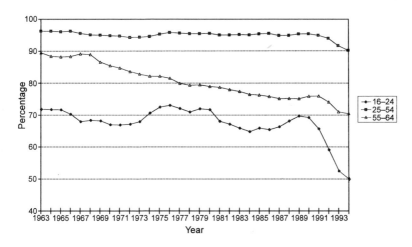

Figure 5.7b   The share of men of working age who participate in the workforce, 1963–94
Source: Labour Market Survey (AKU).

In the 16–24 age group, the participation frequency decreased from
almost 70 per cent in 1990 to 50 per cent in 1994 for both sexes. In
higher age groups, the decrease was moderate, five percentage points
or less. The finding that mainly young people have left the workforce is
in line with the strengthened education incentives provided by the tax
reform.

The number of *weekly hours worked* also decreased for all groups
between 1990 and 1993, but in relative numbers much less than the
participation frequency; see Figure 5.8. The decreases are especially
small – only a couple of per cent for both sexes – for the 25–54 age
group, where workforce participation is highest. For other groups, the
trend is not quite as uniform, and it is difficult to see any clear gender
differences.[25]

The picture of a substantial decrease in participation in the workforce but a moderate decrease of the average number of working hours
is not in conflict with the hypothesis that TR91 has had positive supply
effects. In order to assess this thesis in more detail, it is necessary to
have an understanding of how strong an effect labour market conditions normally have on the number of working hours. We can illustrate
this by a simple regression analysis of time-series from 1963 and 1993
over the average number of weekly working hours for employed men.

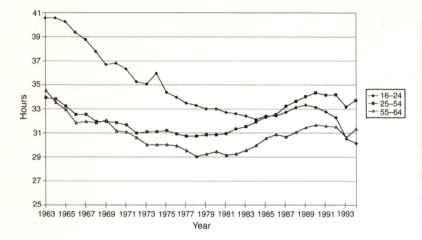

Figure 5.8a   The average number of weekly working hours for women, 1963–94
Source: Labour Market Survey (AKU).

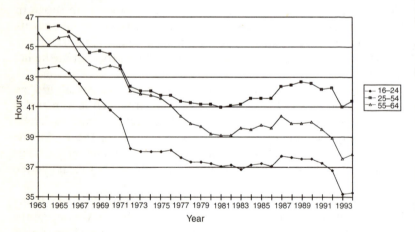

Figure 5.8b   The average number of weekly working hours for men, 1963–94
Source: Labour Market Survey (AKU).

Explanatory variables are the tax wedge for full-time employed industrial workers and open unemployment, which is used to represent the

degree of influence from aggregate labour demand. The results indicate that working hours are very sensitive to labour market conditions. However, changes in the tax wedge also have a significant, if rather moderate, effect. According to the estimated equation, the reduction of the tax wedge by ten percentage points, which took place between 1989 and 1991, should have increased working time by 0.5 hours, or by slightly more than one per cent. At the same time, the effects of the rise in unemployment were greater, so that the net effect was that working hours decreased.[26] The exact numbers, of course, should not be taken too literally. However, they are well in line with a study by Burtless (1987) which presents similar results for a somewhat earlier period.[27]

We have taken special care to examine whether the connection between these variables has changed during the crisis years of the 1990s by estimating the equation on data up to 1990 and using it to predict working hours for the years to come. The forecast captures fairly exactly the decline between 1990 and 1991, but it also predicts a substantial decline between 1991 and 1992, at which time the actual number of working hours did not change at all. The observed decline between 1992 and 1993 is once again captured well by the forecast. Thus, on the whole, the trend for the number of working hours for the population in employment in the crisis years has been less negative than could have been expected from historical patterns. This supports the hypothesis that the lowered marginal tax rates gave rise to positive supply effects.

The incentive to work additional hours has increased more in higher income levels. One would expect trends of working hours to reflect this difference. This hypothesis is illustrated in a rough way in Figures 5.9 and 5.10, which show, for different education levels, the shares of people employed with weekly working hours below 35 hours. Certain differences can be seen here among women as well as men in the expected direction. For highly educated men the share having a short work week is by and large the same before and after 1990, while the share increases substantially after 1990 for those who are poorly educated. For women, the share having a work week below 35 hours decreases for both groups up until 1990, after which the trend turns for those with poor education, but continues for those with higher education.

Another aspect of labour supply is that part which constitutes *overtime*. From Figure 5.11 we see that the amount of overtime has remained roughly unaltered after 1991 for all groups despite the dramatic rise in overall unemployment. When demand started to increase

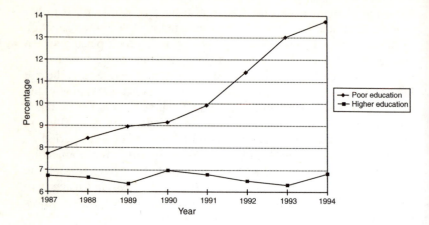

Figure 5.9   The share of people employed who work less than 35 hours per week, men
Source: Labour Market Survey (AKU).

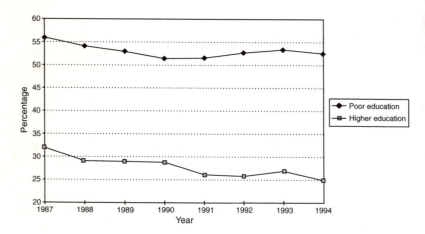

Figure 5.10   The share of people employed who work less than 35 hours per week, women
Source: Labour Market Survey (AKU).

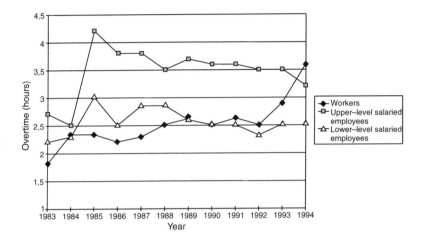

Figure 5.11 The number of overtime hours as a percentage of ordinary
working hours, 1983–94
Source: Swedish Employers' Federation (SAF).

in 1994, overtime increased to historically high levels. This has sometimes been interpreted as a result of overtime becoming economically
more attractive after TR91. If this were the case, one would expect
overtime to have increased much more for those groups which have
received large reductions in marginal tax rates. Actually, the opposite
is the case. The increase in 1993 and 1994 accrues completely to
industrial workers, whose marginal wage rates after tax have increased
relatively little as a result of the reform, while overtime has not
increased at all for upper-level salaried employees, for which the
incentive to work extra hours has increased more.

The conclusions that can be drawn from simple compilations of
aggregate data can never be especially sharp. Still TR91 was such a
big and sudden change that its effects could be expected to dominate
other things that were changed at the same time; it could be viewed as
a natural experiment so that conclusions could be drawn by comparing
'experiment Sweden' after 1991 with 'control Sweden' in the years
prior to the reform. With access to micro-data where the same
panel of individuals are observed before and after the reform one

can examine to what extent differences in marginal tax rate changes across individuals can explain differences in the change in the number of hours worked. In such a study Klevmarken *et al.* (1995) have used data from the HUS panel for 1985 and 1992. The tax reform is captured by dummy variables, one for individuals who have received large reductions in the marginal tax rate (more than 14 percentage points) and one for those with moderate reductions (5–14 per cent). These are used as explanatory variables in addition to changes in income and a number of demographic variables in a regression analysis where the change in the number of hours worked between 1985 and 1992 is the dependent variable. Unfortunately, their analysis does not lead to statistically significant conclusions, although the point estimates indicate rather large positive effects of the reform; the (insignificant) point estimates for the effect of large reductions in the marginal tax rate are around plus 100 hours per year for men and 50 hours for women.

5.9   CONCLUSION

Evaluating the effects of TR91 on the supply of labour in the middle of the most severe unemployment crisis the Swedish economy has faced since the 1930s might appear to be a hopeless enterprise. Our assessments have been based mainly on a combination of *ex ante* econometric studies and *ex post* interpretations of aggregate trends against the background of these studies. The strategy we have used to search for traces of the reform has been based on the idea that supply effects should be different for different groups; greater for high-income earners than for low-income earners, greater for men than for women, greater for middle-aged people than for young people. If the fall in demand does not display the same pattern as the supply effects, then it should be possible to obtain certain indications by quite simply comparing trends in working hours for different groups with each other.

We find hardly anything that contradicts the hypothesis of positive reform effects on the supply of hours worked. On the contrary, the limited decrease in the average number of hours worked for men is well in line with historic patterns. The decrease in the number of working hours since 1991 can be seen as the result of counteracting influences from increasing unemployment and reduced tax wedges. The decrease has actually been less than expected based on historical patterns. In conclusion, however, we must admit that the trend in working hours since 1991 has been so disrupted by other more dramatic events in the economy that we are unable to discern with any precision the effects of TR91 from other factors. This should not induce us to conclude prematurely that it has had no effect on the supply of hours worked in the Swedish economy. On the contrary, our best guess still is that it contributed to increase the aggregate labour supply by a couple of per cent.

6 Stabilization and Tax Revenue

In previous chapters, we discussed behavioural responses to TR91. In this chapter and the two following ones, we will broaden our view and discuss what TR91 has accomplished in terms of the ultimate goals of economic policy. Ever since the classic treatise by Richard Musgrave *The Theory of Public Finance* (1959), it has been common to classify these objectives under the headings of *stabilisation*, *distribution* and *allocational efficiency*, a pedagogical taxonomy to which we ascribe. In this chapter, we present our analysis of the short-term effects of TR91 on the activity level. We also examine to what extent TR91 has contributed to the disastrous decline in government tax revenue in the early 1990s. In the next chapter, we will analyze distributional aspects. Did TR91 attain its goal of not creating new gaps in society? Finally, Chapter 8 discusses how TR91 measures up to the promise that it would give a substantial boost to economic efficiency.

In recent years, Sweden has experienced its most severe economic crisis since the 1930s. In 1991–93, GDP decreased for three consecutive years, with a total drop in production of more than 5 per cent as a very tangible result. Open unemployment, which was 1.6 per cent in 1990, had increased to 8.2 per cent four years later, at the same time as the number of individuals in labour market programmes increased greatly. The mirror image of the imbalances in the real parts of the economy was the deficit in public-sector finances. There was a slight surplus in the government budget for the fiscal year 1989/90. The three following years, there were deficits of 35, 81 and 188 billion kronor, where the last figure corresponds to 13 per cent of GDP.

How much of the deficit is due to TR91? Has TR91 made the recession worse? According to a number of critical voices, some, if not most, of the deficit is due to the fact that TR91 tore big holes on the revenue side of the budget. According to other, more friendly, observers, TR91 has had a negligible effect. Far more important are the effects of the severe recession on various tax bases – a line of reasoning, however, which presupposes that the severe recession is independent of TR91.

When it comes to the effects of TR91 on the macroeconomic activity level, a first observation is that it is important to distinguish between short- and long-term effects, and between effects which affect aggregate supply and those which primarily operate on aggregate demand. As will be seen in Chapter 8, our assessment is that TR91 has created conditions for a more efficient allocation of resources in the long run. In the short run, the picture is different. It is easy to see that TR91 coincided with a rapid and dramatic weakening of the economy. In the late 1980s and early 1990s, the Swedish economy was hit by several interacting macroeconomic shocks. An international recession, combined with high costs of production, led to lost market shares and a fall in demand for Swedish goods and services. The defence of the fixed – but far from credible – exchange rate by the Riksbank, and an emphasis on low inflation as the main goal for monetary policy, led to high nominal interest rates. Combined with a rapid disinflationary process, real interest rates – with some help from German unification – were driven up, which set the stage for a crisis in financial and property markets. In addition, domestic demand was weak. Falling asset prices, combined with weak solidity, gave households the incentive to increase financial saving, an adjustment which was probably strengthened by increased uncertainty about unemployment and the future structure of the social insurance system.

All in all, our diagnosis is that the Swedish crisis gradually deepened from being a traditional cost crisis in the exporting sectors, into a downturn with Keynesian overtones. The change towards a dual economy after the autumn of 1992, when the fall of the krona in one fell swoop eliminated the external cost crisis, is most easily interpreted as a result of a demand-driven process, where a dramatic increase in the financial savings ratio led to lowered capacity utilization in the sheltered sectors. As a consequence, it seems reasonable to analyze the short-term effects of TR91 primarily in terms of aggregate demand: How has TR91 affected the macroeconomic activity level, provided that aggregate demand, and not aggregate supply, is the constraining factor?

In the next section we present a traditional Keynesian analysis of the short-term effects of TR91. We do not claim that this analysis is especially sophisticated. Most people who have come into contact with elementary Keynesian multiplier analysis should have no difficulty orienting themselves. Of course, the shortcomings of this framework are well understood; the supply side of the economy is suppressed, expectations about the future are reduced to constants which are independent of today's economic policies, and so on. However, the crisis of recent years is far from normal, and we believe that an aggregate demand analysis can shed light on the impact of TR91 in a situation characterized by considerable slack capacity. TR91 had both expansionary and contractionary effects on aggregate demand. TR91 – to anticipate some of our results – was underfinanced in the short run; it stimulated spending by increasing household disposable income. But TR91 also contained contractionary impulses, in the form of falling property prices and strengthened incentives for financial savings. The net effect was most likely contractionary, and our numerical examples indicate that TR91 may explain perhaps as much as one-fifth of the drop in Swedish GDP after 1990.

In section 6.2, we use two different methods to analyze how TR91 affected tax revenue. Both methods suggest that TR91 was underfinanced by something like 35 billion kronor per year – equivalent to 2.3 per cent of GDP – in the short run. A large part of this fall in tax revenue can be explained by the fact that most of the financing of TR91 was to take place by levying higher taxes on consumption and personal capital income, two tax bases whose development turned out to be much weaker than expected. It goes without saying that fairly large confidence intervals surround these 35 billion. Our point estimate includes a rough estimate of how that part of the economic downturn, which in our opinion was due to TR91, has affected public sector revenues and expenditures. To the extent that our demand analysis underestimates the contractionary impact of TR91, the underfinancing is even greater. To the extent that we exaggerate the contractionary impact, the underfinancing is smaller.

An underfinancing of 35 billion kronor corresponds to close to 20 per cent of the government's budget deficit for the fiscal year 1992/93. If we add the contribution of TR91 to the budget deficits for the 1991–93 period, and allow for compound interest, it does not take an in-depth analysis to arrive at the conclusion that TR91 may be responsible for increasing the national debt by 110–120 billion kronor, which is between 7.3 and 8 per cent of GDP. In the concluding section, we will discuss how much of this can be blamed on bad luck, and how much can be attributed to circumstances which ought to have been foreseen already when TR91 was designed.

6.1   TR91 AND THE CRISIS OF THE 1990s: AN OLD-FASHIONED ANALYSIS

To analyze the short-term impact of TR91, we choose traditionalism over modernism. We study the effects of TR91 within a simple

Keynesian model, which emphasizes aggregate demand and suppresses all price adjustments. Why? In the first place, as implied above, we believe that traditional Keynesianism may still provide insights about the economic anatomy of a very severe recession. The simple Keynesian model is of limited value for analyzing changes in capacity under normal economic conditions. On the other hand, it seems natural to attach special importance to the role of aggregate demand during periods of substantial excess capacity, like the Great Depression of the 1930s, and the Swedish economic crisis of the early 1990s. Second, our analysis can be seen as an indication of a reasonable upper limit for the short-term contractionary impact of TR91. Since we have chosen a model which gives the greatest possible scope to aggregate demand, and which ignores any expansionary effects via a more efficient supply side, we tend to overestimate the importance of TR91 for the economic downturn.

Let us start from the national income accounts identity, which we can write as

$$Y = C + H + I + G + X - Z \qquad (6.1)$$

where Y = gross domestic product, C = consumption, H = investment in own homes, I = private investment (excluding own homes), G = government purchases, X = exports, and Z = imports. Compared with the usual arrangement of the income identity, we present household investments in own homes separately. With the help of equation (6.1) we can identify two main channels for the short-term impact of TR91. TR91 provided households with a strong incentive to change their savings pattern. Financial savings increased, while 'real' savings in own homes and consumer durables decreased. We can represent this portfolio shift by a decrease in H (by definition, for given consumption and disposable income, a decrease in H implies that household financial savings increase). This contractionary effect is countered by the increase in private spending which may have resulted from the boost to disposable income provided by the underfinancing of TR91. The strength of this expansionary effect depends on the marginal propensity to consume out of current income. When the propensity to consume is small – which we will argue is the plausible case – the expansionary effect is bound to be small as well, which suggests that the contractionary effect dominates.

To proceed, we must complement our bookkeeping with some economic assumptions. First, we assume that the economy finds itself in a position with excess capacity and exogenously given nominal wages and prices. Consequently, the components of aggregate demand determine production. We assume that private investment (I), government purchases (G) and exports (X) are exogenous. Regarding G and X, these were not directly affected by TR91. Private investment may certainly have been affected (broader corporate tax base, lower statutory tax rates), but as we discussed in Chapter 4, there are grounds for arguing that the net impact on aggregate investment incentives was negligible. We assume that imports are determined according to

$$Z = z_C C + z_H H + z_I I + z_G G + z_X X \tag{6.2}$$

Imports depend on the import content for the different components of aggregate demand. For the sake of simplicity, we treat the import shares (z_C, z_H, and so on) as constants.

The remaining demand components are household consumption (C) and housing investment (H); that is, the quantities that are of primary importance in assessing the impact of TR91. Henceforth, we assume that there are two groups of households in the economy. The consumption and investment decisions of *neoclassical households* are based on permanent income considerations, and as a consequence there is no automatic link between current disposable income on the one hand, and consumption (or housing investments) on the other. An increase in disposable income stimulates consumption only to the extent that the increase is seen as being of a more permanent nature. If income increases because of a temporary tax reduction, most of the increase will be saved – the boost to aggregate demand will not materialize. *Keynesian households*, on the other hand, do not save any of their disposable income. Because of credit market regulations, or some deviation from intertemporal optimization behaviour, these households equate current disposable income and current spending on consumption and housing investments. If Keynesian households obtain increased transfers or reduced taxes, the entire income increment will therefore lead to increased spending.

Based on these considerations, C and H may be written as

$$C = \lambda C_K + (1 - \lambda)C_N \tag{6.3}$$

$$H = \lambda H_K + (1 - \lambda)H_N \tag{6.4}$$

where the subscript, $i = K, N$, stands for Keynesian and neoclassical households, respectively, and λ is the share of Keynesian households in the economy. Since our model is static, we cannot analyze how TR91 has affected the consumption and investment decisions of rational and forward-looking neoclassical households. Therefore, we simply assume that

$$C_N = \bar{C}_N \tag{6.5}$$
$$H_N = \bar{H}_N \tag{6.6}$$

that is, C_N and H_N are treated as two exogenous constants.

For Keynesian households, we have

$$C_K = \beta YD \tag{6.7}$$
$$H_K = (1 - \beta)YD \tag{6.8}$$

where YD is disposable income, and β is a parameter that shows how YD is allocated between consumption and spending on housing investment.

If we combine (6.1)–(6.8), we can write the national accounts identity as

$$Y = A + mps\,YD \tag{6.9}$$

where

$$A = (1 - \lambda)[(1 - z_C)\bar{C}_N + (1 - z_H)\bar{H}_N] + I(1 - z_I)$$
$$+ G(1 - z_G) + X(1 - z_X) \tag{6.10}$$

$$mps = \lambda[(1 - z_C)\beta + (1 - z_H)(1 - \beta)] \tag{6.11}$$

The A-term includes the contribution to aggregate demand from all demand components that do not depend on the activity level. As can be seen, we have included consumption and housing investments of neoclassical households in A. The coefficient in front of YD, mps, is the marginal propensity to spend. It indicates how much of a one-krona increment in disposable income that will produce an addition to domestic demand through increased consumption and housing investments. In the special case when $\lambda = 0$, it follows that $mps = 0$; that is, when the economy is populated solely by neoclassical households, aggregate demand is not affected by a temporary increase in current disposable income. To close the model we must define household disposable income as well, and we assume that

$$YD = Y - I - T \tag{6.12}$$

Since firms are assumed to finance investments with ploughed-back profits, we must subtract I from GDP in order to arrive at current disposable income. But we must also account for net taxes and transfers, T. In practice, taxes and transfers depend on the activity level. If GDP increases, so will tax revenue, while transfer payments normally decrease. To capture this connection, we introduce a simple linear tax function

$$T = k + t(Y - I) \tag{6.13}$$

where k is the part of net taxes that is independent of the activity level, and t is the aggregate net marginal tax rate. The tax base is GDP minus firms' investments, that is, we assume that the tax on undistributed profits is zero.

Combining equations (6.9), (6.12) and (6.13), we obtain an expression for GDP in a demand-determined equilibrium

$$Y = m_A A - m_k [I(1 - t) + k] \tag{6.14}$$

where

$$m_A = \frac{1}{1 - (1 - t)mps} \tag{6.15}$$

$$m_k = \frac{mps}{1 - (1 - t)mps} \tag{6.16}$$

Equation (6.14) has the same intuition as all basic multiplier models. The term in front of A, m_A, is the multiplier for autonomous changes in aggregate demand. It tells us how an increase in A by one krona will affect Y, when we allow for all induced demand effects. Correspondingly, m_k is closely related to the conventional transfer multiplier. It tells us how an autonomous increase in household disposable income by one krona affects Y when all induced adjustments in demand have been allowed for.

The multiplier effects in our model are rather small, however. They are dampened in the usual way by import leakage and by the automatic stabilizer effect which follows from income-dependent taxes and transfers. Moreover, we have included households whose consumption is not necessarily affected by changes in disposable income, something that dampens our multipliers even more. For apparently reasonable assumptions about some of the model's key parameters the final change in Y does not differ appreciably from the original change in autonomous demand – m_A is close to one. The transfer multiplier will necessarily be even smaller. In the special case when $\lambda = 0$, we have that $m_A = 1$, and that $m_k = 0$.

Using (6.14), we can illustrate the net effect of the expansionary and contractionary ingredients of TR91. The expansionary effect (from an underfinanced tax reform) works via the transfer multiplier m_k, and the contractionary effect (from decreased housing investment and increased financial savings) works via the autonomous multiplier m_A. In Table 6.1, we present numerical examples, which in a highly stylized manner describe possible outcomes. In order to create a clear reference case, we have calibrated the model to an initial equilibrium which roughly reflects the actual conditions in 1991 regarding consumption, housing investments, exports, import shares, GDP, and so on. We also, less realistically, choose initial values which imply that the household financial savings ratio is zero initially. Since the financial savings of Keynesian households is equal to zero by definition, we adjust consumption and housing investments of neoclassical households so that they match disposable income. Further, the tax rate t is set at 0.74.[1]

We assume throughout that the contractionary effect of TR91 consists of an autonomous fall in housing investment. Regarding the neoclassical households, we assume that H decreases by one-third as a result of TR91. Since, at the same time, we assume that their consumption spending C is not directly affected, this means that financial savings increase, and that aggregate demand decreases. Regarding the Keynesian households, we assume that TR91 leads to a new spending pattern; the share β of disposable income that is consumed increases, and the share $1 - \beta$ that is invested in housing decreases. Since Keynesian households spend all of their disposable income, such a shift does not necessarily affect aggregate demand. However, since the import share is far greater for consumption than for housing investment, the effect will still be contractionary.

In columns 1–4, we present results based on different assumptions about the share of households that react to an underfinanced tax reform by increasing their expenditures to a corresponding extent,

Table 6.1 A multiplier-analysis of TR91

	Fraction of credit rationed households			
	0	*0.15*	*0.3*	*0.5*
mps	0	0.1	0.2	0.33
m_A	1	1.03	1.05	1.09
m_k	0	0.1	0.21	0.36
GDP (change in per cent)	−1.2	−1.0	−0.7	−0.4
Household financial savings ratio (increase in percentage points)	4.2	3.6	3.1	2.3

Sources and method: See text.

that is, we study the effects based on different assumptions about the size of λ. In line with the analysis of the next section, we assume that the reform was underfinanced by 20 billion kronor, *at a given initial tax base*. In terms of household disposable income (more than 800 billion in 1991), this is equivalent to an increase by 2.5 per cent. In our simulations, we have chosen to distribute this additional income by decreasing the intercept, k, in our linear tax function (6.13), at the same time as we assume that t remains unchanged. (In simulations that we do not report, we have investigated how the results are affected if the underfinancing rather is caused by a reduction in t. Although this alternative is the realistic one, it turns out that the results are affected in a negligible way.)

In the first column, we present the results when $\lambda = 0$. Since the expenditure decisions of neoclassical households are unaffected by a temporary income hike, both *mps* and the transfer multiplier m_k are equal to zero. When we have thus short-circuited the expansionary ingredient of TR91, only the contractionary effect via housing investments remains. The autonomous fall in housing investments by one-third corresponds, in absolute terms, to a decrease by 20 billion. Since we assume that the import share for housing investments is 0.1, aggregate demand directed at domestic production decreases by 18 billion (0.9 times 20). As there are no induced demand effects from lower disposable income, the autonomous multiplier m_A is equal to one, which implies that Y also decreases with 18 billion. Since we have calibrated the model so that Y is 1465 billion in the initial equilibrium, GDP decreases by 1.2 per cent.

When we increase the share of Keynesian households in columns 2–4, *mps*, m_A, and m_k increase. The important observation is that m_k increases more rapidly than m_A; the expansionary effect of a temporary addition to disposable income will matter relatively more, as λ increases. When $\lambda = 0.15$, Y falls by around one per cent, when $\lambda = 0.5$ (half of the households are Keynesian, half neoclassical) the fall is only 0.4 per cent. If a sufficiently large majority of households are Keynesians, the expansionary effect will dominate the contractionary one – the increase in consumption more than outweighs the decrease in housing investments.

Another observation is that the increase in financial savings is more modest when we increase the share of households which by definition do not save. When $\lambda = 0$ the financial savings ratio increases by 4.2 percentage points. When $\lambda = 0.5$ the increase is 2.3 percentage points. In Chapter 3 we concluded that TR91 had increased the household financial savings ratio by 3–4 percentage points. As can be seen from the table, the results for $\lambda = 0.15$ are well in line with this analysis.

Through Keynesian eyeglasses, TR91 can be seen as a gigantic, but hardly intentional, fiscal policy experiment in a situation when the Swedish economy was on the brink of the most severe recession since the early 1930s. On the one hand, TR91 entailed a very powerful stimulus to household purchasing power. On the other hand, households were given strong incentives to increase their financial savings and decrease their investments in real assets, above all in property. Our simple numerical examples warrant two conclusions.

First, the contractionary effect has dominated. The drop in the activity level would have been smaller if the old tax system had remained in force. The expansionary part of TR91 had an impact through the marginal propensity to spend. A large spending propensity assumes that a considerable fraction of households, for various reasons (credit rationing, 'rule-of-thumb behaviour'), allow their consumption to be driven by short-term fluctuations in disposable income. This, however, does not appear to be an especially realistic assumption. Some recent Swedish econometric studies indicate that predictable changes in current disposable income is relatively unimportant for contemporaneous consumption; λ could lie somewhere in an interval between 0.1 and 0.3 (see Campbell and Mankiw (1991), Agell, Berg and Edin (1995), and Agell and Berg (1996)).

Our second conclusion has to do with the size of the contractionary effect. With apparently plausible assumptions about import propensities, the aggregate marginal tax rate and the effect of TR91 on housing investment and household financial savings, the effect is bound to be rather modest. Despite the fact that our model is of the simplest Keynesian variety, it provides no support for the claim that TR91 has been a primary factor behind the macroeconomic crisis. In terms of our multiplier analysis in Table 6.1, we believe that the results in columns 2 and 3 represent reasonable magnitudes. In the short-term, TR91 may explain a fall in production of barely one per cent, and it may have increased the household financial savings ratio by between three and four percentage points. To get some perspective on these figures, it should be noted that GDP decreased by three per cent in 1991–2. If GDP had grown in the same way during these years as it did during the 1970s and 1980s, accumulated growth would have been 3.5 per cent; that is, at the end of 1992, there was an accumulated growth gap of 6.5 percentage points. If the contractionary effect of TR91 is one per cent of GDP, about 15 per cent of the growth gap could be attributed to the reform.

Of course, these calculations are subject to unusually large margins of error. It is quite possible to modify some of the assumptions of our analysis in such a way that the contractionary effect becomes larger. Agell, Berg and Edin (1995) present results that indicate that private consumption may have responded adversely to capital losses in the housing market – losses which we linked to TR91 in Chapter 3. Nor have we taken into account the fact that business investments may be negatively affected when aggregate demand decreases. If we incorporate another old-fashioned Keynesian device, an investment accelerator, the fall in the activity level gets larger.

But we have also neglected mechanisms which pull in the opposite direction. According to some observers, a tighter credit rationing in the wake of the severe crisis has meant that current disposable income has been increasingly important for the consumption of many households. If this is correct, we tend to underestimate both the marginal propensity to spend and the expansionary effect from the underfinancing of TR91. Moreover, we ignore the fact that households who believe that TR91 creates long-term gains in efficiency have an incentive to increase their current consumption in anticipation – households which revise their assessment of permanent income upward increase consumption. Finally, we have based our analysis on a macromodel which, by its construction, eliminates all the effects that have an impact through the supply side of the economy. This is perhaps the most serious omission.

6.2   TR91 AND THE FISCAL DEFICIT

TR91 was carried out in two steps, a relatively small one in 1990, and a bigger one in 1991. The total financing estimate for the two steps, according to the original calculations of the Ministry of Finance, is presented in Table 6.2. All figures are in 1991 prices, and they concern the predicted average budget effect for the years 1991–93 for the consolidated public sector. The most burdensome entry on the expense side of TR91 was the revenue loss from the reduced tax rates on earned income, a loss estimated at 89.1 billion. Added to this should be increases in some social transfers (increased child and housing allowances) which were decided on in connection with TR91. These were warranted by distributional concerns and amounted to 8 billion. The main source of financing was a substantial redistribution of the tax burden from taxes on earned income to higher taxes on consumption and personal capital income. In all, about 40 per cent of the financing was to take place through higher taxes on capital, while indirect commodity taxation was to account for 30 per cent. We can also note that the new corporate tax rules played an insignificant role in the financing of the reform. Dynamic revenue gains from a more efficient economy were assumed to contribute rather modestly to the financing. For 1991–93, they were estimated at 2.5, 5.0 and 7.5 billion kronor respectively. In the long run, the dynamic revenue gains were estimated to contribute about 20 billion kronor – equivalent to 1.3 per cent of GDP. An immediate observation is that one can hardly accuse the architects of TR91 of being naive supply-siders.

And, yet, the budget deficit of the central government remains. What went wrong? As we will see, a major part of the rapid erosion of the goverment's finances can be explained by the general recession. Other effects follow from a change in the rules for VAT accounting in municipal, county and state public authorities. However, even if we adjust central government tax revenue for the business cycle and new VAT-accounting procedures, a huge loss of tax revenue remains. In the following we will exploit two methods to assess what fraction of this revenue loss is due to TR91.

The first method, presented in Kristoffersson (1995), is mainly an updating of the original revenue forecast of the Ministry of Finance. The revenue projections in Table 6.2 were based on a simple extrapolation of the development of certain key tax bases after 1988. Since the end of the 1980s was characterized by an overheated economy with

Table 6.2   Revenue consequences of TR91 according to original projections, yearly averages for 1991–93 (in billion kronor and 1991 prices)

Budgetary losses	
Lower tax rates on earned income	89.1
Distributional measures	8.2
Total	97.3
Budgetary gains	
Broader tax base, earned income	12.7
Broader tax base, personal capital income tax	38.6
VAT and other indirect taxes	28.4
Corporate profits tax	1.2
Other revenue gains	9.2
Gains from a generally more efficient economy	5.0
Total	95.1

Source: The Swedish Tax Reform of 1991 (Ministry of Finance, 1991).

soaring asset prices and a consumption boom, this extrapolation pre-supposed that the exceptional boom would continue well into the 1990s. Kristoffersson's revised calculations are based on the same method, but applied on *actual*, rather than *extrapolated*, tax bases. The revised numbers illustrate the consequences for the fisc of carrying out TR91 in a much less favourable macroeconomic climate than predicted.

The second method is based on a time-series analysis of the connection between tax revenue and various macroeconomic aggregates. Based on the historical relation between tax revenue and nominal GDP between 1964 and 1989, we calculate the tax revenue that ought to have materialized in the beginning of the 1990s if TR91 had not taken place. The difference between this forecast and the actual outcome can be seen as a rough indication of the effect of the changes in tax rules which took place during the 1990–93 period.

Method 1

The basic methodology, and the possible sources of error, behind the estimates in Table 6.2 can be described by a simple example. Assume that the government taxes a certain economic activity X (consumption, labour income, and so on) at a rate t. We further assume that X depends on t, as well as on another variable, the 'state of the business cycle'. In more formal terms we have

$$X = X(t, \theta) \tag{6.17}$$

where θ represents the influence of the business cycle on X.[2] The government's revenue from taxing X, T, will thus be $T = tX(t, \theta)$. We assume that θ can assume two values, θ_B and θ_R, where index B stands for boom, and index R for recession. The tax rates before and after TR91 are t_{89} and t_{91}. If we assume that the economy is initially in a boom, tax revenue before TR91 can be written as

$$T_{89} = t_{89}X(t_{89}, \theta_B) \tag{6.18}$$

How is tax revenue affected by the change from t_{89} to t_{91}? If we assume that the new tax system coincides with a recession ($\theta = \theta_R$), we can define the change in tax revenue as

$$\Delta rev = t_{91}X(t_{91}, \theta_R) - t_{89}X(t_{89}, \theta_R) \tag{6.19}$$

The first term on the right-hand side is actual, and observable, tax revenue; it depends on the new tax rate, and on the new state of the business cycle (a recession). The second term, which is not observable, is the tax revenue that would have materialized, if we had had the old tax system *and* the recession.

The original revenue forecast in Table 6.2 was based on a mechanical extrapolation of past trends of tax bases. Given the observed tax base initially (a tax base which in reality was conditioned on the existing boom and the old tax system) one studied the revenue effect of shifting from t_{89} to t_{91}. In our notation the original revenue prediction can be written as

$$\Delta rev_{pred} = (t_{91} - t_{89})X(t_{89}, \theta_B) \tag{6.20}$$

If we compare (6.19) and (6.20), we see that there are two reasons that can explain why the original forecast went astray. In the first place, with some minor exceptions, no account was taken of the fact that TR91 could affect the tax base. Second, it was assumed that the new tax system would go into effect when there was a continued boom; the prediction was conditioned on θ_B and not on θ_R. With hindsight, it is all too easy to ascertain that neither assumption was tenable. The prediction error, that is, the difference between Δrev and Δrev_{pred}, can be written as (after slight rearrangement)

$$\begin{aligned} error = (t_{91} - t_{89})[X(t_{91}, \theta_R) - X(t_{89}, \theta_B)] \\ + t_{89}[X(t_{91}, \theta_R) - X(t_{89}, \theta_R)] \end{aligned} \tag{6.21}$$

The first term on the right-hand side is that part of the forecast error which is directly observable. The expression within brackets is the actual change in the tax base between '89' and '91'. The second term (which cannot be observed) captures the effects of TR91 on behaviour: How does the new tax system affect the tax base, if we keep the macroeconomic situation constant?

Kristoffersson (1995) presents calculations which makes it possible to assess the forecast error which derives from the first term on the right-hand side of (6.21). What would the original forecast, presented in the Spring of 1990, have looked like, if there had been knowledge of the actual tax bases for 1991? Kristoffersson calculates the modified revenue effect of TR91 according to

$$\Delta rev_{mod} = (t_{91} - t_{89})X(t_{91}, \theta_R) \tag{6.22}$$

By comparing the *ex post* forecast in (6.22) with the original *ex ante* forecast in (6.20) we can get an idea of the size of the first part of the forecast error in (6.21).

Table 6.3   Revenue forecast error for 1991 according to revised *ex post*
calculation (in billion kronor and 1991 prices)

	1991
Broader tax base, earned income	−6.0
Broader tax base, personal capital income tax	−6.8
Other revenue gains	−2.5
Corporate profits tax	−3.1
VAT	−2.5
Other indirect taxes	−1.2
Gains from a generally more efficient economy	−2.5
Miscellaneous	1.6
Total forecast error according to revised calculation	−23.0

Source: Kristoffersson (1995).

In Table 6.3, we present the main results of Kristoffersson's revised
revenue estimate for 1991. The total forecast error is large −23 billion
kronor, which is equivalent to about 1.5 per cent of GDP. The decisive
factor, which explains most of the *ex post* revision, is that many of the
tax bases which were supposed to finance TR91 stagnated, or
decreased. The biggest single revision has to do with the revenue
from the new uniform tax on personal capital income. The original
estimate was based on an optimistic extrapolation of various asset
prices from 1987–88. In reality, asset prices increased in a more modest
way. Also the new corporate profits tax yielded a minus, again due to
bearish asset markets, but also to decreased profitability in the corporate sector. Another big minus entry, 6 billion, has to do with the effect
of the reduced tax rates on earned income. Here, the mechanism is the
reverse. Earned income increased faster than expected up until 1991.
If the old, more progressive, tax system still had been in place, there
would therefore have been a revenue bonus.

All in all, our assessment is that these estimates ought to be
regarded as a lower limit for the short-term underfinancing of TR91.
They primarily reflect how the rapid and unexpected deterioration of
the macroeconomic situation affected the financing of TR91. Two
factors suggest that the actual underfinancing was even greater. First,
Kristoffersson's estimates only reflect the forecast error which is linked
to that part of TR91 which was implemented in 1991. The change of
the tax system in 1990, which in quantitative terms consisted of about
one-third of the total reform, is not taken into account. However, since
the 1990-component of TR91 dealt in part with other tax bases than
the one in 1991, we cannot simply apply the results in Table 6.3 and

argue that the 1990 tax changes corresponded to an underfinancing of one-third of the 23 billion.

Second, the revised *ex post* forecast does not account for behavioural responses to TR91. In terms of our decomposition of the total forecast error in equation (6.21), Kristoffersson's estimate does not provide any information about the second term on the right-hand side, which represents the effect of changed behaviour at an unchanged state of the business cycle. Housing demand, household financial savings, and the demand for certain specific commodity groups (for example, tourism services) are examples of activities that have been affected by TR91. A further complicating circumstance is that the macroeconomic situation – our parameter θ – cannot be regarded as independent of TR91. As TR91 reinforced the downturn, the underfinancing increases correspondingly.

With the aid of our aggregate demand analysis of the preceding section, it is easy to illustrate the size of the underfinancing due to the short-term contractionary effect of TR91. Our multiplier analysis suggests that TR91 may have caused an aggregate production loss of barely one per cent of GDP. Converted into kronor (in 1991 prices) this corresponds to 12–15 billion. If we think of the forecast error (6.21) in macroeconomic terms, we can interpret $X(t, \theta)$ as GDP, the term $t_{89}[X(t_{91}, \theta_R) - X(t_{89}, \theta_R)]$ as a measure of the contractionary effect of TR91, and t_{89} and t_{91} as the aggregate marginal tax rates before and after reform.[3] If we assume that the aggregate tax rate is 0.74, we obtain an extra underfinancing of between 8.9 and 11.1 billion – a sum that should be added to Kristoffersson's estimate for 1991.

According to our estimate, the total underfinancing of TR91 is more than 30 billion, most of which (23 billion) is attributed to the revised *ex post* estimate, and the rest (8.9 to 11.1 billion) to the contractionary macroeconomic effect of TR91. Moreover, if we take into account the possible underfinancing that is associated with the first step of TR91, which was implemented in 1990, and revenue losses due to behavioural adjustments on a more disaggregated level (savings composition, consumption patterns, and so on) the effects can be even greater. On the whole, it appears likely that the total underfinancing for 1991 is in the region of 35 billion (2.3 per cent of GDP). It goes without saying that this figure is surrounded by considerable uncertainty.

What can be said about the underfinancing in the next few years, primarily 1992–93? On the basis of the trends of some important tax bases since 1991, we can identify some qualitative mechanisms. A tax base that is very important for TR91, private consumption, decreased (as was discussed in Chapter 3) by slightly less than two per cent in 1992, and by slightly less than four per cent in 1993. This indicates that an *ex post* revision along the lines of Kristoffersson (1995) would give rise to a greater loss of VAT revenue than is shown in Table 6.3 for 1991. On the other hand, other tax bases changed in a more favourable direction, especially after 1992. Share prices started to increase in 1993, and profitability in the corporate sector improved markedly after the fall of the krona in November 1992. As we shall see in the next section, where we study the time series relation between tax revenue and the aggregate tax base, there is reason to believe that the underfinancing of TR91 actually decreased after 1992.

Method 2

In Figure 6.1, we plot central government tax revenue in current prices for the fiscal years 1963/64 through 1993/94. Up to fiscal year 1989/90 we see that there is a steady growth trend. This trend is broken in the first years of the 1990s, when nominal tax revenue decreased four years in a row. We get another perspective on government tax revenue if we compare actual revenue with the tax revenue that would have been

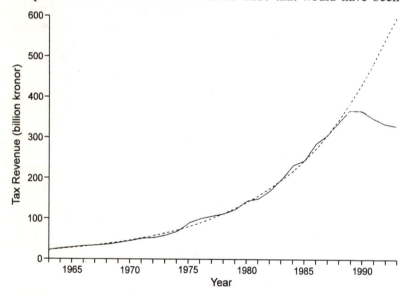

Figure 6.1   Actual and extrapolated tax revenue of the central government for the fiscal years 1963/64–1993/94
Source: Own calculations.

generated in the early 1990s with an unchanged trend. Since tax revenue grew on average by slightly more than 11 per cent per year between 1963/64 and 1989/90, we ought to have observed continued exponential growth. The difference between extrapolated revenue for 1993/94 and actual revenue is more than 250 billion (which is 16.7 per cent of GDP)!

The purpose of our analysis in this section is to try to estimate how large a part of the decreased tax revenue in the 1990s can be attributed to the severe recession and the fast downshifting of the rate of inflation. By estimating econometric models of the relation between tax revenue and various measures of the activity level for the 25 fiscal years that preceded TR91, we can construct a simple forecast model for tax revenue in the early 1990s. What tax revenue should we expect, given the historical relationship between aggregate tax bases and tax revenue? By comparing predictions and outcomes, we obtain residuals indicating the loss of revenue that cannot be attributed to the macro-economic environment. Interpreted with care, these residuals give us an indication of the influence of tax changes in the early 1990s, including TR91.

In our regressions, we try to explain the (logarithmic) change in nominal tax revenue by three macroeconomic variables – change in nominal GDP, change in real GDP, and change in the consumer price index. In order to capture various time lags in the collection of tax revenue, we sometimes try specifications where the change in tax revenue depends not only on changes in the explanatory variables in the same period, but also on changes during the immediately preceding period.

In Figure 6.2 we present the forecast for central government tax revenue for the fiscal years 1990/91–1993/94 according to two of our estimated models. They have been estimated for the 1963/64–1989/90 period, and we have generated the forecast for the following fiscal years by substituting the actual values of the explanatory variables in the estimated equations. The first forecast ('Model 1') is based on a model where the percentage change in nominal tax revenue is correlated with the percentage change in nominal GDP in the same fiscal year.[4] The other forecast ('Model 2') is based on a model which also includes the percentage change in nominal GDP in the previous fiscal year. Since both models are estimated on a rate of change form, we need further assumptions to generate a forecast for the level of tax revenue, a problem which we have solved by assuming that actual and forecasted tax revenue are the same for fiscal year 1989/90.

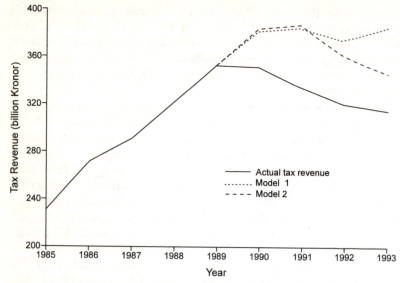

Figure 6.2   Actual and forecasted tax revenue of the central government for
the fiscal years 1985/86–1993/94

Notes: Model 1 regresses the change in nominal tax revenue on a constant and the
percentage change in nominal GDP for the same fiscal year. Model 2 also includes the
percentage change in nominal GDP for the previous fiscal year.

Both forecast models illustrate the fact that central government tax
revenue shows a very high degree of sensitivity to changes in the
activity level.[5] According to Model 1, an increase in nominal GDP by
one per cent implies that tax revenue increases by 1.3 per cent in the
same year. According to Model 2, an increase in nominal GDP by one
per cent during two successive years means that tax revenue increases
by 1.1. per cent in the first year, and by almost 1.9 per cent in the next.
During the greater part of the 1980s, nominal GDP increased by
around 10 per cent per year. In the beginning of the 1990s, there was
a substantial break, and the nominal growth of GDP was limited to
between zero and 3.5 per cent. Against this backdrop, it is not surprising that both models indicate that nominal tax revenue ought to
stagnate, and even decrease.

But Figure 6.2 suggests that nominal tax revenue in reality fell much
more than predicted by the time series relation between tax revenue
and the nominal activity level; for both models, we obtain large negative residuals in the early 1990s. These residuals might depend on
TR91, but they might also be due to many other factors, like the
usual statistical uncertainty, changes in tax rules that cannot be

attributed to TR91, and so on. These confounding influences cumulate over time – the confidence bands around our predicted values increase as time goes by, and as the scope for influences from other policy changes increases. Therefore, the residuals for the early 1990s are no final test of the size of the underfinancing of TR91. On the other hand, we are encouraged by the fact that the residuals are quite consistent with the estimates we presented in the previous section.

For fiscal years 1990/91 and 1991/92, the residuals are of approximately the same size for both models. With Model 1, the residuals are 30 and 51 billion, respectively. With Model 2, the residuals are 32 and 53 billion. These residuals are, at least for fiscal year 1991/92 (when TR91 was fully implemented), considerably larger than the interval for underfinancing which followed from the previous method. However, an important explanation for this is that TR91 was accompanied by new conventions for VAT accounting within various bodies of the public sector. As of 1991, municipalities, counties and various other government authorities were permitted unlimited reimbursement for paid VAT. At the same time, the central government was compensated for this loss of VAT revenue by cuts in grants to municipalities and appropriations to state authorities. In bookkeeping terms, central government VAT revenue decreased, but expenditures were adjusted accordingly.

According to calculations provided by the Ministry of Finance, these accounting operations, which are of no real significance, explain 11 and 28 billion kronor of the revenue losses in the fiscal years 1990/91 and 1991/92. When we adjust our residuals accordingly, the remaining residuals for the same fiscal years are 19 and 23 billion according to Model 1, and 21 and 25 billion according to Model 2. For the fiscal year 1991/92, both residuals are obviously well in accordance with Kristoffersson's revised *ex post* estimates, discussed above. A cautious conclusion of this exercise is that it strengthens our belief in the estimates of the previous section – we find no cause to revise our conclusion that TR91 was underfinanced by around 35 billion in 1991.[6]

The size of the residuals for the fiscal years after 1991/92 obviously differs considerably between the two models. According to Model 2, which we prefer on both economic and statistical grounds, the residual decreases in both 1992/93 and 1993/94. Subject to the provision that this forecast is surrounded by considerable uncertainty, we interpret this as an indication that the underfinancing of TR91 tends to diminish over time.

6.3   CONCLUSION

It is easy to conclude that the timing of TR91 was unfortunate. Even if TR91 is most likely a secondary factor, it did help to deepen the severe macroeconomic crisis. In addition, the adverse influence of the recession on some of the tax bases that were important for the financing of TR91 explains much of the underfinancing we have discovered. In the best of all possible worlds, TR91 would have been implemented in the middle of the 1980s. Then the reform, with its limitations on the deductibility of interest expenses, would have helped to stem the rapid credit expansion after 1985, and it could have dampened the considerable overheating of the economy that took place towards the end of the 1980s. What went wrong?

Tax reforms, especially far-reaching ones, are (and should be) time-consuming processes. In the case of TR91, the time required from the directive to set up a commission, to the introduction of a bill, and the final implementation of the new tax law, was four years. It is no exaggeration to describe the work effort during these years as unusually thorough. Reports from a great number of economists and tax specialists were requested, and many of Sweden's foremost specialists in the field of tax law and public economics were given the opportunity to penetrate a number of different aspects of the tax system. Economic principles and arguments were transformed into technical tax legislation. Finally, conflicting political interests were identified and weighed together in such a way that a parliamentary majority could pass the final reform proposal.

As we all know, it is difficult to make predictions about the future. In the very comprehensive background material, many stones were upturned, but hardly anywhere was there a hint of a discussion about the macroeconomic aspects of TR91. In retrospect, this might appear to be thoughtless. But it should immediately be said that this thoughtlessness was shared by almost all economic observers at the time – no one anticipated that the Swedish economy was in for a rough ride. In the light of this, it is not surprising that the architects of TR91 did not foresee that 'the tax reform of the century' would go into effect when the economy was sliding into its most severe crisis since the 1930s.

Matters are different when we turn to the revenue predictions. The original financing estimate for TR91 was based on unduly optimistic assumptions about important tax bases. Even if we only consider the information actually available at the end of the 1980s, the revenue projections make little sense. At that time, consumption spending exceeded household disposable income, and real asset prices increased very rapidly. By extrapolating tax bases from an unsustainable macro-economic situation, one conveyed an unrealistic picture of the revenue gains from broader tax bases. From a public choice perspective, one could perhaps argue that it is not surprising that it was easier to sell an underfunded reform, where all groups could be portrayed as winners, than a fully financed reform, where some groups would appear as losers.

7 Income Distribution

The goal of an even distribution of income has been central to Swedish tax policy and the debate on tax policy for the greater part of the postwar period. In giving a higher priority to efficiency, the 1991 tax reform reflects the change of opinion which took place in the 1980s. However, the goal of an even income distribution still puts an important restriction on policy, and it was emphasized that TR91 should not systematically change the distribution of income between rich and poor households. The reform was intended to be neutral in terms of income distribution due to a combination of factors. The reduction of the marginal tax rates would primarily benefit high-income earners. But they would tend to lose from the reduction of the tax rate for capital income since the size of interest deductions tend to increase with income. Further, increased child allowances and housing allowances would increase the disposable income of families with children. The estimates presented by the RINK Commission (in SOU 1989:33) indicated that, on average, these effects would cancel out for all income groups. However, this average hid a large spread between winners and losers. Thus, while the reform was judged in advance to be neutral, studies on income distribution by Statistics Sweden have shown that disposable income in fact became more unevenly distributed after 1991. The question is how these two pictures relate to each other. Were the estimates of the commission misleading or incomplete, or have other factors than TR91 been decisive for trends in the 1990s?

In many cases, analyses of income distribution are based on income measures derived from the tax assessments, which may not be the most suitable way to measure income. Therefore, it is natural to begin with a discussion of measurement problems. In section 7.1 we discuss how to take different family sizes into account, how capital income should be measured, and if annual income or average income over a longer period of time is the more relevant concept of income. After this, the distribution of income before and after tax is described in section 7.2. We also discuss, in principle, how one should regard the effects of the tax system on income distribution. One approach is to take the distribution before tax as a given, and to see the difference in distribution before and after tax as a measure of the redistributive effect of the tax system. Although fraught with problems, since the before-tax distribution clearly depends on the tax system to some extent, we chose to follow this approach. Results in section 7.3, based on a definition of income which largely agrees with the one which is used in the official statistics produced by Statistics Sweden, indicate that the role of the *tax system* in redistributing income has decreased since the reform, but that the redistributive effect of the *allowance system* (above all housing allowances and children's allowances) has increased at the same time. On the whole, the difference in the degree of inequality before and after taxes and allowances was about the same in the years following the reform, 1991 and 1992, as in the preceding year, 1989. This conclusion applies over all households in active ages, where households of different sizes are made comparable by so called equivalence scales. In section 7.4, each category of household is treated separately. The degree of redistribution has increased within those groups where allowances are most important, that is, households with several children, while it has decreased for households without children or with one child. Capital income is especially important for the distribution of income since it is so unevenly distributed. At the same time, this income category is particularly difficult to measure in a satisfactory way with the aid of available statistics. In section 7.5 we use some alternative definitions of capital income, but none of them provides a radically different picture of the distributional effects of the tax reform. In section 7.6, we look at the impact of capital gains and losses brought about by the reform.

7.1 WHICH INCOMES?

The goal of an even distribution of income is closely related to ideology and personal values. One interpretation emphasizes fairness in the *process* that generates income. Equality is viewed in terms of the distribution of *opportunities*. This can be interpreted either in terms of constitutional rules and other institutions that define the fundamental rights and obligations of citizens, or in terms of the distribution of economic resources at the start of life, accessibility to education, and other factors. Another interpretation emphasizes the *result* of the process in the form of the distribution of income and welfare. Without taking a stand on this basic question of values, it is natural for us to focus on income, since tax policy has a direct impact on how incomes are distributed, but only an indirect effect on the distribution of opportunities.[1] Income can be measured in many different ways. A natural definition – which in Sweden is associated with economists such as David Davidson (1889) and Erik Lindahl (1939) and has such international proponents as Haig (1921) and Henry Simons (1938) – is to see income as the amount of consumption which the individual or the household can afford without drawing on its future consumption opportunities. Even if we use this definition as our starting-point, a number of practical problems remain in implementing it.

The composition of households

It is most natural that incomes are measured on the household level since the household functions as an economic unit and many allowances go to the household as a whole rather than to any specific individual. At the same time, it is rather obvious that it is the distribution of incomes across individuals which should be of interest, rather than the distribution across households. Therefore, in some way or other, one should take into account household size and composition. The easiest way is to divide the total income of the household by its number of members and look at per capita income. However, this neglects obvious economies of scale; five individuals do not need five times the income of a single person in order to obtain the same consumption standard. Therefore, when dividing, one usually uses equivalence scales based on calculations of the cost of supporting an additional household member. In this way, it is possible to express the size of the household in the number of so-called consumption units.

Even if the transformation from household to individual might appear to be self-evident and natural, it raises problems about the way children are looked upon. With equivalence scales an additional child means a decrease in income, since the family income has to be divided by the equivalence number for a larger household. This reflects the fact that there is one more mouth to feed, but it conflicts with the feeling of most parents that the birth of a child enriches them, rather than makes them poorer. An alternative view would be to only correct incomes for the equivalent number of adult members of the household. The choice to have children would then be seen as one of many decisions about the use of the resources of the household. Here, however, we will mainly follow tradition and divide household income by the equivalent number of consumption units.[2]

The effect of using equivalence scales can be seen from the official income statistics. Here households are divided into decile groups, ranked according to disposable income per consumption unit, from the ten per cent of households which have the lowest income in decile

1 to the ten richest per cent in decile 10. In this ranking, couples without children constitute less than ten per cent of households in deciles 2–4, but as much as 50 per cent in deciles 8 and 9. The average family in deciles 2–4 represents ca. 2.2 consumption units, while the average in deciles 8 and 9 is 1.7 units. If we look at disposable income per household instead of per consumption unit, there is almost no difference between deciles 3 and 8 (ranked according to household disposable income per consumption unit). Since changes in allowances related to the composition of the family (children's allowances and housing allowances) were important parts of TR91, our view about the effects of the reform may be sensitive to the use of equivalence scales. In section 7.4 we deal with this problem by studying the distribution of income within each category of households separately.

Capital income

While employment income can often be measured with reasonable precision, capital income is surrounded by a number of more severe measurement problems. A faithful application of the Davidson–Lind-ahlian definition would be to calculate capital income in real terms, that is to adjust for changes in the value of money, and to include capital gains and losses regardless of whether they are realized or not. Further, the consumption value of owning a home and consumer durables such as automobiles and boats should be included.

In applying this definition of capital income, one encounters great problems since data on household assets would have to be taken from income tax returns, where reporting is incomplete and useful information about changes in market value is missing, other than when assets are sold. In principle, there are two paths to follow. The first is to completely or partially ignore certain items of measured capital income and deficits based on the reasoning that the connection between these entries and actual capital income is probably close to zero, or even negative. It is well known that the total deficit of capital income reported on tax returns has long exceeded total taxable capital income by a wide margin. Reported deficits resulting from large inter-est deductions often coincide with hidden capital income, for example, due to undervalued securities, expensive sailboats or pure and simple neglect to report such items as premium bonds.

The other path to correct measured capital income is to try to estimate the size of the underreported income as well as possible. In certain areas of central importance, for example the returns on owner-occupied homes, this can be done with some precision, but in other areas, for example consumer durables and outright tax avoidance, it is much more difficult. A radical form of imputation is to estimate a comprehensive market value of net wealth and multiply it by an assumed real rate of interest. An alternative is to use actual return rates for different assets, for example, the change in the share price index for the year. Unfortunately, it is not possible to say which method comes closer to the truth. The lack of reliable data about the real distribution of capital income is especially troublesome for our ability to assess TR91, since the equalizing effect of the reform, to a great extent, was to be brought about by a more uniform taxation of capital.

Working hours

The theoretical definition of income is based on the consumption opportunities of the individual. Market income after taxes and allowances measures the opportunities to buy goods on the market. In principle, they are not affected by the individual's choice of consumption pattern; income is the same whether it is spent on black pudding or Russian caviar. On the other hand, market income is obviously dependent on the individual's choice of consumption of leisure; a person who values leisure highly and has few material needs can choose to work less, and by doing so gets less income according to the usual definition. If we are interested in welfare in a broader sense, we ought to use a measure which also takes into account the opportunities to 'buy' leisure by choosing to work less. Such a measure, usually called *full income*, is defined as the income an individual would have at standardized working hours and current hourly wages. This can be a meaningful concept if working hours are freely chosen, and is therefore a valuable complement to more traditional measurements of income. Obviously, it must be applied with extra care in a situation where a large part of the population is involuntarily unemployed.

An earlier study by Hansson and Norrman (1986) indicates that the equalizing effect of the tax system is less, or even non-existent, if account is taken of differences in the consumption of leisure. They use data from the 1982 HINK survey and focus on middle-age households in the ages 45–55. In a first step of the analysis, no account is taken of differences in working hours, but corrections are made for family size and capital income. It turns out that the effective rate of taxation (tax payments as a share of adjusted income) was less than 30 per cent in the bottom second and third decile of the income distribution compared with 40 per cent in the top decile. In a second step they assess household income at a standardized number of working houses. With this adjustment the effective tax rate is almost the same in all income classes. In other words, it appears that the tax system may not have had any redistributive effects before the reform.

The distribution of full income is also calculated in the study by Björklund, Palme and Svensson (1995), based on data for the years 1967, 1981 and 1991 from the *Level of Living Surveys* (*LNU*). They find that full income is considerably more evenly distributed than market income, which is a rather obvious effect of persons with few or no working hours being moved up from the bottom of the income distribution when the value of leisure is taken into account. However, as opposed to Hansson and Norrman, they find that the tax system is redistributive even when full income is used. It is true that in 1967 when only every other woman was in gainful employment, the degree of redistribution, measured by the difference in the Gini coefficient[3] before and after tax, was only half as big measured by full income as it was when it was measured by market income; but in 1991, when women participated in the workforce almost as much as men, there was no such difference.[4] The degree of equalization at that time was the same for both concepts of income.

There are certainly good reasons, in principle, why a distribution study should be based on full income, but in doing this one encounters a number of difficult practical problems. Above all, it is necessary to impute a wage for those who do not have any employment income at all.[5] Since it appears that the redistributive effect of the tax system is now about the same measured by actual as well as full income, one may be on firmer ground if basing the distribution analysis on actual income.[6]

Short or long term?

Measuring income in a single year may be a far too short period of time to give a fair picture of income distribution, since consumption opportunities depend more on lifetime aggregate income than on the income of a single year. Annual income varies considerably from year to year, more for some households than for others. This variation can either be systematic over the life cycle or random from one year to the next. Income profiles differ over the life cycle between different occupational categories. In many blue-collar occupations, wages are largely independent of age. On the other hand, in career occupations and professions which require a higher education, there are considerable differences in annual salaries between the beginning and the end of one's career.[7]

Furthermore, uncertainty means that a single year's income becomes an unreliable indicator of an individual's normal income. This uncertainty may be of a micro-nature and hit households on all income levels, for example the loss of income due to illness. Such uncertainty normally entails a tendency for the spread of annual incomes to systematically overestimate the spread of average income over a longer period of time. Other uncertainty can be systematic, for example, reflecting economic conditions or changes in asset prices. Variations in such macro factors mean that the measured spread in annual income will fluctuate from year to year; for example the income of the rich might be overestimated when the price of financial assets increase, and temporarily increased unemployment might mean that the income of the lowest paid groups tends to be underestimated compared with the average income seen in a longer perspective.

It is easy to realize that the tax system can have other effects on the distribution of lifetime income than on the distribution of annual income. With a proportional tax system, it would not make any difference, but with a progressive system the average tax rate increases with the variability of income. What effect this has on the distribution of lifetime income depends on whether it is high-income or low-income earners who have the most variable incomes.

For obvious reasons, there are few studies that try to measure lifetime incomes. With data from the *Level of Living Survey* (*LNU*) and data from public registers for the years in between, Björklund *et al.* (1995) have followed a sample of individuals over the 1974–91 period. They were between 18 and 47 years of age at the beginning of the period and thus between 35 and 64 at the end of it. The discounted present value for this 18-year period is taken as a measure of lifetime income. For this selection of ageing households, the authors calculate measures of income distribution before and after tax, both for annual income and for lifetime income. They find that the spread of annual income before as well as after tax decreased continually up until the end of the 1980s, just as it did for the population as a whole. Further, they find, like Blomquist (1981), that lifetime income is considerably more evenly distributed than annual income – something which is true for both before- and after-tax income. Using differences in the Gini coefficient before and after tax as measures of the redistributive effect of the tax system, they find that the difference is only slightly lower for 'lifetime income' than the average of the differences for the annual incomes.[8] Thus, the conclusion is that for the generation which has been occupationally active during the great expansion period of the welfare state, with its increase of taxes and allowances, the tax and allowance system has helped level out incomes even when looked at over such a long period of time as 18 years.

Although there are strong reasons to try to look at income distribution in a longer perspective, a big practical problem is that such calculations would necessarily be very uncertain since they must be based not only on knowledge of the existing system but also on expectations about the future changes of the system. It might still be appropriate to make a couple of remarks about the possible effects on income distribution between different generations. TR91 can be seen as a transition from an income tax system to a system characterized more by taxes on consumption. Such a change has a general tendency to discriminate against older individuals since, on average, these have higher consumption in relation to their income than do younger people, that is, older people save less.[9] Secondly, the short-term underfinancing of the reform means that tax payments are postponed to the future, which favours older people in relation to younger generations. These two elements affect the distribution across generations in opposite directions.

7.2 THE TAX SYSTEM AND INCOME DISTRIBUTION

Let us take a look at the composition of income for the aggregate household sector in order to get a picture of the extent of the public tax and transfer system in relation to income generated directly on the market. In Table 7.1 different income entries are expressed as shares of *total factor income*, that is the sum of wages, entrepreneurial income and capital income. The latter item is defined by Statistics Sweden as the sum of *gross* interest and dividend income (that is, without taking interest expenses into account) and *net* positive capital gains (that is, after deductions of losses until the balance is zero). Such a definition, which clearly conflicts with all definitions of income grounded in theory, may be motivated by the fact that interest expenses and capital losses signal unreported or underreported capital income, and that one therefore may get closer to the truth by ignoring them.[10] After adding allowances and deducting taxes from factor income, one arrives at

Table 7.1   Income structure as a share of aggregate household factor income, per cent

	1980	1985	1989	1991	1992
(1) Wages	89.6	87.3	85.7	87.1	88.9
(2) Entrepreneurial income	3.4	3.8	3.0	2.2	2.0
(3) Interest and dividends	6.2	7.8	6.3	5.8	6.7
(4) Realized capital gains	0.8	1.0	5.1	4.9	2.2
(5) Factor income	100.0	100.0	100.0	100.0	100.0
(6) Sickness benefits	4.9	4.7	6.2	5.6	3.7
(7) Pensions and life annuities	20.4	24.5	24.2	26.1	28.3
(8) Parents' allowances, etc.	2.3	3.0	3.2	3.8	4.3
(9) Unemployment allowances	1.2	2.0	1.4	2.5	5.4
(10) Factor income, incl. work-related transfers	128.8	134.2	135.0	138.0	141.7
(11) Children's and housing allowances	3.8	3.6	3.0	4.1	4.3
(12) Other transfers	2.0	1.7	1.7	2.3	2.6
(13) Taxes	37.6	39.6	43.2	37.4	37.7
(14) Disposable income	97.1	99.8	96.5	107.0	110.8
(15) Normal return on net wealth	7.5	7.3	8.5	7.9	7.2
(16) Deficits	9.4	9.9	9.9	8.9	10.1
(17) Accrued capital gains	−13.1	2.0	22.3	−3.9	−23.2
(18) Indirect taxes	23.6	27.6	25.2	27.6	25.8

Notes: The entries for wages, interest and dividends, and capital gains are adjusted for 1980, 1985 and 1989 in order to reflect the broadening of the tax bases from 1991. The numbers for 1980 and 1985 are adjusted upwards by the same percentage as Statistics Sweden has used to adjust 1989 income upwards. The entry, normal return, is calculated as three per cent of net wealth.
Sources: Income distribution survey 1992; Be21 SM 9401, Table 2. Accrued capital gains from Berg (1994b).

disposable income. Among the transfers are those of an insurance kind where the benefits are entirely or partially linked to participation in the workforce, including pensions. Outside this category fall such transfers as housing and children's allowances.

   Under the line in the table, three items are presented which help put the definition of capital income in perspective. 'Normal return' in line 15 is based on an assessment of net wealth at market prices multiplied by an assumed real rate of interest of three per cent. This measure ends up on about the same level as gross interest and dividends on line 3. Line 16 shows that net deductions consistently exceed the sum of interest and dividends; even after TR91 there is a negative tax on household capital income. Line 17 shows that the accrued capital gains and losses come up to large and variable sums in relation to the normal return on net wealth as well as the sum of interest and dividends. Finally, line 18 shows that indirect taxes, which affect the purchasing power of disposable income, comes to about two thirds of income taxes.

On average, disposable and factor income lie on the same level; that is, transfer payments are about as big as the direct taxes households pay. However, the fact that the levels of both income concepts lie so close to each other is a coincidence. There is no reason *a priori* that this should be so. On the one hand, the use of resources by the public sector has to be financed by taxes, which means that factor income has to exceed disposable income if the latter takes all taxes into account. On the other hand, the calculation of disposable income in accordance with line 14 does not take into account other sources of financing public sector activities, above all not commodity taxes and corporate taxes. In the years prior to the reform, disposable income was a couple of percentage points lower than factor income; after the reform it was suddenly about ten per cent higher.[11] This swing is partially explained by increased indirect taxes, which can be seen from the last line of the table. However, it also reflects the real underfinancing of the reform which we discussed in Chapter 6. The entries which are directly attributable to TR91 (housing allowances and children's allowances, and direct and indirect taxes) together account for an increase in household disposable income of 5.1 per cent of factor income, or 36.8 billion kronor. This lies close to our estimate of the underfinancing of the reform by ca. 35 billion kronor, which we arrived at from completely different starting points.

From Table 7.1 we see that 40 per cent of disposable income is channelled through the public sector or the public insurance system. To what extent does this redistribute income between rich and poor households? One answer is given by the ratios between disposable and factor income as presented in Figure 7.1 (lines 14 and 5 in Table 7.1), with households divided into deciles according to employment income per consumption unit.[12] The figures only refer to households in the active age groups, defined here by the head of the household being between 18 and 64 years of age. The tax and allowance system is redistributive in the sense that households with low incomes (up through and including deciles 3, 4 and 5) receive larger sums in transfers than they pay in taxes; the ratio between disposable income and factor income is greater than one, while the opposite applies in higher income brackets. It is also apparent that disposable income has

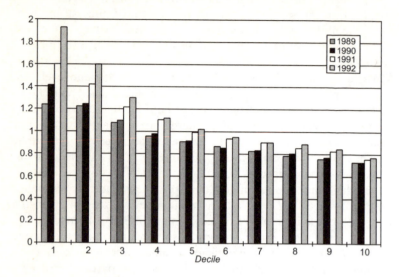

Figure 7.1   The ratio between disposable income and factor income exclusive
work-related transfers for different income deciles 1989–92, head
of household 18–64 years
Source: The HINK study and authors' calculations.

increased in relation to factor income for all groups since the tax
reform, but it has increased most in the lower income brackets. In
the next to lowest decile, decile 2, the ratio between disposable income
and factor income increased from 1.2 in 1989 and 1990 to 1.6 in 1992.
At the same time, the ratio increased only insignificantly in the next
highest decile, decile 9, from ca. 0.75 in 1989 and 1990 to barely more
than 0.80 in 1991 and 1992.[13] Measured this way, the tax system has
become more redistributive since the reform. Despite this, the spread
in disposable income increased in this period. Between 1989 and 1992,
disposable income decreased by 20 per cent in decile 1 and by 1 per
cent in decile 2 while it increased by five per cent in the three highest
deciles.

In Figure 7.1, only market incomes are counted as factor income.
This may give a misleading picture of how the degree of redistribution
has changed over time. In particular, unemployment benefits have
increased considerably during the 1990s at the same time as employment income has decreased. In decile 2, unemployment benefits
increased from 3.6 per cent of factor income in 1989 to 8.0 per cent
in 1992, while the corresponding increase in decile 9 was less, from 0.9

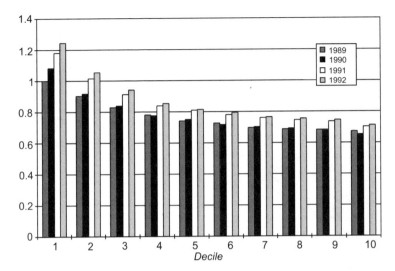

Figure 7.2 The ratio between disposable income and factor income inclusive
work-related transfers for different income deciles 1989–92, head
of household 18–64 years
Source: The HINK study and authors' calculations.

per cent to 3.4 per cent. If unemployment benefits are included in taxes
and allowances, as in Figure 7.1, the picture is one of a considerably
increased before-tax spread of income which was counteracted by an
almost equally big increase in redistribution through taxes and allowances. If, instead, unemployment benefits are included in before-tax
income, the picture is one of a moderate increase in the spread of
income both before and after tax. Figure 7.2 is based on the latter view,
with factor income calculated inclusive of work-related transfers
(unemployment benefits and parents' insurance). Even measured this
way the ratio of disposable income to factor income is consistently
larger in the deciles below the median. However, the difference
between the years before and after the reform is somewhat less clear
using this definition of income.

The amount of redistribution can also be illustrated by a Lorenz
diagram, where all households (or individuals) are ranked according to
income. The vertical axis gives the share of total income which accrues
to households below a certain position in the distribution of income. If
the distribution of income was completely equal, the Lorenz curve
would describe a straight 45-degree line. The more unequal income

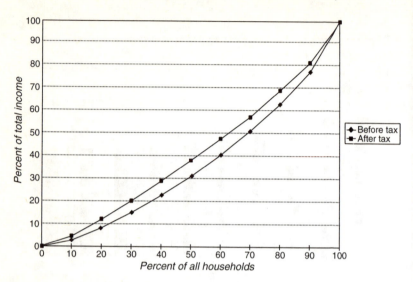

Figure 7.3   The share of the total sum of income for households below a certain position in the distribution of income
Source: The HINK study and our own calculations.

is distributed, the further below the 45-degree line lies the Lorenz curve. An example based on income for 1989 is presented in Figure 7.3. The curve for after-tax income clearly lies closer to the 45-degree line than the before-tax curve. This confirms the conclusion that the tax and allowance system helps bring about a more even distribution of annual income. A summary measurement is the Gini coefficient, defined as the ratio between two areas, namely, the area between the Lorenz curve and the 45-degree line and the entire triangle area under the 45-degree line. It can assume values between zero, when all incomes are equal, and one, when all income accrues to one individual. The Gini coefficient can also be interpreted as half the mean value of the absolute difference between all incomes expressed as a fraction of average income. This means that if two randomly chosen individuals meet, the Gini coefficient says how much (as a share of average income in society) the richer person has to give the poorer one, on average, in order for them to be equally rich. In Sweden, typical Gini coefficients for disposable income lie around 0.20. This means that the expected income difference between an arbitrary couple of households is about 40 per cent of average income. In other developed market economies the Gini coefficients often lie somewhat higher, between 0.25 and 0.30.

How should we assess the effects of TR91 on income distribution? One way is to choose a summary measure of the redistributive capacity of the tax system and compare it before and after the reform. This is what we have done when we have interpreted the relative height of the bars in Figures 7.1 and 7.2 as indicators of how the degree of redistribution has been changed. In a similar way we could compare the difference in the Gini coefficient before and after tax at two different points in time, before and after the reform. A problem is that such comparisons implicitly assume that before-tax income does not depend on tax rules, which apparently conflicts with the fact that the purpose of the reform was to affect the behaviour of households. Therefore, one should in principle try to attribute a certain part of the change in income distribution before tax to the reform. However, such a comparison must be based on credible estimates of the behaviour effects. Keeping in mind that, in general, we have found rather small short-term effects of the current tax reform on labour supply, saving, and wage formation, it hardly has any great practical significance for the *distribution* estimate whether or not we take into account behavioural effects. On the other hand, as we will discuss in more detail in the next chapter, the gains in social *efficiency* can be substantial even if the changes in behaviour are rather small. Even if we were to disregard behavioural responses and consider income distribution before tax as being exogenous, the question arises as to what income distribution before tax should be used as a basis for the estimates. The different alternatives can be presented in a simple figure.

		Income distribution before tax	
		Before TR 91	*After TR 91*
Tax system	*Before TR 91*	1	2
	After TR 91	3	4

The estimates presented before the reform by the RINK Commission represent a comparison of squares 1 and 3, while our discussion based on Figures 7.1 and 7.2 corresponds to comparing the degree of redistribution in squares 1 and 4. In what follows we will largely keep to comparisons of the latter kind, using the actual before-tax income distributions. It is true that a comparison between 1 and 3 (or 2 and 4) can be said to isolate the effect of the tax system; however, one problem is that it requires very detailed calculations of the tax and allowance rules.

A more fundamental problem is that one and the same distribution of factor income before tax can give rise to different distributions of taxable income depending on how heavily the different incomes are taxed, largely reflecting portfolio transactions for tax reasons or attempts to change employment income into capital income or vice versa. Most of the studies which compare squares 1 and 3 (or 2 and 4) completely ignore such links, and assume that high-income earners would keep making large interest payments despite the fact that the value of interest deductions had decreased. Corresponding problems become less serious when comparisons are made between squares 1 and 4, where it is possible to compare directly the distribution of factor income before tax with distribution after tax, without specifying how much of the difference depends on the fact that taxable income deviates from factor income and how much depends on the different tax rates themselves.

7.3   THE REDISTRIBUTION OF ANNUAL INCOME BEFORE AND AFTER TR91

Did the redistributive effect of the tax system change as a result of TR91? We will try to answer this question by comparing the Gini coefficients before and after tax calculated for different definitions of income by Björklund *et al.* (1995). In this study, which is based on data from the HINK surveys, the change in degree of redistribution is analyzed in relation to the actual income distribution before tax at different times, that is, comparing squares 1 and 4. In Figure 7.4 the Gini coefficient for the distribution of *annual income* is given per consumer unit before and after tax from 1967 onward for households

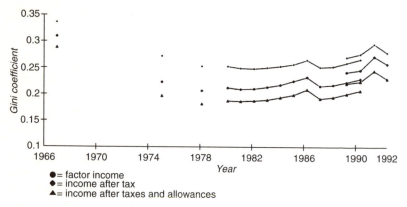

● = factor income
◆ = income after tax
▲ = income after taxes and allowances

Figure 7.4   Gini coefficients for factor income, income after taxes, and income after taxes and allowances
Source: Björklund *et al.* (1995), Figure 3a.

where the head of household is between 25 and 64 years of age.[14] Farmers and entrepreneurs are excluded because problems of measurement are especially great for these groups.

Annual income before tax largely corresponds to factor income including work-related transfers, that is, line 10 in Table 7.1. Since unemployment benefits and other work-related transfers are included here in income before tax, we avoid the problem of growing unemployment distorting the comparison over time. The broadening of the tax bases in connection with the tax reform makes it difficult to compare income before and after 1991. Therefore, there are two different income measures for the two years preceding the reform, one of which includes estimated values for various fringe benefits that became subject to tax as of 1991. In Figure 7.4 the Gini coefficients are given for both measures for 1989 and 1990. We see that the measure of before tax inequality increases when previously untaxed fringe benefits are included.

Figure 7.4 confirms – despite differences in income concepts, population, etc. – the picture from other studies using HINK statistics (for example, Jansson and Sandqvist (1993)) of a relatively weak, but still visible trend throughout the 1980s and into the 1990s toward a more uneven distribution of income after as well as before tax. From 1980 to 1990, the Gini coefficient increased from 0.251 to 0.263 for factor income and from 0.186 to 0.204 for disposable income.[15] Although the figures after 1990 are not comparable, we see that the Gini coefficient for factor income continues to increase between 1990 and 1991 but turns back between 1991 and 1992. The picture of an increased inequality also agrees with the fact that the wage distribution gradually widened from the middle of the 1980s; see for example Edin and Holmlund (1995).[16] If unemployment benefits had been included among transfers, increased unemployment would have been reflected much more strongly in an increased spread of income before tax, and in the difference between the before- and after-tax trend being much bigger.

Figure 7.5 shows the difference between the Gini coefficients before and after taxes and allowances. In the 1980s, the tax system helped lower the Gini coefficient by 3–4 percentage points while allowances added slightly more than an additional two per cent decrease. In the beginning of the 1990s, after the reform, the redistributive effect of the tax system had decreased to just more than two per cent, while the effect of allowances had increased to almost three per cent, that is, the total redistributive effect remained largely constant; the tax system

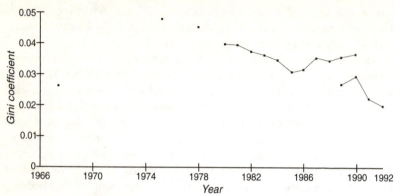

Figure 7.5a   The difference between the Gini coefficient before taxes and allowances and after taxes

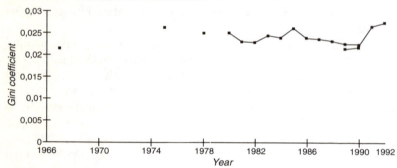

Figure 7.5b   The difference between the Gini coefficient before and after allowances

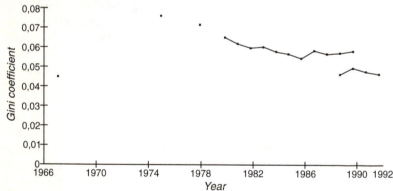

Figure 7.5c   The difference between the Gini coefficient before taxes and allowances and after taxes and allowances

Source: Björklund *et al*. (1995), Figure 3c–3e.

became less redistributive, but this was counteracted by increases in childrens' allowances and housing allowances. Before we draw our final conclusions, we ought to investigate how sensitive this picture is to alternative definitions of income.

7.4 FAMILY COMPOSITION

When one makes use of equivalence scales and calculates disposable income per consumption unit, families with children will be strongly overrepresented in the lower deciles. This explains why households in the lower regions of the income distribution (per consumption unit) were favoured most by the increase of allowances made in connection with TR91. In decile 2, children's allowances and housing allowances increased from 10.3 per cent of disposable income in 1989 to 12.7 per cent in 1992. In decile 9, the corresponding increase was from 0.6 to 0.8 per cent. This indicates that the tax and allowances reform was redistributive to the advantage of families with children, and it is natural to look at the distribution within each category of households by itself; see Table 7.2.

Table 7.2   The Gini coefficients before and after taxes and allowances for different categories of households, 1989 and 1992

		Before tax	Taxes redistr.	After tax	Allow. redistr.	After tax and allow.	Total redistr.
Single,	1989	0.2563	0.0310	0.2254	0.0077	0.2176	0.0387
without children	1992	0.2643	0.0214	0.2430	0.0096	0.2334	0.0309
Cohabiting,	1989	0.2159	0.0225	0.1934	0.0010	0.1924	0.0235
without children	1992	0.2110	0.0193	0.1917	0.0010	0.1907	0.0203
Cohabiting,	1989	0.2175	0.0269	0.1906	0.0063	0.1843	0.0332
one child	1992	0.2097	0.0190	0.1907	0.0091	0.1816	0.0281
Cohabiting,	1989	0.1887	0.0192	0.1694	0.0110	0.1584	0.0303
two children	1992	0.1992	0.0183	0.1809	0.0160	0.1649	0.0343
Cohabiting,	1989	0.2387	0.0271	0.2116	0.0393	0.1723	0.0664
more than two	1992	0.2557	0.0213	0.2345	0.0501	0.1844	0.0713
children							

Note: The redistribution of taxes is equal to the difference between the Gini coefficient before and after taxes and allowances. The redistribution of allowances is the difference between the Gini coefficient after taxes and after taxes and allowances. The total redistribution is the sum of the redistribution of both taxes and allowances.
Source: Björklund *et al.* (1995), Table B4.

If we first read the table horizontally, we see that allowances are redistributive within each household category. Since the same amount of children's allowances is paid regardless of income it constitutes a larger share of the disposable income of low income-earners and helps to reduce the Gini coefficients. Housing allowances, which are based on income, have a strong redistributive effect. If we read the table vertically, we see large differences between the different categories of households regarding the effect of these allowances. They have a greater redistributive effect than taxes for families with more than two children. They have also increased in importance after the reform for all groups. The increase in the redistributive effect of allowances throughout the entire population noted in previous sections, is thus not only a result of redistribution to families with children from other categories of households.

Adding together the effects of taxes and allowances, we see that the overall effects of the reform differ depending on the number of children. On the one hand, the redistributive effect has increased for the category 'cohabiting with two or more children'. On the other hand, for the categories, 'single people', and 'cohabiting without children or with one child', the degree of equalization has decreased.[17] Comparing the size of the different groups in the population, we see that, taken together, the groups where equalization has diminished are almost twice as large as those where equalization within the group has increased. The reform led to a decreased redistribution between most households with the same number of people to support, but this has been counteracted by an increased redistribution in favour of households with a large number of people to support. For the entire population, these two effects largely cancel out.

7.5   CAPITAL INCOME

Wealth, and hence capital income, is more unevenly distributed than employment income. At the same time, measurement and periodization problems are especially great here. With data based on income tax returns it is possible to measure interest and dividends rather well, but one misses returns in kind from property and consumer durables as well as a large share of returns on unregistered financial assets. Further, there is a considerable periodization problem with capital gains since they are not seen in the statistics until they are realized. In order to illuminate the sensitivity to alternative definitions, Table 7.3

Table 7.3 Different measurements of capital income as a share of factor income (inclusive work-related transfers)

	Decile									
	1	*2*	*3*	*4*	*5*	*6*	*7*	*8*	*9*	*10*
Real normal rate of return										
1989	14.8	4.0	3.7	3.2	3.6	4.1	4.3	4.6	5.7	8.3
1990	9.1	4.0	3.6	3.2	4.1	3.8	4.4	4.7	5.2	9.0
1991	9.9	3.2	3.2	3.1	3.4	3.7	4.2	4.1	4.8	6.7
1992	10.3	3.7	2.6	3.0	2.6	2.9	3.3	4.0	4.4	5.6
Gross interest and dividends										
1989	7.0	3.1	2.7	2.5	2.7	0.9	3.1	3.0	3.7	6.7
1990	6.6	3.4	2.7	2.4	2.9	2.7	3.2	2.8	3.7	6.9
1991	9.0	2.7	2.3	2.3	2.2	2.2	2.4	2.7	3.2	5.6
1992	9.9	3.3	2.8	2.7	2.6	2.8	3.2	3.3	3.7	6.1
Net positive capital gains										
1989	2.1	0.3	0.4	0.5	0.3	0.7	1.0	0.6	1.4	13.8
1990	0.5	0.3	0.5	0.3	0.7	0.9	1.0	0.8	1.3	14.9
1991	1.0	0.5	0.4	0.3	0.6	1.0	0.9	1.2	1.8	14.0
1992	0.8	0.3	0.2	0.2	0.2	0.4	0.7	0.5	0.6	6.4
Net interest and dividends										
1989	0.8	−4.8	−6.1	−7.1	−6.0	−5.9	−5.0	−5.9	−6.2	−6.5
1990	−2.0	−4.4	−7.3	−7.8	−7.4	−6.3	−5.9	−6.5	−6.5	−6.1
1991	−4.7	−6.3	−7.4	−7.6	−7.6	−7.1	−6.6	−6.0	−6.3	−4.7
1992	−8.7	−6.1	−8.4	−8.0	−7.8	−7.9	−7.1	−6.4	−6.7	−5.0

Source: The HINK studies and the authors' calculations.

shows the distribution of four categories of capital income over different deciles for the years 1989–92, expressed as a share of factor income inclusive of work-related transfers. The first measure takes the household's market valued net wealth times a three per cent real interest rate. This can be seen as a measurement of *normal capital income* calculated on the assumption that everyone invests their wealth at the same expected real rate of return.[18] According to this measure, capital income increases as a share of factor income starting with decile 4. In the highest decile it is twice as big a share of factor income as in the middle of the income distribution.

The second and third blocks in the table represent the two items which are a part of capital income as it is defined in the official statistics on income distribution. We see that gross *interest and dividend income* are rather evenly distributed except in the extreme deciles. *Capital gains*, which are calculated net to the extent they are positive, are extremely concentrated in the highest decile, where they would constitute around 5 per cent of income, even if taxes on capital gains were taken into account. In the other income groups they are largely negligible. If interest and dividends and capital gains are added together, one comes quite close to the normal capital income for all deciles except the highest and the lowest. Seen in this way, the aggregate picture which the statistics on income distribution give of capital income is not so misleading, except that these statistics exaggerate capital income at the top of income distribution.

The fact that capital gains carry great weight in the top decile is a result of disposable income being so defined as to include capital gains; even an average-income earner can end up in the highest decile in the year in which their house is sold. The size of capital gains varies considerably from year to year depending on price trends as well as turnover on the market for shares and owner-occupied homes. In connection with TR91, there was an incentive to realize profits on owner-occupied homes under the old system, but to wait with reporting capital gains on shares until the new system had gone into effect.[19] In other words, a measurement of income which includes realized capital gains is especially problematic in connection with the transition between two systems which treat capital gains differently. Therefore, an imputed measure of capital income is to be preferred.

Finally, net *interest and dividends* are stated – that is, the capital income which appears on the income tax return after deductions for interest payments. This item is consistently negative in all deciles despite the fact that average net wealth is positive. Therefore, it appears to be an unreasonable measurement of capital income. However, the negative balance is about proportional to income, constituting between four and eight per cent of factor income.

Calculations reported by the RINK Commission assumed that the portfolio pattern from 1989, with heavy borrowing of higher income households, would remain. Therefore, these groups in high marginal tax brackets initially would be hit especially hard by the transition to a more uniform taxation of capital income at lower tax rates. The assumption of an unchanged portfolio pattern might appear unrealistic, but the figures in Table 7.3 do not show any dramatic reduction of interest deductions in the highest deciles, even if there is a slight decrease in decile 10. However, we judge this decile to be less reliable than the other ones, where there is an increased or unchanged deficit. It should be remembered, however, that the gap between deposit rates and lending rates increased substantially in the wake of the financial

Table 7.4 Gini coefficients for income before tax and differences in Gini coefficients before and after taxes and allowances for different definitions of capital income

	1. Standard definition			2. Without capital gains			3. Imputed		
	Gini	Taxes	Allow.	Gini	Taxes	Allow.	Gini	Taxes	Allow.
1989	0.2672	0.0280	0.0212	0.2493	0.0271	0.0212	0.2494	0.0251	0.0211
1991	0.2917	0.0233	0.0270	0.2652	0.0236	0.0272	0.2653	0.0215	0.0265
1992	0.2754	0.0213	0.0279	0.2665	0.0213	0.0281	0.2668	0.0203	0.0283

Note: 1. According to the standard definition, capital income consists of the sum of interest income, dividends and positive capital gains.
2. Capital income is defined according to the standard definition, but exclusive of capital gains.
3. Capital income is defined as three per cent of net wealth valued at market prices.
Source: Björklund *et al.* (1995), Table 4a.

crisis. The impression that TR91 does not seem to have had any greater immediate effect on household financial transactions is also strengthened by the study that Agell, Berg and Edin (1995) carried out with panel data from HINK for 1989 and 1992, which finds no correlation between changes in tax rates and portfolio adjustments.

A study of Table 7.3 can suggest how the measurement of income distribution is affected by different definitions of capital income, but it does not say how the measurement of the redistributive effects of taxes and allowances is affected. That question is answered in Table 7.4 which contains Gini coefficients before taxes and the difference in the Gini coefficients before and after taxes and allowances for two alternative definitions of capital income.[20] First, we have the previously used standard definition of disposable income which only includes positive interest income and capital gains. In the second definition, capital gains have been excluded (but positive interest and dividends remain). This reduces the measured unevenness of factor income; the Gini coefficient before taxes and allowances is considerably lower than when the standard definition is used. In the third definition, capital income is measured by the imputed measure of normal capital income. This definition gives about the same picture as the second definition.

The choice of definition of capital income has some significance for our view of what happened in connection with the tax reform. Looking at normal income, in the third block of the table, it appears that the 1991 and 1992 tax and allowance system is somewhat *more* equalizing than the 1989 system. This is probably due to the new definition of taxable capital income, with a more symmetric treatment of different types of capital income, being closer to the standard calculation of capital income. Keeping in mind the fundamental problems of measurement which exist regarding capital income, there is no reason to draw far-reaching conclusions from this. Rather, it is striking that three different measurements, all with weaknesses of their own, indicate that the tax and allowance system taken in its entirety helps to redistribute income about as much after the reform as before.

7.6   CAPITAL GAINS AND LOSSES

As capital gains vary considerably from year to year, it is unsuitable to add realized gains to one year's income since they are the result of long-term price trends. For example, income statistics register large capital gains in 1992, despite the fact that prices of shares and owner-occupied homes fell during the year. A consistent application of the Davidson–Lindahlian definition of income would instead treat capital gains as income in the year they accrued rather than when the asset was sold. From Table 7.1 it can be seen that the increases and decreases in asset values in certain years corresponded to more than 20 per cent of disposable income for the average household. Keeping in mind that ownership is more unevenly distributed than income, it is easy to realize that taking into account capital gains has great potential importance for our picture of income distribution.

In order to shed light on the importance of capital gains for the years surrounding TR91, our calculations have combined data from the HINK surveys with Lennart Berg's (1994b) figures over the household sector's total accrued capital gains on shares and owner-occupied homes and summer cottages respectively. We have assumed that the total capital gains from shares have been distributed across income deciles in the same proportion as the holdings of financial assets, and that the gains from owner-occupied homes and summer cottages have been distributed analogously. The result for the 1989–92 period, given in Figures 7.6 and 7.7, shows that the picture of income distribution for a single year would be completely reversed if accrued capital gains on shares were counted fully as a part of annual income. This would mean that for 1990, when households suffered substantial losses, the income for the highest decile would be cut by more than 50 percent, which would place it on a level with the third or fourth decile in income distribution.

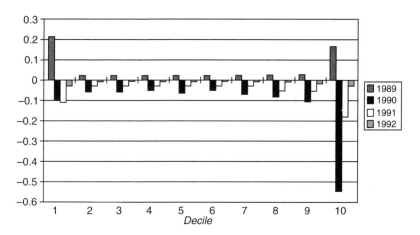

Figure 7.6 Real accrued capital gains on shares as a share of disposable income

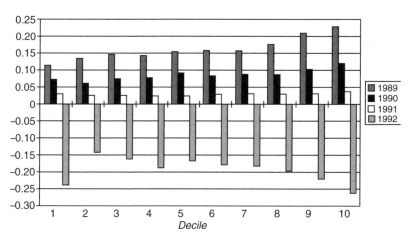

Figure 7.7 Real accrued capital gains on home ownership and summer cottages as a share of disposable income
Source: The HINK surveys and our own calculations.

Capital gains on owner-occupied homes and summer cottages are more evenly distributed than gains on shares. Still they are almost twice as big in relation to disposable income in deciles 9 and 10 as in decile 2. For 1992, when substantial losses were suffered, disposable income would have been 15–25 per cent lower if losses from the fall in housing prices had been included. However, since a person's planning horizon when purchasing a house or making financial investments is much longer than a year, annual figures have limited relevance, and looking at the average of the four years in the diagram reduces the distributional impact of capital gains substantially; gains one year are counteracted by losses in another. Therefore, if one wishes to capture capital gains for an average year it might be reasonable to see them as a part of a normal rate of return on capital.

It is important to distinguish between the capital gains and losses which normally occur as a result of changes in business conditions and unexpected events in the economy, and such gains and losses that can be directly attributable to the tax reform. While it is reasonable to even out the former category of 'normal' gains and losses over a longer period of time, the latter category should of course be included directly in the analysis of the distribution effects of the reform. In what way were the prices of different assets affected by the reform?

The value of an asset can in principle be seen as the discounted current value of the future income which the asset generates. The question is how the reform has affected the numerator (future income) and the denominator (the discount rate) in such a calculation. The relevant discount rate is interest after tax for a representative investor. For shares and other financial assets which are priced on the international market, it is unlikely that the Swedish tax reform affected the discount rate to any appreciable extent. The question, then, is how it affected future earnings flows. For shares, the answer depends on the impact of the reform on the performance of the Swedish economy. If the reform was seen as good news from a growth perspective, it ought to have created expectations about higher dividends in the future, which ought to have helped force up share prices. The magnitude of this, however, is difficult to judge.

For owner-occupied homes, in contrast, the representative owner is a Swedish household, and by lowering tax rates, the reform led to an increase in the discount rate when assessing house values. The effects of this increase were not counteracted to the same extent by increased expected returns. Our estimates in Chapter 3 indicate a probable immediate fall in real prices of the order of 15 per cent as a result of the reform, that is, just as much as house prices fell in 1992. For the average homeowner, this corresponds to around 20 per cent of disposable income. It is easy to read the distribution profile straight from Figure 7.7 which shows that capital losses on owner-occupied homes in 1992 corresponded to nine per cent more of disposable income in decile 9 compared to decile 2. Keeping in mind that the average homeowner lives in his or her house for perhaps a decade, it may be reasonable to spread the capital losses over such a long period of time. The conclusion, then, is that decile 9 lost little more than one per cent of annual disposable income during ten years' time in relation to decile 2.

Focusing on home owners creates a biased picture if one does not also look at the costs for those in the rented sector. Tied to TR91 was a reduction of interest subsidies for newly built apartment houses in order to maintain parity between different forms of tenure. It is a complicated matter to determine the incidence of the reduced subsidies on rent levels. In theory, one should not really expect any greater short-term impact since the stock of flats is given, and rents should be determined by demand rather than by the costs of landlords. However, this is not what has happened. Instead, rent per square metre rose dramatically, and the lack of demand expressed itself in increased vacancies. Between 1989 and 1991, average real rent per square metre rose by approximately 18 per cent. According to calculations presented in Englund *et al.* (1995), this meant that the cost of housing for the average renter increased from 23 to 29 per cent of disposable income. The authors suggest that at least half of this can be attributed to TR91, corresponding to three per cent of annual disposable income. If such large rent increases were to become permanent, this would entail a greater loss for renters than the single capital loss of 20 per cent of annual income which TR91 caused owners of owner-occupied homes. However, there are grounds to question the possibility of retaining such a high level of rent if the prices of owner-occupied homes were to remain on the lower level.

The above discussion has dealt with capital gains and losses caused by the *transition* from the old to the new tax system. Another question is whether the new tax system, when it is fully implemented, will generate capital gains to a greater or lesser extent than the old system. Certain capital gains are unavoidable reflections of new information about technology, competition and other matters. Other capital gains are generated by economic policy. A tax reform is one such example. Variations in inflation which affect the price of assets through nominal interest rates are another example. In a small, open economy with floating exchange rates, it is reasonable to see the *real interest rate before tax* as being determined outside the country's borders. This means that the Swedish nominal interest rate before tax reflects the domestic inflation rate. Prices of owner-occupied homes, and other assets priced by Swedish owners, are determined by the Swedish real interest rate *after* tax. It will be more sensitive to inflation the higher the tax rate on capital income is. In other words, the lower level on capital taxation ought to have the positive effect of making prices of assets held mainly by Swedish owners, for example, owner-occupied homes, less sensitive to variations in the rate of inflation. Our conclusion is that we have obtained a better tax system in this respect.

7.7   CONCLUSION

Did TR91 succeed in its aim of not leading to a more uneven distribution of income? We have tried to answer this question by comparing the income distribution before tax (which has been taken as given), with the distribution after taxes and allowances. Measured in this way, the equalization effect of the *tax system* decreased noticeably; the broadening of the various tax bases and the limitation of the value of the deficit deductions do not outweigh the effects of the lower marginal tax rates. However, taking into account differences in household size, this is counteracted by an increased equalization effect from *children's allowances and housing allowances*. Thus, the total equalization effect of taxes and allowances, when income is calculated per consumption unit, was just as good in the years immediately after the reform, in 1991 and 1992, as it was the year before, in 1989.

Given the importance of allowances aimed at families with children, it is natural to look at redistribution within homogeneous groups of households. Here, one can see that the degree of redistribution *within* groups of *households without children or with one child* has decreased, while the degree of redistribution *within* groups of *households with two or more children* has increased. At the same time, there has been increased redistribution *between* the different groups, from single individuals and couples without children to families with children. Thus, allowances have come to play a more significant role in the redistribution process. A negative aspect of this is that housing allowances are a contributing factor to tax wedges on employment income still being very high for large numbers of households with low incomes. The goal of income distribution has been secured at the price of continued high marginal effects for young people, and low-paid and part-time workers.

At the same time, we know that the distribution of disposable income has become more uneven as a result of income before tax becoming more unevenly distributed. This can be attributed to unemployment and an increased wage dispersion. The question is what role TR91 has played in this respect. Our conclusion is that the opinion which is sometimes advanced in Sweden about TR91 being one of the main reasons for the unemployment crisis is strongly exaggerated. The increased wage dispersion appears to be the continuation of a trend that has been going on since the middle of the 1980s, for which TR91 can hardly have had any decisive importance.

The biggest weakness in our analysis is its fundamentally static perspective. Using actual yearly income is particularly problematic since the reform was not fully financed. Our assessment, made in the previous chapter, is that the underfinancing amounts to around 4 per cent of household disposable income. If the future funding needed to eliminate this deficit turns out to be regressive, for example, due to cutbacks in public spending, this, of course, could change our picture of the distribution effects of the reform. However, we can only guess about this. We can state with greater certainty that the underfinancing of TR91 favours today's active generation at the expense of future taxpayers. Among other dynamic effects are the strong incentive effects on decisions about education and saving, which will no doubt have an impact on the distribution of income. However, a discussion at this time about what direction these effects might take would be largely speculative.

8 Efficiency

An important reason for the introduction of TR91 was the view that the old tax system hampered productive activity. High tax wedges on labour income and nonuniform taxation of capital led to a mismanagement of economic resources. In this concluding chapter, we shall see whether the hopes for a more efficient Swedish economy were justified. An important problem in this context is that many of the desired effects of TR91 are of a decidedly long-term nature. Labour market legislation and the nature of employment contracts mean that a majority of employees cannot make overnight changes in their working hours. It takes several years before improved incentives for higher education are converted into social productivity gains. Added to this – and something which is of decisive importance – is that the severe recession of the 1990s put a wet blanket on the supply side of the economy. As a result, not even a die-hard supply-sider ought to expect rapid and easily detectable effects. It will not be possible to pass a more final efficiency verdict on TR91 until the beginning of the next century.

Our discussion in this chapter will therefore largely be a critical review of the analyses which formed the intellectual basis for TR91. Was the thinking about the reform right? Has new information come to light which means that we should revise our view of the old tax system? Paradoxically, our answer is yes to both questions. Previous analyses of the efficiency losses associated with high marginal tax rates on earned income were often based on somewhat dated empirical studies, which seemed to indicate that taxes played a very important role for labour supply. As should be clear from our discussion in Chapter 5, there are now quite a few studies which indicate that taxes play a relatively minor role. Consequently, at least *one* of the problems of the old tax system may have been exaggerated. Even so, we conclude that the philosophy behind TR91 makes sense. Before TR91, tax wedges were so high that even a small supply response could be translated into a large loss in social efficiency. On many counts, the new tax system seems considerably more reasonable than the old one.

We devote the next section to an introduction to the methods and concepts used by economists to analyze the effects of taxes on allocational efficiency. The reason for this, quite elementary, discussion is our belief that economists and the public at large too often and quite unnecessarily misunderstand each other. In the popular debate,

190

efficiency is often interpreted as a synonym for various easy-to-observe responses, like increased labour supply, higher savings and a lasting increase in economic growth. For an economist, however, efficiency is defined in terms of areas which are not directly observable, between compensated demand and supply curves, and there is no simple relation between tax distortions and magnitudes of behavioural response. The same goes for the relation between efficiency and economic growth. According to the standard neoclassical growth model, a badly designed tax system may create important negative level effects on potential consumption, without the long-term rate of growth being affected.

In section 8.2, we move closer to reality and discuss studies which have tried to put a 'price tag' on the efficiency losses of the old tax system. In the sections thereafter, we present our own analysis of how TR91 has affected different dimensions of allocational efficiency. In section 8.3, we invoke behavioural findings from recent labour supply studies to assess the gains from lower marginal tax rates on earned income. In section 8.4, we discuss how the new, more uniform, capital income tax affects the allocation of capital across production sectors. In section 8.5, we turn to the international aspects and discuss how TR91 has affected the incentives for capital and labour to move across borders. In section 8.6, we examine the efficiency gains which follow from a tax system which is simple, and difficult to manipulate for tax arbitrage purposes. Finally, in section 8.7 we try to clarify the connection between taxes, growth and economic efficiency.

8.1   TAX WEDGES AND ECONOMIC EFFICIENCY: A VERY SIMPLE INTRODUCTION

To a greater or lesser extent, all taxes affect economic behaviour. Sometimes, it is a matter of taxes which improve efficiency. Nowadays, many countries impose special taxes on energy products which are hazardous to the environment. Another example is the high tax on alcohol in Norway and Sweden. Besides from generating tax revenue, the main purpose of this tax is to bring about a reduction in the consumption of alcoholic beverages. The vast majority of taxes, however, have other tasks than improving economic efficiency. Main purposes of the tax system are to finance the public sector and – depending on political preferences – to redistribute income. The common denominator of these taxes, however, is that they are likely to have undesirable side-effects on the way the economy functions.

A fundamental problem with many taxes is that they drive a wedge between social and private returns. Income taxation implies that real take-home pay falls short of the production value created by the worker. Taxes on capital income imply that the saver's net return is less than the profitability of the investment which was financed by the same saver. Commodity taxes increase the price of the consumer above the cost of the producer. These kinds of tax wedges worsen the ability of the price system to provide information about the demand patterns of households and the costs of producers. Since the decisions of economic actors are guided by prices after tax, while social costs and benefits depend on prices before tax, tax wedges tend to lead to inefficient use of scarce economic means.

A classic example of undesirable side-effects from taxation is the special window tax, levied in England towards the end of the seventeenth-century. The more windows a house had, the higher the tax. The window tax drove a wedge between the production costs of the artisan and the price of new windows paid by house owners. As a result, people started to build houses with few (or no) windows. The contribution of the window tax to the state coffers was modest, and it had unintended side-effects. In addition to the direct cost of paying the tax, an extra cost was created in the form of dark homes: The window tax created an *excess burden*. In principle, it is possible to measure the excess burden of a tax in monetary terms. Assume that a typical home-owner pays ten pounds in window tax. How much would that person be willing to pay to avoid the tax in the first place? Obviously, *at least as much* as the tax revenue. Besides the ten pounds, the homeowner pays an extra psychological cost in the form of a poorly lit home. Let us, for the sake of argument, assume that the homeowner assesses this psychological cost at five pounds. In total, he would therefore be willing to pay a maximum of fifteen pounds to escape the window tax. Thus, the excess burden is five pounds, or fifty per cent of the tax paid.

Let us now discuss other, more modern, examples. Assume a closed economy where a fixed pool of investment resources is to be divided between two production sectors – a housing sector and a corporate sector. Assume also that investments in both sectors are subject to diminishing rates of return – the marginal return to capital decreases when investment increases. If there are no taxes, a competitive capital market allocates investments in such a way that marginal returns become the same in both sectors (we ignore risk premia due to differences in risks). Now, assume that the government introduces a corporate income tax. Capital owners then find that the rate of return after-tax is higher in the housing sector than in the corporate sector. As a result, investments are redirected from the corporate sector to the housing sector. But since capital formation takes place under diminishing rates of return, profitability falls in the housing sector, while it rises in the corporate sector. This process continues until the owners of capital once again receive the same rate of return *after tax* in both sectors. In the new equilibrium, profitability before tax, therefore, will be higher in the corporate sector than in the housing sector, a difference in profitability which is of exactly the same size as the tax wedge.

It is this discrepancy which explains why there is an excess burden. The average profitability from investments in the economy, and thus total production as well, would increase if there was a way of transferring capital from the less productive housing sector to the more productive corporate sector. But the tax wedge prevents market forces from doing this on their own. In this particular example, we can note that it would actually be possible to reduce excess burden if the government also levied a tax on housing returns. Then there would be an incentive to bring back capital to the corporate sector. If the government chooses to impose the same tax rates in both sectors, the excess burden is eliminated outright. Capital flows back to the corporate sector until pre-tax returns are the same in both sectors, and since we have a system with uniform tax rates, owners of capital will receive the same after-tax returns regardless of where they have invested their capital.[1]

Our next example concerns the effects of taxes on labour supply. In Figure 8.1 overleaf, we illustrate an individual's choice between goods consumption (vertical axis) and leisure consumption (horizontal axis). The budget constraint before taxation is given by line W_0. Its slope depends on the size of the real wage, which is assumed to be a constant w. If the individual consumes more leisure (supplies less labour), income and goods consumption decrease. Initially, the individual has chosen an optimal consumption mix E_0, which is given by the point where the budget line is tangent to the indifference curve I_0.

We next introduce a proportional income tax at rate t. The tax reduces the rate of return on an extra hour worked from w to $w(1-t)$. As a result the budget line changes. The intercept on the horizontal axis is the same as before; if the individual chooses only to consume leisure, he or she pays no tax. For any given positive quantity of labour supply, however, disposable income will fall. The new budget constraint is given by line W_1, which has a smaller slope than W_0. The new equilibrium is given by point E_1. As we have drawn the

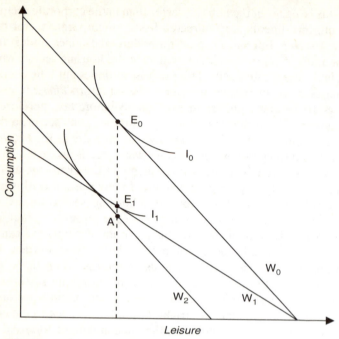

Figure 8.1   Excess burden of an income tax

indifference curves, the tax does not affect the consumption of leisure – despite the tax, labour supply is the same as initially. The explanation is that the tax has both a substitution and an income effect. Since the tax reduces real wages after tax, the opportunity cost of not working is reduced. This makes it cheaper to be at home, which tends to decrease labour supply. But the income effect counteracts this substitution effect. Since the tax makes the individual poorer, he or she will normally cut back on the consumption of goods and leisure, that is, labour supply tends to increase. We have drawn the figure so as to make the substitution and income effects just as large, implying a zero net effect on labour supply.

Government tax revenue is given by the difference between budget line W_0 and W_1 at the leisure consumption of the post-tax equilibrium – that is, the difference between E_0 and E_1. A trivial conclusion is that the tax reduces individual welfare, since disposable income decreases. The interesting question is if this reduction in welfare is larger than direct tax revenue. If this is so, the tax has an excess burden.

Just as was the case with the window tax, we may ask how much the individual is willing to pay to prevent the tax from being levied. To study this question, we return to the original budget line, W_0. We measure the willingness to pay to avoid the tax by examining how much this budget line can shift downwards – in a parallel manner – without the individual getting lower welfare than would have been the case with the income tax. We represent this hypothetical experiment by the budget line W_2. With this budget line the individual achieves the same utility, represented by indifference curve I_1, as when the income tax is in place. The difference between W_0 and W_2 is the willingness to pay to avoid the tax altogether. It is easy to see that willingness to pay is greater than direct tax revenue. The income tax has an excess burden, which is given by the distance between E_1 and A.

In popular debate, it is often argued that taxes with no effect on economic behaviour are of no consequence for economic efficiency. This is a misunderstanding. In our example, the tax does not affect labour supply, but it still creates an excess burden. The explanation, quite simply, is that the effect of the tax on labour supply is determined by counteracting substitution and income effects, while the effect on the excess burden (and thus on efficiency) depends only on the substitution effect. It is the substitution effect that reflects to what extent the tax wedge distorts the choice between leisure and goods consumption. The income effect only reflects the fact that the tax reduces disposable income, which all taxes do. A tax which has only an income effect, and does not create a tax wedge which distorts the price system, is of the lump-sum variety. Since a lump-sum tax is imposed regardless of the taxpayer's economic circumstances (wealth, income, and so on), it does not create a substitution effect.[2]

8.2 THE 'PRICE TAG' ON THE OLD TAX SYSTEM

The view that the old tax system created large excess burdens was an important source of inspiration for TR91. The tax system was supposed to have an indirect price tag, which went over and beyond the revenue accounts of the tax collector. As we saw in Chapter 5, the combination of narrow tax bases, income-dependent allowances and benefits, and a highly progressive tax schedule implied that extra work effort could trigger a very large marginal tax wedge. In addition, the progressive income tax tended to harm individuals with an uneven distribution of income over their lifecycle. The tax wedge between

pre- and post-tax returns on education for many university programmes could be considerable.

Other unwarranted effects were claimed to follow from various
asymmetries of capital income taxation. As implied by our simple
example, efficient allocation assumes that capital is distributed
between different production sectors in such a way that the rate of
return before tax is the same in all sectors. However, the asymmetries
of the personal and corporate tax codes implied that return requirements for new investments differed a lot between the corporate sector
and the housing sector. A closely related problem had to do with the
fact that the tax code was based on an *ad hoc* mixture of nominal and
real taxation principles. In Chapter 3, we showed that increased inflation led to a dramatic spread in the effective tax rates on different
forms of saving, something which meant that the rate of inflation
became very important for savings composition.

In recent years, many economists have tried to estimate the magnitudes of the excess burdens from different tax instruments; see
Browning (1976) for a pioneer study. This, however, is no easy task.
It is not enough to measure the size of tax wedges in order to gain an
understanding of the distorting effect of the tax system. We also need
information about supply and demand conditions in the different markets. How elastic is the supply of labour? What determines the demand
for labour? How does a change in capital costs affect investments?
Despite the great strides of econometric research in recent decades,
there is – as is evident in several parts of this book – considerable
uncertainty about the answers to these and many similar questions.

A further complication is that a quantitative assessment of excess
burdens typically requires that we account for the interaction between
different markets. In Figure 8.1 we limited ourselves to study the
excess burden of a tax on labour income in a model of *partial equilibrium*. But, as can be inferred from our example of capital allocation in
an economy with two production sectors, a partial equilibrium analysis
can easily lead in the wrong direction. To analyze the effect on efficiency from a tax on housing capital, we must allow for the fact that
capital formation is affected in the corporate sector also. Economists
therefore often use *general equilibrium models* which take into account
the mutual dependency between different parts of the economy.

Interesting general equilibrium evaluations of the excess burden
associated with the old Swedish tax system are Hansson (1984)
and Hansson and Stuart (1985). Hansson and Stuart develop highly
stylized – in the sense that they include a very limited number of

markets – general equilibrium models and put figures on important behavioural relations by combining econometric results from other sources with an aggregate description of the Swedish tax system at the end of the 1970s. According to Hansson (1984), some of the most important taxes gave rise to considerable excess burdens. Measures that increased the progressivity of income taxation could lead to an excess burden several times larger than the additional tax revenue; an additional krona of tax revenue could imply an extra excess burden of up to six kronor. On the other hand, the excess burden associated with an increase in proportional taxes, like VAT and payroll taxes, was much more modest; the efficiency price tag on an additional krona's tax revenue was in the range 0.5–1 krona.

These estimates imply that great efficiency gains could be had by redistributing the tax burden. If progressive income taxes were lowered by one krona, and this was financed by a corresponding increase in VAT, the excess burden could be reduced by up to five kronor (we might gain an entire six kronor from lowering the income tax, but we might lose around one krona by increasing VAT). Another interesting result of Hansson and Stuart (1985) was that higher taxes (or decreased subsidies) on housing capital was associated with a *negative* excess burden. Higher taxes on housing seemed to promote efficiency, a possibility which was implied in our simple example above. If these calculations are realistic, they undoubtedly suggest that TR91 ought to be conducive to efficient resource allocation. The reduced progressivity of the income tax creates an efficiency gain which is greater than the cost which is generated by increased VAT. The increase in capital taxation, which largely meant tougher taxation of housing, creates conditions for a more efficient intersectoral allocation of capital.

How reasonable is this analysis? To estimate the size of excess burdens, by necessity we need a simplified model of the economy, its institutions and market structures. Most studies, in Sweden and elsewhere, are based on the assumption that all markets (including the labour market) are characterized by a high degree of competition, and that the public sector affects household behaviour mainly through taxation. These assumptions clearly leave something to be desired. Wages are determined, at least in Sweden, mainly by negotiations between firms and unions. We also know that for many parents with small children, labour supply is affected by access to municipal child care. If we ignore these mechanisms, there is a risk that we will over-estimate the efficiency losses from taxation. As is discussed by Holmlund and Kolm (1995), there is some empirical support for the hypothesis that progressive income taxation can actually help to dampen the wage claims of unions and to reduce unemployment – potential gains for society that should be set against the excess burden from the distortion of workers' leisure choice. Moreover, to the extent that increased income taxes are used to subsidize child care, any negative disincentive effects on labour supply must be set against the positive effect of subsidized child care on the labour force participation of parents with small children.

Another complication follows from the fact that the excess burden in a very sensitive way depends on the exact assumptions we make about a few key parameters. As is discussed by Browing (1987), who uses a partial equilibrium model of the labour market to estimate the size of the marginal excess burden associated with the US income tax, small changes in parameter assumptions can have dramatic effects. By experimenting with different parameter combinations, Browning shows that the marginal excess burden may vary from ten per cent to more than 300 per cent of the additional tax revenue. Browning's own conclusion is that it is not possible to measure the excess burden of the US tax system with any great precision. Nevertheless, he concludes that plausible assumptions about certain parameter values are consistent with a marginal excess burden of between 32 and 47 per cent for an extra dollar's tax revenue.

Since excess burdens are not directly observable, all calculations must be based on a chain of assumptions, a chain that is no stronger than its weakest link. In the remainder of this chapter we will try to give (by simple mathematical examples and intuitive reasoning) what is by necessity a somewhat impressionistic analysis of how some central ingredients of TR91 (lower marginal tax rates, uniform capital taxation) have affected efficiency. In the next section, we report a number of numerical simulations of the excess burden associated with the marginal tax wedge on earned income. Our starting-point is a model of labour supply, and like Browning (1987) we explore how marginal excess burden depends on certain parameter assumptions, primarily the size of the tax wedge and the compensated labour supply elasticity.

Like Browning, we find that the excess burden is very sensitive to small changes in parameter assumptions. However, we also find that the excess burden of the old Swedish tax system was far from negligible for seemingly reasonable assumptions about the compensated wage elasticity. Even if we accept the view that labour supply is quite inelastic, it is difficult to avoid the conclusion that the old tax system imposed nontrivial efficiency costs. The reason is that the marginal tax wedge, which here includes income, payroll and indirect taxes, used to be very high. Since the difference between social and private marginal returns used to be so huge, also a modest reduction in labour supply was compatible with a large efficiency loss. Although our simulations should be interpreted with a grain of salt, they clearly indicate that TR91 has helped bring down the tax wedge to a level where the marginal excess burden is less troublesome.

8.3 TR91 AND THE MARGINAL EXCESS BURDEN

In Section 8.1 we analyzed how an income tax affects the choice between leisure and goods consumption, and we demonstrated how one can construct a graphical measure of the excess burden. In this section, we conduct a similar analysis in numerical terms. By assuming a specific utility function and choosing realistic values of the marginal tax wedge before and after TR91, we compute the size of the excess burden. The primary advantage of a partial equilibrium approach is that it is transparent. The simple nature of the model means that it is both easy to understand what drives the results and also to isolate the effects of alternative assumptions.[3] Readers who have another opinion as to what constitutes a reasonable calibration can easily carry out their own sensitivity analysis.

We focus our interest on the *marginal excess burden* of the income tax. How does the excess burden change if we increase the marginal tax rate? When we divide the marginal excess burden, *MEB*, by the extra tax revenue generated by the higher marginal tax rate, ΔT, we obtain the *marginal excess burden per revenue unit*, $MEB/\Delta T$. This measure is useful in two ways. First, it provides information which can be used for a cost–benefit analysis of public spending programmes. To ascertain whether a tax-financed expansion of public spending is desirable, it is not enough to compare the usefulness of the increased public spending with the direct cost for the taxpayers. If the spending increase is to be socially warranted, the benefits must be at least as large as the sum of direct tax revenue and *MEB*. Second, it can help us to analyze the structure of the tax system. When the *MEB*'s per revenue unit differ across tax instruments, there is an efficiency case for redistributing the tax burden.

How does the government use the increased tax revenue? Hansson and Stuart (1985) study the case when tax revenue is returned to the individual in the form of a lump-sum transfer, and the case when revenue is used to finance public consumption which does not directly affect labour supply. Henceforth, we will limit ourselves to the experiment where revenue is used to finance a lump-sum transfer. Since we thus eliminate the income effect from a tax hike, it is only the substitution effect which matters for the behavioural response. A higher marginal tax rate then has a clear-cut negative effect on labour supply.

In Chapter 5, we tried – based on recent econometric studies – to arrive at a reasonable interval for the compensated labour supply elasticity. By choosing different values for a parameter in the individual's utility function, we calibrate our model in such a way that it generates elasticities within this interval.[4] In our first specification, which is well in line with the basic cases in Hansson (1984) and Hansson and Stuart (1985), the compensated supply elasticity is 0.25. This elasticity, which represents our most optimistic scenario concerning supply responsiveness, might possibly have some relevance for certain special categories in the labour market (single women are a possible example). However, as a description of the behaviour of a typical Swede, it is probably too high. Our second case is a wage elasticity of 0.11, an elasticity which is rather typical for Swedish studies of the labour supply of married prime-age males. Our third alternative is a wage elasticity of 0.05, which is in line with the findings in Ackum Agell and Meghir (1995), who study a panel of blue-collar workers. Considered as a representative elasticity for the average wage earner, it is probably too low.

Another important parameter is the size of the marginal tax wedge. Labour income is taxed in many stages, and the income tax is only one component of the tax wedge. The difference between the marginal product of a worker and real take-home pay also depends on payroll taxes, indirect taxes and the extent of income-dependent social benefits. According to the calculations of Du Rietz (1994), which however ignore the role of income-dependent benefits, the marginal tax wedge for an individual with the income of an average blue-collar worker was 70.5 per cent in the late 1980s. For an average white-collar worker, it was slightly less than 80 per cent, and for a senior white-collar worker it was 85.5 per cent. TR91 reduced the marginal tax wedge for all categories. According to the 1991 tax rules, the tax wedge was 62 per cent for the blue-collar worker and 71.5 per cent for both categories of white-collar workers. An alternative calculation of the marginal tax wedge is provided in SOU (1992: 19). Unlike the estimates of Du Rietz, this calculation deals with the marginal tax wedge on average earned income, a tax wedge which includes income-dependent

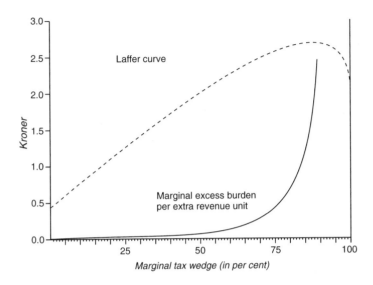

Figure 8.2 Marginal excess burden per extra revenue unit (left scale), and the Laffer curve

benefits. According to the Ministry of Finance, the marginal tax wedge was 73 per cent in 1988. After TR91 it decreased to 63 per cent.

In Figure 8.2 we plot *MEB* as a fraction of the additional tax revenue generated by a small increase in the tax wedge when the compensated wage elasticity is 0.11, that is, an elasticity which is fairly typical of many Swedish econometric studies. We also plot the Laffer curve, which shows the relation between the tax wedge and total tax revenue. Given our assumptions, the Laffer curve peaks at a tax wedge of 89 per cent; at higher tax rates, the tax base (the number of hours worked times a constant wage rate) is eroded to such an extent that revenue declines. Clearly, the tax wedges that were typical at the end of the 1980s, 70–85 per cent, were a little below the tax wedge which maximizes revenue.[5]

Regarding the marginal excess burden, we find a familiar pattern. For a broad interval of tax wedges, *MEB* is modest. When the tax wedge is 30 per cent, *MEB* is four per cent of the extra revenue. When we repeat the same experiment at a tax wedge of 40 per cent, the marginal efficiency cost increases to seven per cent of the extra revenue. At tax wedges above 65 per cent, the picture changes dramatically; *MEB* now grows very rapidly. With a tax wedge of 70 per cent, *MEB* is 31 per cent of extra revenue; with a tax wedge of 85 per cent, the price tag has risen to 169 per cent.

Two effects explain why the price tag on additional tax revenue starts to grow so rapidly. The first has to do with the numerator in *MEB*/ΔT. The change in *MEB* when the tax wedge increases depends on the induced decrease in (compensated) labour supply, and on how much the reduced labour supply costs in efficiency terms. When the difference between pre-tax productivity and after-tax wage is huge, lower labour supply implies a large social production loss, but a small private loss. The important observation is that this suggests that the social efficiency loss can be large even if labour supply is inelastic. If the tax wedge decreases by five percentage points from 75 to 70 per cent, the individual's net wage increases by 20 per cent. With a compensated wage elasticity of 0.11, labour supply increases by 2.2 per cent. But because of the high marginal tax wedge, the social efficiency gain is still considerable. In fact, the total excess burden decreases by 20.1 per cent; that is, a change which is more than nine times as large as the percentage change in labour supply! The second effect has to do with the denominator, or the change in tax revenue. When the tax wedge exceeds 70 per cent, the Laffer curve levels out. The additional tax revenue, ΔT, which is generated when the marginal tax wedge increases is less and less. We will, therefore, divide *MEB* by a smaller and smaller number. As we approach the peak of the Laffer curve, marginal excess burden as a share of extra tax revenue goes to infinity.

In Table 8.1 we present a sensitivity analysis of how the marginal excess burden per extra revenue unit depends on labour supply elasticities and marginal tax wedges. Like Browning (1987), we find that the results are exceptionally sensitive to our precise assumptions. If we confine attention to the result for the marginal tax wedge of the average Swede under the 1988 tax rules (row 5) the marginal welfare cost per revenue unit varies from 14.6 to 175 per cent. A tempting conclusion (which we, however, believe is an erroneous one) is that the results are so imprecise that we cannot draw any conclusions about the efficiency losses from the Swedish tax system.

The weakest link in our chain of circumstantial evidence is the one concerning the size of the compensated wage elasticity – a link which is no stronger than the econometric results in the field. If for a moment we regard our simulations as an attempt to measure the marginal excess burden for the typical Swedish wage earner, we believe that an elasticity of 0.11 is reasonable.[6] If we compare the marginal excess

Table 8.1 Marginal excess burden per unit of extra tax revenue (in per cent)

	Compensated labour supply elasticity		
	0.05	0.11	0.25
Marginal tax wedge (in per cent):			
62 (average blue-collar worker, 1991)	8.2	19.0	54.7
63 (average earned income, 1991)	8.6	20.1	59.0
70.5 (average blue-collar worker, 1988)	12.7	31.6	121.8
71.5 (average white-collar worker, 1991)	13.4	33.9	139.1
73 (average earned income, 1988)	14.6	37.8	175.0
79 (average white-collar worker, 1988)	22.0	65.3	2280.0
85.5 (average senior white-collar worker, 1988)	41.0	192.5	—
Tax rate which maximizes tax revenue	94.5	89.5	79.5

Source: See Appendix.

burden before and after TR91 (we compare the results for marginal tax wedges of 73 and 63 per cent) we see that it decreases from 37.8 to 20.1 per cent. The invisible price tag on an extra revenue unit has been reduced by 47 per cent.

An analysis, however, of the representative individual can easily lead in the wrong direction. In reality, both behavioural responses and tax wedges differ between different types of households. Since the relation between marginal excess burden and underlying parameters are highly non-linear, an analysis of the average individual will underestimate the efficiency loss.

Assume, for the sake of argument, that there are three groups of employees, which differ regarding the wage elasticity but not the tax wedge. For most of the individuals, 70 per cent, the elasticity is 0.11, for 20 per cent it is 0.05, and for 10 per cent it is 0.25. As a result, the average wage elasticity is again 0.11. But since $MEB/\Delta T$ is an increasing (and convex) function of the wage elasticity, the average efficiency loss will be larger than would have been the case if all individuals were alike. At a marginal tax wedge of 73 per cent, the average $MEB/\Delta T$ for our three groups of employees is 46.9 per cent. When the marginal tax wedge drops to 63 per cent, average $MEB/\Delta T$ decreases to 21.7 per cent. According to this estimate, which in a rudimentary way allows for worker heterogeneity, TR91 leads to a larger efficiency gain. The average $MEB/\Delta T$ decreases by 54 per cent, as opposed to 47 per cent when everyone was the same. If we had taken into account heterogeneity regarding wage elasticity *and* initial tax wedge, the efficiency gain would have been even greater.[7] Even if only a minority of employees is characterized by a large wage elasticity and a high marginal tax wedge, the size of the efficiency loss for this group may still matter a lot for the calculation of the average excess burden for the population.

Any computation of the efficiency cost of taxation is fraught with a number of problems, and our results should be interpreted cautiously. Nonetheless, we believe that they convey a plausible message about the effects of TR91 on the labour/leisure incentive margin. Although available empirical studies do not allow a more definite opinion about the size of compensated wage elasticities, the results in most studies are compatible with the idea that marginal tax wedges on a par with those which were typical before TR91 create considerable marginal excess burdens. A country that lets the total marginal tax wedge on earned income rise to 70–80 per cent will most likely not suffer an economic collapse. On the other hand, in our view, such a country exposes itself to unnecessary risks; the confidence intervals for the compensated wage elasticity reported in recent studies mean that we can by no means rule out the possibility that the efficiency price tag on the old tax system was considerable.

Seen from this perspective, the marginal tax wedges which resulted from TR91 seem less risky. For broad groups of full-time employees, marginal excess burdens have most likely decreased considerably. The mathematical logic of the marginal excess burden means that a reduction of the marginal tax wedge by a few percentage points can be very important – TR91 reduced the tax wedge by ten percentage points for an average employment income. At the same time, many households find themselves in a situation with very high marginal tax wedges after TR91 as well. The interaction of the tax system with income-dependent transfers (like housing allowances) and fees (like child-care fees) means that some households still are confronted with marginal tax wedges of far more than 80 per cent.[8] These blemishes illustrate that tax wedges cannot be discussed separate from distribution policy in general. There are no simple technical modifications which can remedy all incentive problems of taxes and benefits without renouncing political goals about an equitable income distribution.

8.4   TR91 AND CAPITAL ALLOCATION

Much of the Swedish tax debate in the 1980s centred on the possible discrimination of investments in the corporate sector relative to investments in the housing sector. In this section, we will try to clarify to what extent TR91 has helped level the playing field as far as tax incentives are concerned. In Chapters 3 and 4, we discussed how TR91 affected the cost of capital for investments in own homes and corporate assets. We will now put the pieces of the puzzle together.

To create a clear benchmark, we will assume (as we did in Chapter 4) that the real rate of interest is internationally determined and equal to four per cent. Regarding corporate investments, this real rate of interest corresponds to the rate of return required by investors *after* corporate taxes, but *before* personal taxes; that is, we treat capital costs in the corporate sector as independent of taxes on personal capital income. As we discussed in Chapter 4, this is consistent with the idea that investment incentives for tax purposes in a small open economy with perfect capital mobility depends only on the corporate income tax. We further assume that corporate investments are financed by loans, new issues and retained earnings to the extent which actually applied in the 1980s, and that they follow the actual distribution between machinery, buildings and inventories. Average capital costs under the old and the new tax rules have already been presented in Tables 4.1 and 4.2 in Chapter 4, and in Table 8.2 we reproduce these results.

Regarding capital costs in the housing sector, we base our discussion on the user cost calculations for owner-occupied housing which we presented in Chapter 3. But since we then defined user costs as including operating and maintenance expenses, this definition is not directly comparable to the measure of capital costs which we adopt for corporate investments. Therefore, the calculations which we present in Table 8.2 only include the costs for the homeowner in the form of interest on loans, foregone return on owner's equity, and taxes.[9] Since the homeowner combines the functions of financier and investor in the same person, the tax on personal capital income will matter for capital costs. We have set the share of loans in the housing sector at 35 per cent.

Table 8.2 Real cost of capital for new investments (in per cent)

	1985 tax rules				1991 tax rules			
Inflation (%)	0	4	8	10	0	4	8	10
Corporate investment	4.5	4.5	4.3	4.2	4.4	4.5	4.6	4.6
Housing investment	3.6	1.7	−0.6	−1.4	3.9	3.0	1.5	0.8

Source: See text.

Under the old tax system, and with the inflation rates which were typical of the 1980s (close to ten per cent), capital costs in the housing sector were actually negative. Since the real interest rate before tax is assumed constant, and since nominal interest income is taxed while nominal interest expenses are deductible, inflation forces down both the real after-tax interest rate on loans and the real after-tax rate of return on owner's equity. If we compare capital costs in the corporate sector and the housing sector, we see that housing investments were given an extremely generous tax treatment. With the new tax system, the distortions of investment incentives appear far more modest. Capital costs in the housing sector still decrease with inflation, but since the tax rate is lower now, the effect is softened. At low inflation rates, the difference in investment incentives across sectors is small.

On the whole, it is hard to avoid the conclusion that TR91 created conditions for a more efficient allocation of capital. However, these gains from levelling the playing field only materialize in the long run. In the short run, as discussed in Chapter 3, TR91 caused severe transitional problems. Many homeowners and renters who had adapted their portfolios and housing consumption to the old tax rules suffered considerable losses. Also, as discussed in Chapter 6, the transition to a more uniform capital income tax served to deepen the macroeconomic crisis of the early 1990s. These observations illustrate that tax reforms raise important issues of their own. The long-term gains from a more efficient tax system must be set against the risk that the reform itself will create injustices and macroeconomic imbalances.[10] A possible way to mitigate these conflicts over goals would be to have flexible transition rules, or to phase-in the new tax system under a succession of years. A government that wants to minimize the extent of arbitrary windfall gains and losses in asset markets, and to honour the principle of horizontal equity, should provide households with a sufficient amount of time to adjust. However, an obvious problem in this context – which may explain (but not excuse) why the architects of TR91 treated the transition problem with such ease – is that long phasing-in periods presuppose that the parliamentary process is characterized by an unusual amount of stability and long-term vision.

8.5   INTERNATIONAL ASPECTS

So far, our analysis has been guided primarily by the possibility of bringing forth quantitative evidence, and we have not gone beyond the narrow search-light provided by our formal models. But TR91 affected many incentive margins other than labour supply and intersectoral capital allocation. In this and the following sections, we will discuss some of these broader issues. The common denominator for our discussion is that we deal with issues of potentially great importance, but for which hard evidence is hard to come by.

How has TR91 affected efficiency in the allocation of resources between Sweden and the rest of the world? In a closed economy, an efficient allocation of capital assumes that pre-tax returns are the same in all production sectors. In an open economy, where capital can move freely across borders, investments should be allocated in such a way that pre-tax returns are the same as the real interest rate in the rest of the world. A country which taxes new investments drives a wedge between the international real interest rate and the return on new investments in the own country. Since this means that investments will flow out of the country, there will be an excess burden due to the fact that the domestic capital stock is too small. From an efficiency perspective, the tax rate on new investments in an open economy should be zero.[11]

What bearing does this discussion have on Swedish tax policy? As could be seen from our discussion in Chapter 4, it is important to distinguish between taxes which burden Swedish savers, and those which burden investments in Sweden. In Sweden, as in most other countries, personal income taxation is based on the *residence principle*. Taxes are paid on capital income in the country of residence of the taxpayer, regardless of whether income derives from domestic or foreign assets. Therefore, the personal capital income tax is a tax on the savings of domestic households. On the other hand, it does not matter for investment incentives in Swedish industry. The tax which primarily affects investments is the tax on corporate profits. The Swedish corporate income tax follows the *source principle*, which means that all profits which are generated in a country are subject to tax regardless of the nationality of the owner. As a result, the corporate income tax is – in theory – a harmful tax which drives a wedge between the international real interest rate and the marginal returns on investments in Sweden.

Swedish tax policy has for a long time centred on the idea that productive capital is an internationally mobile production factor, and that the corporate income tax must be internationally competitive. Indeed, as could be seen from our cost of capital calculations in Chapter 4, Sweden lies pretty close to the textbook ideal regarding the corporate income tax in an open economy. The effective corporate tax wedge on an average marginal investment is close to zero, both before and after TR91. Our assessment therefore is that TR91 did not alter the international competitiveness of the Swedish corporate income tax. The tax on new investments in the corporate sector was low by international standards before TR91 (see also OECD, 1991), and the same is true today.

When it comes to taxation of earned income, the picture is more complicated. Sweden's participation in the ongoing process of European integration – Sweden is a member of the European Union since 1995 – has helped increase the potential mobility of labour across borders. No longer are there any rules which prevent Swedes from entering the European labour market. For a country with a large public sector and high ambitions concerning income distribution, this raises a number of disturbing questions. In many respects, the 'Swedish model' has been based to a very large extent on the ability to tax and redistribute labour income. Even if the accuracy of distribution policy has sometimes been questioned, available studies indicate that taxes and benefits have helped to bring about a considerable equalization of incomes between individuals in different socioeconomic groups. The losers have been persons with a high education and a 'marked upper-class background'; see Björklund (1991, pp. 107–9).

The possibility of conducting an independent distribution policy depends crucially on whether the losers choose to migrate to countries with higher wages, or lower taxes, for the highly educated. Historically, cross-country differences in taxes and wages have hardly caused great waves of migration; cf. Lundborg (1992). According to the results from a major research project on Scandinavian migration patterns in the 1980s, the propensity to migrate seems to increase with the level of education.[12] Another result is that the migration pattern of people with higher education depends primarily on differences in pay levels, while the migration pattern of people with poor education depends primarily on unemployment levels. In absolute figures, however, migration flows seem to be quite modest.

However, it is not at all clear that these experiences can be extrapolated. Knowledge about the opportunities that result from a common European labour market ought to increase gradually. The internationalization of big companies and the growth of subsidiaries in other countries have expanded the scope for international labour mobility *within* firms. Another indication of potential future labour mobility is the rapidly increasing number of students enrolled in foreign exchange programmes. Nowadays, spending a semester at a foreign university is a normal part of the education of many Swedes. Although ties in the form of family, culture and language may remain more important than differences in taxes and wages for the vast majority of highly educated people, the fact remains that the threshold to migrate has become lower. While there is little reason to believe that there will be a very extensive migration of persons with higher education and other specialist competence, mobility will most likely increase.

How has TR91 affected migration incentives? In a closed economy, the *marginal tax rate* on earned income is of central importance for evaluating the incentive effects of the tax system. In an open economy with unrestricted labour mobility, however, the *average tax rate* is of interest as well. Somewhat loosely put, the marginal tax rate affects the incentive to choose working hours, while the average tax rate affects the incentive to migrate (or the decision to participate in the labour force).[13] If the average tax on a person's labour income is high, and if she does not feel that public sector benefits provide sufficient compensation, there is an incentive to migrate.

The average tax rate on labour income is high after TR91 as well.[14] The purpose of TR91 was to reduce marginal tax wedges, but to maintain the total tax burden. Another central starting-point was that the reform would not alter the distribution of income. Net taxes were not supposed to change in different income deciles. Our analysis in Chapter 7 indicates that TR91 probably achieved this goal, in the short term, when we group households according to disposable income. Net taxes for individuals in the highest deciles have not changed relative to other groups. Since there is an obvious connection between income and education, we interpret this as a rough indication that TR91 has not had a very strong direct effect on the incentive to migrate for individuals with a higher education.[15]

8.6 SIMPLICITY AND TAX AVOIDANCE

Other potential efficiency gains have to do with the transaction complexity of the old tax system. It was difficult to fill in tax returns, even for taxpayers with normal economic transactions. Moreover, as we discussed in Chapter 2, under the old tax system a number of financial and organizational transactions were carried out only because they were profitable for tax purposes. These transactions covered everything from outright tax fraud and quite legal tax planning within the family, to the investment choice of firms, the choice of organizational form for small businesses, and the type of compensation (fringe benefits versus ordinary salary) chosen by employees. The tax system also affected when transactions were carried out. Interest expenses were paid in advance, and realizations of capital gains took place at a point in time which minimized tax payments.

The common denominator for all these activities is that they did not have any real economic substance, apart from reducing tax payments. Nonetheless, they were associated with real resource costs, or excess burdens, for all parties involved. These burdens included not only direct costs of tax administration and auditing, but also taxpayer costs in the form of time and money spent on filling in tax forms and hiring tax advisors.

As could be seen in Chapter 2, we believe that TR91 has lessened these problems. The tax system became simpler, and the gain from investing in tax avoidance activities became less than before. Although it is difficult to translate these effects into quantitative terms, certain indications are given in Malmer and Persson (1994). They report survey evidence suggesting that the time households spend on filing returns decreased substantially in connection with TR91. Based on certain assumptions about the opportunity cost of household time use, Malmer and Persson found that the simplification of the tax code saved households the equivalent of 800 million kronor a year (which is a little more than 0.5 per cent of GDP). On the other hand, there were increased costs for employers, something which seems to depend solely on changes in tax rules implemented *after* TR91. Finally, Malmer and Persson conclude that TR91 had beneficial effects for the work done by the tax authorities.

8.7   IS THERE A GROWTH BONUS?

Against the backdrop of high unemployment and imbalances in public-sector finances, it is natural that the issue of economic growth has caught the political limelight. In this context, it is also natural that great expectations have been linked to TR91 as a dynamo for higher long-term growth. However, neither established theory nor available econometric evidence seem to provide the basis for a more definite answer to the question of how TR91 affects long-term growth.[16] One could even argue that the question is put incorrectly. The long-term growth rate is not necessarily a very reliable indicator of the effects of

TR91 on the excess burden of the tax system. It is quite possible, and in fact rather likely, that TR91 will enhance economic efficiency *without* the long-term growth rate being affected.

The basic neoclassical model of growth, which until the mid-1980s was the workhorse model when academic economists discussed growth, emphasizes the importance of savings and capital formation for the rate of growth in a short- or medium-term perspective.[17] In the long run, on the other hand, the growth rate is reduced to a constant, which depends on factors which are determined outside the model. In the short run, increased saving results in greater capital formation and higher growth, but since capital intensity also increases, the marginal return to capital tends to fall. But when this happens, growth is also checked, both because a given amount of savings now yields a lower return, and because a lower return in itself tends to decrease savings. As a result, savings can never function as a long-term growth engine in the neoclassical model. The stock of capital cannot grow faster in the long run than the *effective* supply of labour, a quantity which depends on two exogenous variables in the model, the size of population and the technical skills of the workforce.

This characteristic is of decisive importance for a discussion about economic policy. The model explains why different economic policies can change the *level* of the economy's long-term growth path; a good policy shifts the path upwards; a bad one shifts it downwards. On the other hand, the slope of the path, the growth rate, is not affected. Of course, this does not mean that tax wedges lack importance for economic efficiency. In the first place, transition effects matter. In the medium term, when the economy is on its way from one growth path to another, a tax reform which stimulates capital formation can lead to a temporary increase in the growth rate.[18] Second, level effects are also important. A country with an inefficient tax system grows as fast in the long run as a country with an efficient tax system, but the consumption level is permanently lower. We can interpret this level effect as a measure of the excess burden associated with an inefficient tax system. The tax system creates a welfare loss, which at least in principle can be measured along the lines discussed in previous sections.[19]

Most of the potential efficiency gains which we have identified in this chapter are most easily thought of as level effects. However, it is considerably more difficult to find arguments to support the claim that these gains somehow will lead to higher long-term growth. Let us study some examples.

A potential efficiency gain, which we have discussed in gruesome detail, is the decreased excess burden from lower tax wedges on labour income. The other side of the coin, as discussed in Chapter 5, is a modest increase in labour supply. As discussed above, a small supply response may come hand-in-hand with a several times larger decrease in excess burden. If we only wanted to study efficiency, we could have ended our discussion here. If we want to understand the effect on growth, we have to take the argument one step further. When labour supply increases, capital intensity tends to decrease, which tends to drive up the return on new investments. But when this happens, there is an incentive to increase savings and capital formation, which in the short run will lead to increased growth.[20] However, the growth effect will most likely be modest – remember that the primary growth impulse is a small increase in labour supply. After a period of perhaps ten years, the neoclassical brake, in the form of decreasing returns to new investments, has done its job. In the new steady state, growth is the same as it was initially, before the tax reform. But the consumption level is nevertheless higher than it would have been without the reform. The gain in the form of a lower excess burden has not disappeared along the way.

Another example concerns educational incentives. In Chapter 5, we found that TR91 has implied higher returns on investments in education. Based on the historical relation between educational returns and university enrolment, we arrived at the conclusion that TR91 may boost the share of persons with higher education. In the neoclassical growth model, we can interpret such a shift in the educational composition of the workforce as a one-time increase in labour supply in efficiency units; on average, workers produce more than before. Regarding growth, the argument is analogous to our previous example. When labour supply increases in efficient terms, the return on saving and investment also increases, which creates a temporary growth effect. In the long run, production is permanently higher, but growth is the same as it was initially.

In our examples so far, the transitory growth effect is explained by an *indirect* effect on capital formation caused by responsive labour supply. According to many observers, TR91 was expected to have a *direct* effect on capital formation also, through strengthened incentives for savings and investments. However, regarding the response of households, we concluded in Chapter 3 that TR91 primarily seems to have affected the composition of savings. Savings in non-financial outlets like own homes and consumer durables have decreased, and financial saving has increased. Regarding the response of firms, we concluded in Chapter 4 that TR91 did little to alter investment incentives for the average firm. Nonetheless, in this chapter we arrived at the conclusion that TR91 has created conditions for a more efficient allocation of capital across sectors. How does this argument hang together?

Since the capital stock in the corporate sector can be taken to be determined by an internationally given return requirement, the additional financial savings in the household sector will be channelled abroad. Household holdings of foreign assets increase, and foreign debts decrease. At the same time, the previously tax-favoured housing stock shrinks. But when investments in housing decrease, total domestic production tends to decrease as well – in the short run there is a tendency for *lower* economic growth. Despite this, social efficiency increases. Since subsidies and generous tax incentives used to imply that capital cost for new investments in the housing sector was far below the (international) real rate of interest, each krona's worth of investment which is moved from the housing sector to investments abroad means that national income increases. Production tends to decrease, at the same time as national income – which includes net interest income from abroad – increases.

Is there then no theory that is compatible with the intuitively reasonable idea that tax policy can affect long run growth? Yes, there is. In the last decade, research on *endogenous* growth has come to challenge the traditional neoclassical growth model.[21] As the name implies, this theory deals with a class of models which, as opposed to the neoclassical one, determines long-term growth within the model.

A central idea in the literature on endogenous growth is that production requires more than investments in physical capital combined with labour. Investments in knowledge and human capital, R&D and in public infrastructure are important as well. With this expanded concept of capital, it might seem reasonable to abandon the assumption of diminishing returns on savings and new investment, that is, to release the neoclassical brake on growth. Constant, or even increasing, returns to those production factors which can be reproduced by savings and investments is the fundamental, long-term growth mechanism in many endogenous growth models. The long-term rate of growth thus becomes endogenous, in the sense that it depends on investment decisions which are determined within the framework of the model.

An important implication is that economic policy can now play a role for long-term growth as well. A number of researchers have studied by what mechanisms trade policies, taxes and public consumption can lead to permanent growth effects. Just as in the neoclassical model, tax wedges lower economic efficiency. But we can also obtain permanent negative growth effects. Simulations of how taxes can hinder growth have produced mixed results, from relatively small effects (Lucas, 1990) to very large ones (Jones, Manuelli and Rossi, 1993). This wide scope of results is not especially surprising since different models emphasize alternative growth mechanisms, and thus different incentive margins where tax wedges come into play.[22]

Compared with the neoclassical growth model, endogenous growth in many ways provides a richer analysis of the growth process, and it has quickly reached the status of a theoretical construction with political appeal. The rich flora of alternative approaches means that most consumers of endogenous growth literature can find at least some model which agrees with their own particular vision of the world, and with their own opinion about how economic policy should be designed. At the same time, it is important to keep in mind that many of the central assumptions should be seen as preliminary hypotheses, often of unclear empirical relevance. Our view is that endogenous growth is a too disparate and empirically untested body of literature to serve as a solid basis for analyzing TR91.

In the popular debate it is often claimed, for example, that endogenous growth lends support to the idea that huge investments in higher education and 'competence development' can have a lasting growth effect. In a narrow sense this line of reasoning is unassailable – it certainly possible to find theoretical studies that emphasize the positive growth externalities from human capital formation. But it is also possible to find analyses where human capital and educational incentives are less important.

What type of institutions and economic policy create a favourable climate for growth? There is hardly any area where the discrepancy between beliefs and facts is so great. Whoever believes that TR91 is a cure-all for the Swedish growth problem will probably be disappointed. But our concluding point is that it should be possible to swallow this pill of disappointment. Even if TR91 only stimulates the annual growth rate by some figure in the first decimal for perhaps a decade, it can attain its goal of giving a substantial contribution to a better-functioning economy.

APPENDIX: A MODEL OF EXCESS BURDEN

We consider the atemporal leisure choice of an individual who has a utility function characterized by constant elasticity of substitution:

$$U(y, H) = \delta \frac{y^{1-\rho}}{1 - \rho} + (1 - \delta) \frac{(T - H)^{1-\rho}}{1 - \rho} \qquad (A8.1)$$

where y is disposable income (which is equal to consumption of market goods), T is the time endowment, H is labour supply, and δ and ρ are parameters which characterize the properties of the utility function $(\rho > 0, 0 < \delta < 1)$. The budget constraint is

$$y = (1 - t)wH + k \qquad (A8.2)$$

where w is the wage, t is a constant marginal tax rate, and k is a lump-sum transfer.

Maximizing (A8.1) subject to (A8.2) produces the first order condition

$$\delta[(1 - t)wH + k]^{-\rho} w(1 - t) = (1 - \delta)(T - H)^{-\rho} \qquad (A8.3)$$

which defines optimal labour supply, H^*.

In our simulations, we assume that tax revenue is returned as a lump-sum transfer, $k = twH$. Without loss of generality, we normalize the wage and set $w = 1$. The distribution parameter, δ, is set at 0.5. Finally, we assume that the time endowment is sixteen hours a day (we subtract eight hours sleep). As a result, we obtain

$$H^* = [1 + (1 - t)^{-\sigma}]^{-1} 16 \qquad (A8.4)$$

where $\sigma = 1/\rho$. Equation (A8.4) implies an eight-hour workday when $t = 0$.

Combining these equations, we can derive indirect utility, V, as a function of the marginal tax rate:

$$V = V(t) \qquad (A8.5)$$

It is easy to show that V decreases with t. We compute the excess burden of a given tax rate t by comparing indirect utility with and without taxes: At tax rate t, what addition, EB, to disposable income is required to make the worker just as well off as when $t = 0$? Relating *EB* to total revenue, tH^*, we obtain a measure of the average excess burden per revenue unit. Relating the change in *EB* to the change in tax revenue when t increases marginally provides a measure of the marginal excess burden per extra revenue unit.

Notes and References

1. INTRODUCTION

1. See Auerbach and Slemrod (1997) for an extensive discussion of the arguments put forth in the context of TR91.
2. See Sørensen (1994) for further discussion.
3. From the point of view of evaluation research, the timing of TRA86 was more fortunate. As discussed by Auerbach and Slemrod (1997), the US macroeconomy was well-behaved in the years surrounding TRA86.
4. For an overview of the Swedish macroeconomic experience, see Calmfors (1993).
5. However, compared with the international recession, and the non-accommodative exchange rate policy, TR91 was most likely a less decisive factor. A back-of-the-envelope calculation, presented in Chapter 6, suggests that TR91 may explain about one-fifth of the sharp decline in Swedish GDP between 1991 and 93.
6. For a discussion of consumption behavior in Sweden, see Berg (1994a).
7. A complication in assessing the effects of TR91 on intertemporal incentives stems from the fact that TR91 contained provisions with counteracting effects on the real after-tax interest rate. The lower statutory tax rate on capital income strengthened incentives, but some of the base-broadening ingredients, like the abolishment of the favorable treatment of long-term capital gains, worked in the opposite direction. On balance, however, it seems reasonable to conclude that TR91 implied lower effective marginal tax rates for a majority of households. This can be contrasted to the case of TRA86, where the conclusion seems to be that the impact on savings incentives was of an ambiguous sign; see Auerbach and Slemrod (1997).
8. A more likely factor in a drop in permanent labour income is the sharp increase in unemployment after 1991. While higher unemployment may induce consumers to revise their expectations of future labour income, it may also boost precautionary savings. When consumers are prudent, more uncertain earnings prospects can have strong negative effects on current consumption; see e.g. Caballero (1991). Although we believe that part of the increase in unemployment can be explained by the short-term contractionary impact of TR91, the major impulses should – as already discussed – be sought elsewhere.
9. According to the National Accounts of Statistics Sweden, household net lending is defined as the sum of borrowing and lending in the credit market, net purchases of corporate shares, individual insurance savings, and savings in other interest bearing assets.
10. The latter advantage, however, was offset by special interest subsidies at high rates to housing constructed after 1975.

217

11. Though data is still scant, preliminary observations seem to confirm this assumption.
12. Measuring pre-tax income by the sum of taxable labour income and an imputed measure of capital income (net wealth times a 3 per cent real interest rate) and using the square-root equivalence scale to adjust for differences in household composition, the Gini coefficient based on yearly pre-tax income was around 0.25 during the 1980s, a quite low number by international standards. After taxes and housing and child allowances, the coefficient was around 0.20, i.e. a sizeable redistribution.
13. It should also be pointed out that the calculations reported above are confined to personal income taxes and disregard the incidence of the corporate income tax. However, as is seen from Table 1.1, corporate tax revenues did not change much as a result of TR91, and assumptions about corporate tax incidence should not be crucial.
14. The drastic increase in household financial savings in the early 1990s was accompanied by a rapid improvement of the current account.

2 TAX PLANNING

1. See, for example, Lindencrona (1993) and Mutén (1995).
2. Tax-favoured forms of saving were kept to a certain extent even after TR91; see further below.
3. See, for example, Lindencrona (1993) for a more detailed acount of this phenomenon.
4. Bill 1993/94: 50, Appendix 3, p. 427.
5. See Mutén (1995) for a detailed analysis of international tax planning, especially in relation to the 1991 tax reform.
6. See Mutén (1994).

3 SAVINGS AND CONSUMPTION

1. While we believe that there is some truth in this, we should note that some forces, not accounted for in Table 3.1, operated in the opposite direction. First, as Sweden removed most of its foreign exchange controls during the 1980s, many firms were no longer confined to raise capital domestically. Second, much of the financial resources that went to the corporate sector were channelled through various financial intermediaries (such as tax-exempt institutions, and insurance companies), which were subject to preferential tax treatment; see Södersten (1993) for further discussion. Third, to the extent that a preferential tax treatment of housing gets capitalized in house prices and aggregate net wealth, the conventional assumption that asset demands are homogeneous of degree one in net wealth implies the existence of positive spillover effects in the markets for corporate assets; see Agell (1989).

2. The idea that a large and rapidly increasing government deficit may induce consumers to reduce spending is developed in some detail by Giavazzi and Pagano (1990, 1996). They also make the related point that a severe fiscal contraction may actually boost consumer confidence and private spending.

3. In a recent paper, Attanasio and Weber (1994) present evidence which suggests that the UK consumer boom in the late 1980s may have about as much to do with permanent income dynamics as with financial liberalization. For a related analysis of the Swedish consumption boom, see Agell and Berg (1996).

4. See e.g. Hall (1988). For Swedish evidence on the intertemporal elasticity of substitution, see Campbell and Mankiw (1991), and Agell, Berg and Edin (1995).

5. A complication in assessing the effects of TR91 on intertemporal incentives stems from the fact that TR91 contained provisions with counteracting effects on the real after-tax interest rate. The lower statutory tax rate on capital income strengthened incentives, but some of the base broadening ingredients, like the abolishment of the favourable treatment of long-term capital gains, worked in the opposite direction. On balance, however, it seems reasonable to conclude that TR91 strengthened savings incentives for a majority of households. This can be contrasted to the case of TRA86, where the conclusion seems to be that the impact on savings incentives was of an ambiguous sign; see Auerbach and Slemrod (1996).

6. A more likely factor in rationalizing a drop in permanent labour income is – as already discussed – the sharp increase in unemployment after 1991. While higher unemployment may induce consumers to revise their expectations of future labour income, it may also boost precautionary savings. When consumers are prudent, more uncertain earnings prospects can have strong negative effects on current consumption; for example, see Caballero (1991).

7. Several foreign studies have found a negative relation between consumption and unemployment; cf. Lattimore (1994) and Muellbauer (1994).

8. For related findings for other countries, see King and Leape (1984) and Hubbard (1985).

9. These theoretical price effects probably overestimate the actual outcome, since they presume that consumers do not decrease demand for the product in question. If this happens, part of the tax hike is shifted on to producers.

10. In this section, we will focus on the response of the market for owner-occupied housing. This demarcation does not mean that the rental market in Sweden is less important. In 1990, 40 per cent of households lived in small houses, 15 per cent in cooperative housing and 45 per cent in rental flats. Instead, our demarcation reflects the fact that our knowledge of the workings of the regulated rental market is very incomplete.

11. For a discussion of tax expenditures in Sweden, see Mattsson (1992).

12. In equation (3.2), we have not taken into account the effects of government interest subsidies (which were of less importance for marginal

investments). Moreover, we ignore the wealth tax (which in practice only applied to a limited number of owner-occupiers), and the taxation of capital gains on single-family homes (if we transform the capital gains tax to an equivalent tax on accrued capital gains, the equivalent tax rate is close to zero for reasonable assumptions about the discount rate and holding time).

13. In 1990, 40 per cent of households were homeowners. If this share decreases to 36 per cent, and the households which move over to the rental market own single-family houses of average size, the total demand for single-family homes would decrease by 10 per cent.

4 THE CORPORATE RESPONSE

1. Economic depreciation is calculated on the written-down price-adjusted replacement cost of real capital, taking into account an estimated economic life.
2. Denmark and the Anglo-Saxon countries do not have this connection.
3. Forsling (1995) measures utilization rate as a share of the maximum available tax allowances actually used by companies. The share of tax-paying companies for the ten-year period of 1979–88 has been calculated by letting each company and year be an observation.
4. Assuming that the inventory volume does not decrease.
5. Corresponding calculations may be made for the taxes which are paid by the company's owners and lenders. See the Swedish country chapter in King and Fullerton (1984) for examples of such calculations.
6. The effective marginal tax rate is the tax wedge divided by the pre-tax rate of return on investment. See further King and Fullerton (1984), for a thorough analysis of the incentive effects of capital taxation based on calculations of the effective marginal tax rate.
7. In Table 3.2 in Chapter 3, the starting-point for corresponding calculations is instead that the household shall receive a real return of 2 per cent after *all* taxes.
8. The weights in Tables 4.1 and 4.2 reflect conditions within manufacturing in 1988. An average new investment is made up of 28 per cent inventories, 37 per cent machinery and 35 per cent buildings. The financing weights are 59 per cent for retained earnings, 5 per cent for new equity and 37 per cent for debt.
9. See the report of the Commission, SOU 1993:29.
10. See Apel and Södersten (1995) for a more detailed discussion.
11. See for example King (1975).
12. This conclusion is qualified below. The cost of new share issues can be affected by taxation when there is a tax on dividends as well.
13. The equivalence between a tax on dividends and a tax on expenditure can be demonstrated in the following manner: Let D = dividend, BV = operating surplus, iB = interest expenses (financial net expenses), ΔB = new borrowing, I = investments, S = payment of taxes. The budget constraint of the company gives $D = BV - iB + \Delta B - I - S$. In the

case of a tax on dividends with a tax rate of T, $S = TD/(1 - T)$. This gives $S = T(BV - iB + \Delta B - I)$. Thus, the tax basis in the case of a tax on dividends corresponds to the tax basis in the case of (a variant of) an expenditure tax.

14. The dividend constraint which we have given as an explanation as to why companies have refrained from taking advantage of the existing consolidation possibilities does not limit use of the Annell deduction, since this deduction is made directly on the company's tax return and is thus not limited by a requirement to report after-tax book profits.

15. See, for example, Bradley, Jarrell and Kim (1984) for a thorough discussion with further references.

16. See MacKie-Mason (1990).

17. By using accelerated depreciation and contributions to inventory reserves and investment funds, the company defers corporate tax payments, that is, it acquires tax debt. See Kanniainen and Södersten (1994) for further explanation.

18. See Taylor (1982).

19. See Södersten (1989) for an in-depth study of the incentive effects of the investments funds system. A less technical analysis can be found in Bergström and Södersten (1984). See also Auerbach, Hassett and Södersten (1995).

20. As was the case in Tables 4.1 and 4.2, the calculations have been made using conventional methods for capital cost analysis, which are based on present-value calculations of profits and tax payments from hypothetical investment objects. In Figure 4.6, a risk premium has been added, assuming that the cost of equity funds corresponds to 1.5 times the interest rate on bonds. See Bergström and Södersten (1984) for a detailed account.

21. See Eliasson (1965) and Rudberg and Öhman (1971).

22. See Praski (1978), Kanis (1979) and Bergström (1982).

23. The study is based on two-digit data from the National Accounts. After aggregating, three main industries are studied: mining, manufacturing and construction.

24. The authors distinguish between short-term and long-term incentive effects. The short-term effects include company expectations about future changes in the tax system. The long-term effects assume that the existing tax rules remain in the future.

25. Our estimations in Table 4.2 show a certain amount of subsidization of investments in machinery under the new tax system. Auerbach *et al.* (1995), however, ignore the Annell deduction.

5 THE SUPPLY OF LABOUR

1. The HINK survey is conducted yearly by Statistics Sweden based on tax returns and survey information from around 10,000 households.

2. However, see Stafford and Sundström (1992) for an analysis of how parents' allowances have affected labour supply and the number of births of women.

3. If this is a proper characterization depends, above all, on what demands are made, in practice, on participating in the workforce; see Gustafsson, Hydén and Salonen (1994) for a study of how social welfare benefits are actually implemented.

4. HUS is a data base with comprehensive information about a panel of Swedish households from 1984 and onwards; see Klevmarken and Olovsson (1993) for a description.

5. Aronsson and Walker (1995) present changes in budget restrictions between 1981 and 1991 for a number of different types of household.

6. See Klevmarken *et al.* (1995) for corresponding figures for other categories of households where allowances are taken into account.

7. The curves give the difference between income levels at the same number of working hours $I_{92}(L) - I_{85}(L)$ where I signifies income and L working hours. The slope is $[I_{92}(L+1) - I_{85}(L+1)]$ $-[I_{92}(L) - I_{85}(L)] = [I_{92}(L+1) - I_{92}(L)] - [I_{85}(L+1) - I_{85}(L)]$, which is the very difference in marginal effect between two points in time. This similarity obviously applies only on the condition that it is the same household at different numbers of working hours.

8. The increased differences in *employment income* after tax can be compatible with an unaffected income distribution after tax, since the effective taxation of the *capital income* of high-income earners also increased as a part of TR91; see further the distribution analysis in Chapter 7.

9. It appears less unlikely that a tax reform could be self-financing if it only lowers the marginal tax rate at higher incomes; see the simulations in Blomquist (1989).

10. An alternative to tax increases is, of course, to reduce public expenditures. This would normally give rise to income effects. In this case, however, we are not talking about a pure tax reform, but a structural reform with a reduced public sector.

11. Methods which are based on maximization of a likelihood function and a complete modelling of the budget restriction, represented, for example, by Blomquist (1983), have generally obtained small positive compensated wage elasticities. Studies which are based on instrumental variable methods, for example Flood and MaCurdy (1993), have reported negative elasticities in some cases. The same applies to the preliminary studies by Flood (1995) and Hansen (1995) for HINK data from 1984 to 1992 which indicate such results for large groups of households. However, such results raise the question of how negative compensated elasticities should be interpreted.

12. By wage or income elasticity is meant the percentage change in labour supply per percentage change in wage and income. These concepts are well defined when wages after tax are independent of the number of hours worked, that is, at linear budget restrictions, but not otherwise. The figures which are presented in the text are elasticities regarding wages after tax and so called linearized income assessed at the mean value in the respective data base.

13. An estimation in Flood and MaCurdy (1993) which produces a negative compensated wage elasticity is not included here.

14. The large differences depend in part on the elasticities being evaluated at different numbers of working hours. The elasticities in the lower part of the interval are calculated at typical working hours for women.
15. See also Aaberge *et al.* (1989).
16. The *Level of Living Survey* (*LNU*) is based on data on approximately 6000 individuals interviewed in 1968, 1974, 1981 and 1991. See Eriksson and Åberg (1987) for a more detailed description.
17. Aaberge *et al.* (1989) also take rationing into account in the sense that they assume that the supply of work opportunities is concentrated to full-and part-time work. However, they analyse HINK data where information about what individuals are rationed is lacking.
18. They also estimate two models which follow directly from the life-cycle model with perfect capital markets, which implies that the rate of wage increase minus the interest rate is the central explanatory variable. Both these models produce low and statistically insignificant elasticities, of 0.02 and 0.05 respectively. See Ackum Agell and Meghir (1995), Table 2.
19. Another dynamic effect is the pension decision. This has been studied jointly with labour supply in different ages within the framework of a life-cycle model by Hansson Brusewitz (1992). His main result is that the choice of age for full or partial pension seems to be insensitive to wages after tax. Labour supply elasticities for men in occupationally active ages are on a level with those found in other studies (around 0.1) whereas he finds a somewhat greater elasticity (around 0.32) for men above retirement age.
20. Expressed technically, it is assumed that the behaviour of households can be represented by the maximization of a constant-elasticity-of-substitution utility function. Based on assumptions about values of substitution elasticities between the leisure of men and women and commodity consumption, it is possible to uniquely determine the other parameters in the utility function so that the observed choices of households of working hours in the base year of 1985 can be replicated exactly.
21. The corresponding result for the underfinanced reform is that labour supply is ca. three per cent lower. This relatively big difference is an indication that the model assumes income elasticities that (in absolute numbers) lie a bit above those which have been reported in most of the econometric studies.
22. See Sørensen (1993) for an analysis and discussion of taxes and household work.
23. This conclusion is analogous to a cash-flow based corporate tax, regardless of its level, not affecting the profitability of an investment.
24. Corresponding elasticities for the share of registered students (not just first-year students) is lower, 1.8 and −0.8 respectively.
25. These data refer to contracted working hours. On the other hand, the actual number of hours worked per employee – calculated as the number of hours worked according to the National Accounts divided by the number of people employed according to AKU – increased by ca. five per cent between 1990 and 1994. Decreased absence due to illness is one explanation for this. Several studies, for example Johansson and Palme

(1996) and Brose (1995), indicate that absence due to illness is sensitive to economic incentives.

26. These statements are based on an estimated equation for the 1964–90 period. Hours are the average number of weekly working hours for men between the ages of 25 and 54 (from Figure 5.8b). The tax wedges are taken from Figure 5.2. Unemployment is the average open unemployment in the entire economy during the year (in per cent). The equation is specified in differences, that is Δ refers to change in relation to the preceding year. The result with standard error in parenthesis is:

$$\Delta \text{ Hours} = - \underset{(0.074)}{0.122} - \underset{(2.30)}{4.81} \cdot \Delta\text{tax wedge} - \underset{(17.67)}{46.44} \cdot \Delta\text{unemployment};$$
$$\bar{R}^2 = 0.27, DW = 1.69$$

When the equation is estimated on data for the entire 1964–93 period, the coefficient for the tax wedge is by and large unchanged, while the coefficient for unemployment is halved.

27. Burtless' result is based on after-tax wages instead of the tax wedge. If public expenditures neutralize the income effects of taxation, the specification we use here captures the substitution effect as opposed to Burtless' specification, which also includes income effects from the general wage trend.

6 STABILIZATION AND TAX REVENUE

1. This figure includes a rough estimate of the total marginal tax wedge (including income taxes, indirect taxes and certain income-dependent allowances) which was levied on labour income at the end of the 1980s. For a similar estimate, cf. SOU 1992: 19. (1992, p. 329).
2. Whoever wishes, may assume that X, t, and θ are vectors.
3. The business cycle parameter θ should now be understood as an indicator of that part of the cycle which does *not* depend on the tax system.
4. Since we measure tax revenue per budget year (and not per calendar year), we have used quarterly data to calculate the change in nominal GDP.
5. This is also borne out in the study of Ohlsson and Vredin (1994), which relies on a time-series analysis quite similar to our own.
6. In order to arrive at a figure for the total revenue loss, we must, just as before, make an addition for the contractionary macroeconomic impact of TR91.

7 INCOME DISTRIBUTION

1. This description, of course, is not without its exceptions. An obvious exception is inheritance taxation. Children's allowances are another. A third could perhaps be said to be the taxation of investments in educa-

tion. Thus, the dividing line between the two interpretations, in practice, is not a strict one.

2. In one case, it appears that equivalence scales should be used, namely, if one is interested in the income distribution between children in society. See Björklund and Freeman (1995), Table 3.

3. See section 7.2 for a presentation of the Gini coefficient as a measurement of differences in income distribution.

4. Here, the household is regarded as a unit of income. When the individual is used as the income unit it appears that the tax system does not redistribute full income. See also Björklund *et al.* (1995), section 6 for a discussion of possible explanations as to why their results differ from those of Hansson and Norrman (1986).

5. Björklund *et al.* (1995) deal with this problem by using a predicted wage and by correcting for sample selection.

6. Since the tax reform aims at increasing the supply of labour, and the incentive to work more has increased more for high-income earners, it can be misleading to look at the distribution of ordinary incomes without taking into account the value of leisure. According to Aronsson and Palme (1994), the tax reform would uniformly increase the spread of annual wage income since high-income earners who received the biggest marginal tax rate reductions increase their working hours the most, while the spread of a utility index that also takes into account the value of leisure remains largely unaffected after the reform.

7. Estimations of wage equations made from the 1992 HINK data by Bertil Holmlund confirm these differences. The estimated equations indicate that a salaried employee has a 54 per cent higher salary after 30 years of work compared with his original starting salary. The corresponding figure for a blue-collar worker is 22 per cent.

8. The Gini coefficient for total discounted income for the entire period is 0.272 before and 0.240 after tax. The average value of the Gini coefficients for annual incomes is 0.306 and 0.277 respectively.

9. See, for example, Auerbach and Kotlikoff (1987).

10. In keeping with this view, no attempt has been made to include the consumption value of homeownership under income.

11. A corresponding pattern is found in the National Accounts. GNP decreased by 3.4 per cent from 1990 to 1992. At the same time household disposable income increased by 7.2 per cent.

12. The figures in this section are based on compilations of the HINK statistics which were presented in more detail in SOU 1995: 104, appendix 4.

13. We often choose to look at deciles 2 and 9 rather than 1 and 10 since the extreme deciles consist largely of households whose income conditions are not representative for their normal incomes. Among other things, the lowest decile contains a large share of entrepreneurs with low incomes or losses in their business activities.

14. Note that the data presented in section 7.2 apply to ages 18–64.

15. The deviation from trend in 1986 is probably in part an expression of random error. The temporary increase in income distribution for this

year can be attributed mainly to the entry, 'income from interest and dividends'.

16.   Holmlund and Kolm (1995) analyze the connection between the progression of taxes and the spread of wages before tax within the framework of a bargaining model, but find nothing to support the claim that decreased progression leads to a more uneven distribution of wages.

17.   Corresponding calculations for single households show an analogous pattern. The overall equalization effect has decreased among single people with one child, but has increased among single people with several children; see Björklund *et al.* (1995), Table B4. These groups, however, are so small that calculations are fraught with especially great statistical uncertainty.

18.   Return should be understood here in a broad sense, where for example, the rate of return from a bank account not only consists of interest, which is quite low, but also of the value of various transaction services.

19.   See Lundborg and Skedinger (1995) for an analysis of the importance of the tax on capital gains for turnover on the market for owner-occupied homes.

20.   Note that Table 7.4 comes from Björklund *et al.* (1995) and is thus based on a more narrowly demarcated selection from the HINK survey than Table 7.3.

8   EFFICIENCY

1.   The reason that a uniform capital income tax creates no excess burden in our example is the assumption that the total pool of investment resources is unaffected by the tax. If we had taken into account effects via new savings, the result would have been different. Since all taxes on capital drive a wedge between the rate of return of the saver and the rate of return on investments, we will normally get an *intertemporal* excess burden.

2.   It should immediately be said that the weakness of economists for lump-sum taxes is mainly due to pedagogical and analytical-technical reasons. Despite their good efficiency characteristics, they are hardly a realistic alternative for actual tax policy. Since a lump-sum tax does not take into account either the taxpayers' ability to pay, or utility from tax-financed public spending, it is contrary to established principles for fair taxation.

3.   As is discussed by Browning (1987), it is not obvious that a general equilibrium analysis would have much to add. Browning's analysis indicates that most of the different conclusions from different studies of the excess burden of the US income tax can be attributed to different assumptions about the size of a few parameters – the choice between partial and general equilibrium is less important.

4.   The utility function is of the CES type, and for each value of the substitution parameter we can calculate a corresponding compensated supply elasticity. All values of the elasticity that are given in the text have

been evaluated at a marginal tax wedge of 70 per cent. See the appendix for a description of the model.

5. We can note here, however, that the tax wedges calculated by Du Rietz for senior white-collar workers at the end of the 1970s (90.5 per cent in 1979) are above the revenue-maximizing level.

6. In the Swedish debate on tax policy, reference is often made to the estimates of Hansson (1984) and Hansson and Stuart (1985) as supporting the idea that the marginal excess burden per extra revenue unit was at least 100 per cent under the old tax system. The result in our third column is based on the same labour supply elasticity, 0.25, as Hansson and Stuart used (on the basis of a very thorough survey of the then available labour supply literature) in their base case. Despite the fact that there is a great difference in the choice of analytic method (partial versus general equilibrium), it is noteworthy that our results in the third column are well in line with those presented by Hansson and Stuart (line 1, Table 3, p. 346). In their reference case, the Laffer curve peaks at a tax wedge of 80 per cent. The corresponding tax wedge in our case is 79.5 per cent. At tax wedges of 60 and 70 per cent respectively, they report marginal excess burdens per extra revenue unit of 53 and 129 per cent respectively, which can be compared with 47 and 115 per cent in our partial equilibrium model.

7. A proper analysis of heterogeneity among households requires that we use a microsimulation approach. Such an analysis is presented in Aronsson and Palme (1994). They do not present an analysis of the marginal excess burden, but choose instead to study the effect of TR91 on the *total* excess burden. Their result implies that excess burden decreased by at least 25 per cent because of TR91.

8. See Andersson and Gustafsson (1992).

9. A detailed description of the calculations can be found in a separate appendix that can be obtained from the authors upon request.

10. The crucial distinction between the process of tax reform and *de novo* tax design is discussed in Feldstein (1976).

11. This standard optimal taxation result does not hold generally. In the case of monopoly rents tied to domestic capital, there is a case for taxing corporate profits.

12. See Pedersen and Schröder (1996).

13. For a discussion of taxation and labour mobility in the open economy, see Christiansen, Hagen and Sandmo (1994).

14. Here, some clarification is appropriate. TR91 meant that lower taxes on labour income would be financed by higher taxes on consumption and personal capital income. Since taxes on consumption and personal capital income can be avoided by migration, it is the sum of taxes on earned income, personal capital income and consumption that is important for the incentive to migrate.

15. If we also take into account indirect behavioural adjustments as a result of the reform, the picture is rather that the incentive to migrate has decreased. Our analysis of marginal excess burdens in Section 8.3 indicated that efficiency costs have decreased for many individuals with high

labour incomes, which affects migration incentives in an advantageous manner for Sweden.

16. For overviews of the evidence on the link between the public sector and economic growth, see Atkinson (1995), Slemrod (1995) and Agell, Lindh and Ohlsson (1997).

17. If not otherwise stated, we assume in the following that we study a closed economy.

18. However, simulations of the neoclassical growth model indicate that the period of transitional growth is fairly brief, perhaps a decade; see King and Rebelo (1993). The analysis of King and Rebelo is based on a version of the neoclassical growth model that incorporates optimizing savings behaviour. Simulations of an older version of the model, which somewhat unrealistically assumes that the household savings ratio is an exogenous constant, imply that it takes much longer before the growth effects subside; see Sato (1963).

19. For an interesting analysis of how the US tax system affects efficiency in a neoclassical growth model, see Jorgenson and Yun (1990).

20. In a small open economy, the adjustment of the capital stock would take the form of an inflow of foreign investment. For some experiments with an intertemporal simulation model of the Swedish economy, see Söderlind (1989).

21. For two pioneering articles, see Romer (1986) and Lucas (1988). For a recent exposition, see Barro and Sala-i-Martin (1995).

22. See also Stokey and Rebelo (1995) and Nordblom (1996).

Bibliography

Aaberge, R., S. Ström and T. Wennemo (1989) 'Skatt, arbeidstilbud og inntekts-fordelning i Sverige' ('Taxes, labour supply and income distribution in Sweden') in SOU 1989:33.

Ackum Agell, S. and C. Meghir (1995) 'Male labour supply in Sweden: Are incentives important?', *Swedish Economic Policy Review*, vol. 2, 391–418.

Ackum Agell, S. and M. Apel (1993) 'Female labor supply and taxes in Sweden – A comparison of estimation approaches', in *Essays on Work and Pay*, Ackum Agell, S., Economic Studies 15, Department of Economics, Uppsala University.

Agell, J. (1989) 'Inflation, taxes and asset prices. A note on wealth effects and asset complementarity', *Journal of Public Economics*, vol. 40, 151–7.

Agell, J. and L. Berg (1996) 'Does financial deregulation cause a consumption boom?', *Scandinavian Journal of Economics*, vol. 98, 579–601.

Agell, J., L. Berg and P.-A. Edin (1995) 'The Swedish boom to bust cycle: Tax reform, consumption and asset structure', *Swedish Economic Policy Review*, vol. 2, 271–314.

Agell, J. and P.-A. Edin (1989) 'Tax reform and individual investor response: Evidence from Swedish tax return data', *Public Finance*, vol. 44, 183–203.

Agell, J. and P.-A. Edin (1990) 'Marginal taxes and the asset portfolios of Swedish households', *Scandinavian Journal of Economics*, vol. 92, 47–64.

Agell, J., P. Englund and J. Södersten (1995) *Svensk skattepolitik i teori och praktik. 1991 års skattereform* (*Swedish tax policy in theory and practice. The 1991 tax reform*) (Fritzes: Stockholm).

Agell, J., P. Englund, and J. Södersten (1996) 'Tax reform of the century – the Swedish experiment', *National Tax Journal*, vol. 49, 643–64.

Agell, J., T. Lindh and H. Ohlsson (1997) 'Growth and the public sector: A critical review essay', *European Journal of Political Economy*, vol. 13, 33–52.

Andersson, I. and B. Gustafsson (1992) *Fattigdomsfällor (Poverty traps)*, Ds 1992:25 (Stockholm: Fritzes).

Angelin, K. and L.P. Jennergren (1995) 'Partner leasing in Sweden', Tax Reform Evaluation Report No. 4 (Stockholm: National Institute of Economic Research).

Apel, M. and J. Södersten (1995) 'Personal taxation and investment incentives in a small open economy', Working Paper 1995:21, Department of Economics, Uppsala University.

Aronsson, T. (1991) 'Nonlinear taxes and minimum hours constraints in a model of women's labor supply', Umeå Economic Studies, No. 256.

Aronsson, T. and M. Palme (1994) 'A decade of tax and benefit reforms in Sweden – effects on labour supply, welfare and inequality', Tax Reform Evaluation Report No. 3 (Stockholm: National Institute of Economic Research).

Aronsson, T. and J.R. Walker (1995) 'The effects of Sweden's welfare state on labor supply incentives', SNS Occasional Paper No. 64, Stockholm.

229

Åsberg and Åsbrink (1994) 'Capitalisation effects in the market for owner-occupied housing: A dynamic approach', Tax Reform Evaluation Report No. 2, (Stockholm: National Institute of Economic Research).

Atkinson, A. (1995) 'The welfare state and economic performance', *National Tax Journal*, vol. 48, 171–98.

Attanasio, O.P. and G. Weber (1994) 'The UK consumption boom of the late 1980s: Aggregate implications of microeconomic evidence', *Economic Journal*, vol. 104, 1269–302.

Auerbach, A.J. (1979) 'Wealth maximization and the cost of capital', *Quarterly Journal of Economics*, vol. 93, 433–46.

Auerbach, A.J. and K. Hassett (1992) 'Tax policy and business fixed investment in the United States', *Journal of Public Economics*, vol. 47, 141–70.

Auerbach, A.J., K. Hassett and J. Södersten (1995) 'Taxation and corporate investment: The impact of the 1991 Swedish Tax Reform', *Swedish Economic Policy Review*, vol. 2, 361–83.

Auerbach, A.J. and L.J. Kotlikoff (1987) *Dynamic fiscal policy* (Cambridge: Cambridge University Press).

Auerbach, A.J. and J. Slemrod (1997) 'The economic effects of the tax reform act of 1986', *Journal of Economic Literature*, vol. 35, 589–632.

Barot, B. (1995) 'The role of wealth in the aggregate consumption function using an error correction approach: Swedish evidence from the years 1970–1993', licentiat dissertation, Department of Economics, Uppsala University.

Barro, R. and X. Sala-i-Martin (1995) *Economic growth* (New York: McGraw-Hill).

Berg, L. (1988) *Hushållens sparande och konsumtion (Household savings and consumption)* (Stockholm: Allmänna förlaget).

Berg, L. (1994a) 'Household savings and debts: The experience of the Nordic countries', *Oxford Review of Economic Policy*, vol. 10, 42–53.

Berg, L. (1994b) 'Kapitalvinster, hushållens konsumtion och sparande' ('Capital gains, household consumption, and savings'), *Ekonomisk Debatt*, vol. 22, 427–32.

Berg, L. and R. Bergström (1995) 'Housing and financial wealth, financial deregulation, and consumption – the Swedish case', *Scandinavian Journal of Economics*, vol. 97, 421–39.

Bergström, V. (1982) *Studies in Swedish post-war industrial investments* (Almqvist & Wiksell: Uppsala).

Bergström, V. and J. Södersten (1984) 'Do tax allowances stimulate investment?', *Scandinavian Journal of Economics*, vol. 86, 244–68.

Björklund, A. (1991) 'Inkomstfördelningens utveckling' ('The development of the distribution of income'), in *Ekonomi och samhälle 1 – skatter och offentlig sektor (Economy and society 1 – taxes and the public sector)* (Stockholm: SNS Förlag).

Björklund, A. and R. Freeman (1995) 'Generating equality and eliminating poverty – the Swedish way', SNS Occasional Paper No. 60, Stockholm.

Björklund, A., M. Palme, and I. Svensson (1995) 'Tax reforms and income distribution: An assessment using different income concepts', *Swedish Economic Policy Review*, vol. 2, 229–66.

Blomquist, N.S. (1981) 'A comparison of distributions of annual and lifetime income: Sweden around 1970', *Review of Income and Wealth*, vol. 2, 243–64.

Blomquist, N.S. (1983) 'The effect of income taxation on the labor supply of married men in Sweden', *Journal of Public Economics*, vol. 22, 169–97.

Blomquist, N.S. (1989) 'Beskattningens effekter på arbetsutbudet' ('Effects of taxes on labour supply'), in SOU 1989:33, part IV.

Blomquist, N.S. (1995) 'Restrictions in labor supply estimation: Is the MaCurdy critique correct?', *Economics Letters*, vol. 47, 229–35.

Blomquist, N.S. (1996) 'Estimation methods for male labor supply functions. How to take account of nonlinear taxes', *Journal of Econometrics*, vol. 70, 383–405.

Blomquist, N.S. and U. Hansson-Brusewitz (1990) 'The effect of taxes on male and female labor supply in Sweden', *Journal of Human Resources*, vol. 25, 317–57.

Bradley, M., G.A. Jarrell and E.H. Kim, (1984) 'On the existence of an optimal capital structure: Theory and evidence', *Journal of Finance*, vol. 39, 857–78.

Brose, P. (1995) 'Sickness absence: An empirical analysis of the HUS panel', Working Paper 1995: 12, Department of Economics, Uppsala University.

Browning, E.K. (1976) 'The marginal cost of public funds', *Journal of Political Economy*, vol. 84, 283–98.

Browning, E.K. (1987) 'On the marginal welfare cost of taxation', *American Economic Review*, vol. 77, 11–23.

Brownstone D. and P. Englund (1991) 'The demand for housing in Sweden: equilibrium choice of tenure and type of dwelling', *Journal of Urban Economics*, vol. 29, 267–81.

Brownstone D., P. Englund and M. Persson (1985) 'Effects of the Swedish 1983–85 tax reform on the demand for owner-occupied housing: a microsimulation approach', *Scandinavian Journal of Economics*, vol. 87, 625–46.

Brownstone D., P. Englund and M. Persson (1988) 'A microsimulation model of Swedish housing demand', *Journal of Urban Economics*, vol. 23, 179–98.

Burtless G. (1987) 'Taxes, transfers and labor supply', in B. Bosworth and A. Rivlin (eds), *The Swedish Economy* (Washington, DC: Brookings Institution).

Caballero, R. (1991) 'Earnings uncertainty and aggregate wealth accumulation', *American Economic Review*, vol. 81, 859–71.

Calmfors, L. (1993) 'Lessons from the macroeconomic experience of Sweden', *European Journal of Political Economy*, vol. 9, 25–72.

Campbell, J.Y. and N.G. Mankiw (1991) 'The response of consumption to income. A cross-country investigation', *European Economic Review*, vol. 35, 723–67.

Christiansen, V., K.P. Hagen and A. Sandmo (1994) 'The scope for taxation and public expenditure in an open economy', *Scandinavian Journal of Economics*, vol. 96, 289–309.

Davidson, D. (1889) *Om beskattningsnormen vid inkomstbeskattningen* (*On the norm of taxation in the taxation of income*) (Uppsala: Almqvist & Wicksell).

Du Rietz, G. (1994) *Välfärdsstatens finansiering* (*Funding the welfare state*) (Stockholm: City University Press).

Dufwenberg, M., H. Koskenkylä and J. Södersten (1994) 'Manufacturing investment and taxation in the Nordic countries', *Scandinavian Journal of Economics*, vol. 96, 443–61.

Edin, P.-A. and B. Holmlund (1995) 'The Swedish wage structure: The rise and fall of solidarity wage policy in Sweden', in R. Freeman and L. Katz (eds), *Differences and Changes in Wage Structure* (Chicago: University of Chicago Press).

Ekman, E. (1995) 'Taxation and corporate financial policy', Tax Reform Evaluation Report No. 6 (Stockholm: National Institute of Economic Research).

Eliasson, G. (1965) 'Investment funds in operation', Occasional Paper 2 (Stockholm: Konjunkturinstitutet).

Englund, P., P.H. Hendershott, and B. Turner (1995) 'The tax reform and the housing market', *Swedish Economic Policy Review*, vol. 2, 319–56.

Englund, P. and M. Persson (1982) 'Housing prices and tenure choice with asymmetric taxes and progressivity', *Journal of Public Economics*, vol. 19, 271–90.

Eriksson, R. and R. Åberg (1987) *Welfare in Transition. A Survey of Living Conditions in Sweden 1968–1981*, Clarendon Press Oxford.

Feldstein, M. (1976), 'On the theory of tax reform', *Journal of Public Economics*, vol. 6, 77–106.

Flood, L. (1988) 'Effects of taxes on non-market work – The Swedish case', *Journal of Public Economics*, vol. 36, 259–67.

Flood, L. (1995) 'The structure of the tax system and the estimation of labor supply models: A note', mimeo, Department of Economics, Gothenburg University.

Flood, L. and U. Gråsjö (1995) 'Changes in time spent at work and leisure: The Swedish experience 1984–1993', mimeo, Department of Economics, Gothenburg University.

Flood, L. and A. Klevmarken (1990) 'Effekter på den privata konsumtionen av de indirekta skatternas höjning' ('Effects on private consumption of the indirect tax hikes'), in J. Agell, J. Södersten and K.-G. Mäler (eds), *Ekonomiska perspektiv på skattereformen* (*Economic perspectives on the tax reform*) (Stockholm: Ekonomiska Rådet).

Flood, L.R. and T. MaCurdy (1993) 'Work disincentive effects of taxes: An empirical analysis of Swedish men', *Carnegie–Rochester Conference Series on Public Policy*, vol. 37, 239–77.

Forsling, G. (1995) 'Utilization of tax allowances: A survey of Swedish corporate firms, 1979–93', Tax Reform Evaluation Report No. 22 (Stockholm: National Institute of Economic Research).

Frederiksen, N.K., P.R. Hansen, H. Jacobsen and P.B. Sørensen (1995) 'Subsidising consumer services – effects on employment, welfare and the informal economy', *Fiscal Studies*, vol. 16, 71–93.

Fredriksson, P. (1994) 'The demand for higher education in Sweden', Working Paper 1994:14, Department of Economics, Uppsala University.

Giavazzi, F. and M. Pagano (1990) 'Can severe fiscal contractions be expansionary? Tales of two small European countries', *NBER Macroeconomics Annual*, 75–116.

Giavazzi, F. and M. Pagano (1996) 'Non-keynesian effects of fiscal policy changes: More international evidence', *Swedish Economic Policy Review*, vol. 3, 67–103.

Gustafsson, B., L. Hydén and T. Salonen (1994) 'Decision-making on social assistance in major Swedish cities', *Scandinavian Journal of Social Welfare*, vol. 2, 197–203.

Haig, R.M. (1921) *The federal income tax* (New York: Columbia University Press).

Hall, R. (1988) 'Intertemporal substitution in consumption', *Journal of Political Economy*, vol. 96, 339–57.

Halleröd, B. (1993), '"Dynamiska effekter" – har 1991 års skattereform påverkat arbetskraftsutbudet?' ('"Dynamic effects" – did the 1991 tax reform affect the supply of labour?'), *Ekonomisk Debatt*, vol. 21, 347–54.

Hansen, J. (1995) 'The labor supply of young people in Sweden: Controlling for unemployment in a double-hurdle framework', mimeo, Department of Economics, University of Gothenburg.

Hansson, I. (1984) 'Marginal cost of public funds for different tax instruments and government expenditures', *Scandinavian Journal of Economics*, vol. 86, 115–130.

Hansson, I. and E. Norrman (1986) 'Fördelningseffekter av inkomstskatt och utgiftsskatt' ('Distributional effects of income tax and expenditure tax'), in SOU 1986:40.

Hansson, I. and C. Stuart (1985) 'Tax revenue and the marginal cost of public funds in Sweden', *Journal of Public Economics*, vol. 27, 331–53.

Hansson Brusewitz, U. (1992) *Labor supply of elderly men. Do taxes and pension systems matter?*, Doctoral dissertation, Department of Economics, Uppsala University.

Hausman, J. and J. Poterba (1987) 'Household behavior and the tax reform act of 1986', *Journal of Economic Perspectives*, vol. 1, 101–19.

Holmlund, B. and A.-S. Kolm (1995) 'Progressive taxation, wage setting, and unemployment – theory and Swedish evidence', *Swedish Economic Policy Review*, vol. 2, 423–60.

Hubbard, R.G. (1985) 'Personal taxation, pension wealth, and portfolio composition', *Review of Economics and Statistics*, vol. 67, 53–60.

Hultkrantz, L. (1995) 'On determinants of Swedish recreational domestic and outbound travel', Tax Reform Evaluation Report No. 7 (Stockholm: National Institute of Economic Research).

Jansson, K. and A. Sandqvist (1993) *Inkomstfördelningen under 1980-talet* (*Income distribution in the 1980s*), appendix 19 to the 1992 Medium-Term Survey (Stockholm: Fritzes).

Johansson, P. and M. Palme (1996) 'The effect of economic incentives on worker absenteeism: An empirical study using Swedish micro data', *Journal of Public Economics*, vol. 59, 195–218.

Jones, L.E., R.E. Manuelli and P.E. Rossi (1993) 'Optimal taxation in models of endogenous growth', *Journal of Political Economy*, vol. 101, 485–517.

Jorgenson, D. and K.-Y. Yun (1990) 'Tax reform and U.S. economic growth', *Journal of Political Economy*, vol. 98, 151–93.

Juster, F.T. and F.P. Stafford (1991) 'The allocation of time: Empirical findings, behavioral models, and problems of measurement', *Journal of Economic Literature*, vol. 29, 471–522.

Kanis, A. (1979), *Demand for factors of production. An interrelated model of Swedish mining and manufacturing industry*, Stockholm.

Kanniainen, V. and J. Södersten (1994) 'Costs of monitoring and corporate taxation', *Journal of Public Economics*, vol. 55, 307–21.

King, M.A. (1975) 'Taxation, corporate financial policy, and the cost of capital. A comment', *Journal of Public Economics*, vol. 4, 271–9.

King, M.A. and D. Fullerton (eds) (1984) *The taxation of income from capital – A comparative study of the United States, the United Kingdom, Sweden and West Germany* (Chicago: Chicago University Press).

King, M.A. and J. Leape (1984) 'Wealth and portfolio composition: Theory and evidence', Economic and Social Research Council Programme in Taxation, Incentives, and the Distribution of Income, No. 68, London.

King, R. and S. Rebelo (1993) 'Transitional dynamics and economic growth in the neoclassical model', *American Economic Review*, vol. 83, 908–31.

Klevmarken, A. (1996) 'Did the tax cuts increase hours of work? A pre-post analysis of Swedish panel data', mimeo, Department of Economics, Uppsala University.

Klevmarken, A., I. Andersson, P. Brose, E. Grönqvist, P. Olovsson, and M. Stoltenberg-Hansen (1995) 'Labor supply responses to Swedish tax reforms 1985–1992', Tax Reform Evaluation Report No. 11 (Stockholm: National Institute of Economic Research).

Klevmarken, A. and P. Olovsson (1993) *Household market and non-market activities. Procedures and codes 1984–1991* (Stochholm: The Industrial Institute for Economic and Social Research).

Koskela, E. and M. Virén (1992) 'Capital markets and household saving in the Nordic countries', *Scandinavian Journal of Economics*, vol. 94, 215–27.

Kristoffersson, A. (1995) 'Was the tax reform fully financed?', Tax Reform Evaluation Report No. 23 (Stockholm: National Institute of Economic Research).

Lattimore, R. (1994) 'Australian consumption and saving', *Oxford Review of Economic Policy*, vol. 10, 54–70.

Lindahl, E. (1939) *Studies in the theory of money and capital* (London: Farrar & Rinehart).

Lindencrona, G. (1993) 'The taxation of financial capital and the prevention of tax avoidance', in *Nordic council for tax research, 1973–1993 Tax reform in the Nordic countries*, (Gothenburg: Jubilee Publication).

Ljungqvist, L. and T.J. Sargent (1995) 'Taxes and subsidies in Swedish unemployment', SNS Occasional Paper No. 66, Stockholm.

Lucas, R. (1988) 'On the mechanics of economic development', *Journal of Monetary Economics*, vol. 22, 3–42.

Lucas, R. (1990) 'Supply-side economics: an analytical review', *Oxford Economic Papers*, vol. 42, 293–316.

Lundborg, P. (1992) *Svensk ekonomi och den fria arbetskraftsrörligheten* (*The Swedish economy and the unrestricted international mobility of labour*) (Stockholm: Allmänna Förlaget).

Lundborg, P. and P. Skedinger (1995) 'Capital gains taxation and residential mobility in the Swedish housing market', Tax Reform Evaluation Report No. 18 (Stockholm: National Institute of Economic Research).

MacKie-Mason, J.K. (1990) 'Do taxes affect corporate financing decisions?', *Journal of Finance*, vol. 45, 1471–493.

Malmer, H. and A. Persson (1994) 'Skattereformens effekter på skattesystemets driftskostnader, skatteplanering och skattefusk', ('The effects of the tax reform on compliance costs, tax planning, and tax fraud'), in H. Malmer, A. Persson and Å. Tengblad (eds), *Århundradets skattereform* (Tax reform of the century) (Stockholm: Fritzes).

Mattsson, N. (1992) *Skatteförmåner och andra särregler i inkomst-och mervärdesskatten* (*Tax expenditures in the income tax and the value added tax*), Ds 1992:6 (Stockholm: Allmänna Förlaget).

Miller, M. (1977) 'Debt and taxes', *Journal of Finance*, vol. 32, 261–75.

Ministry of Finance (1991) *The Swedish tax reform of 1991* (Stockholm: Allmänna förlaget).

Modigliani, F. and M. Miller (1958) 'The cost of capital, corporation finance and the theory of investment', *American Economic Review*, vol. 48, 261–97.

Muellbauer, J. (1994) 'The assessment: Consumer expenditure', *Oxford Review of Economic Policy*, vol. 10, 1–41.

Musgrave, R.A. (1959) *The theory of public finance* (New York: McGraw-Hill).

Mutén, L. (1994) 'International experience of how taxes influence the movement of private capital', *Tax Notes International*, vol. 8, 743.

Mutén, L. (1995) 'Tax reform and international tax planning', Tax Reform Evaluation Report No. 5 (Stockholm: National Institute of Economic Research).

Myrdal, G. (1978) 'Dags för ett nytt skattesystem!' ('Time for a new tax system'), *Ekonomisk Debatt*, vol. 6, 493–506.

Nordblom, K. (1996) 'How harmful is the Swedish tax system to economic growth?', Working Paper 1996:16, Department of Economics, Uppsala University.

OECD (1991) *Taxing profits in a global economy* (Paris: OECD).

Ohlsson, H. and A. Vredin (1994) *Finanspolitik, konjunkturer och ekonomisk integration (Fiscal policy, business cycles, and economic integration)* (Stockholm: Fritzes).

Palmer, E. E. (1984) 'Hushållssparandet' ('Household savings'), Annex 3 to *The 1984 medium-term economic survey* (Stockholm: Allmänna Förlaget).

Pedersen, P. and L. Schröder (1996) 'Summary and conclusions', in P. Pedersen (ed.), *Scandinavians without borders – skill migration and the European integration process* (Amsterdam: North-Holland).

Poterba, J. (1984) 'Tax subsidies to owner-occupied housing', *Quarterly Journal of Economics*, vol. 99, 729–52.

Poterba, J. (1990) 'Taxation and housing markets: Preliminary evidence on the effects of the recent tax reform', in J. Slemrod (ed.), *Do Taxes Matter? The Impact of the Tax Reform Act of 1986* (Cambridge, MA: MIT Press).

Praski, S. (1978) *Econometric investment functions and an attempt to evaluate the investment policy in Sweden 1960–73* (Uppsala: Almqvist & Wiksell).

Romer, P. (1986) 'Increasing returns and long run growth', *Journal of Political Economy*, vol. 94, 1002–37.

Rudberg, K. and C. Öhman (1971) 'Investment funds – The release of 1967', Konjunkturinstitutet Occasional Paper No. 5, Stockholm.

Sacklén, H. (1995) 'Labor supply, income taxes and hours constraints in Sweden', Working Paper 1995:2, Department of Economics, Uppsala University.

Sato, R. (1963) 'Fiscal policy in a neoclassical growth model: an analysis of the time required for equilibrating adjustment', *Review of Economic Studies*, vol.30, 16–23.

Simons, H. C. (1938) *Personal income taxation* (Chicago: University of Chicago Press).

Slemrod, J. (1992) 'Do taxes matter? Lessons from the 1980's', *American Economic Review*, vol. 82, 250–6.

Slemrod, J. (1995) 'What do cross-country studies teach about government involvement, prosperity, and economic growth', *Brookings Papers on Economic Activity*, vol. 2, 373–431.

Söderlind, P. (1989) 'MAMTAX. A dynamic CGE model for tax reform simulations', Working Paper, Economic Council: Stockholm.

Södersten, J. (1989) 'The investment funds system reconsidered', *Scandinavian Journal of Economics*, vol. 91, 671–87.

Södersten, J. (1993) 'Sweden', in D.W. Jorgenson and R. Landau (eds), *Tax reform and the cost of capital. An international comparison* (Washington, DC: The Brookings Institution).

Sørensen, P. B. (1994) 'From the global income tax to the dual income tax: Recent tax reforms in the Nordic countries', *International Tax and Public Finance*, vol.1, 57–79.

Sørensen, P. B. (1995) 'Changing views of the corporate income tax', *National Tax Journal*, vol.48, 279–94.

Stafford, F. and M. Sundström (1992) 'Female labour force participation, fertility and public policy', *European Journal of Population*, vol.8, 199–215.

Stokey, N. and S. Rebelo. (1995), 'Growth effects of flat-rate taxes,' *Journal of Political Economy*, vol. 103, 519–550.

Taylor, J. (1982) 'The Swedish investment funds system as a stabilization policy rule', *Brookings Papers on Economic Activity*, vol.13, 57–99.

GOVERNMENT COMMITTEE REPORTS

SOU 1982:1   *Real beskattning (Real taxation)*.

SOU 1986:40   *Utgiftsskatt. Teknik och effekter (Expenditure taxation. Technique and effects)*.

SOU 1989:33   *Reformerad Inkomstbeskattning (Reformed income taxation)*.

SOU 1989:34   *Reformerad företagsbeskattning (Reformed corporate taxation)*.

SOU 1992:19   *Långtidsutredningen 1992 (1992 Medium-term survey)*.

SOU 1993:29   *Fortsatt reformering av företagsbeskattningen. Del 2, Den ekonomiska dubbelbeskattningen (Continued reform of corporate taxation. Part 2: Economic double taxation)*

TAX REFORM EVALUATION REPORTS

Editors: Jonas Agell, Peter Englund and Jan Södersten

Number	Author	Title	Date
1	Apel, Mikael	An Expenditure-based Estimate of Tax Evasion in Sweden	11/94
2	Åsberg, Per and Stefan Åsbrink	Capitalisation Effects in the Market for Owner-occupied Housing – A Dynamic Approach	11/94
3	Aronsson, Thomas and Mårten Palme	A Decade of Tax and Benefit Reforms in Sweden – Effects on Labour Supply, Welfare and Inequality	11/94
4	Angelin, Ken and L. Peter Jennergren	Partner Leasing in Sweden	3/95
5	Mutén, Leif	Tax Reform and International Tax Planning	3/95
6	Ekman, Erik	Taxation and Corporate Financial Policy	3/95
7	Hultkrantz, Lars	On Determinants of Swedish Recreational Domestic and Outbound Travel, 1989–1993	3/95
8	Auerbach, Alan J., Kevin Hassett and Jan Södersten	Taxation and Corporate Investment: The Impact of the 1991 Swedish Tax Reform	6/95
9	De Ridder, Adri and Tomas Sörensson	Ex-Dividend Day Behavior and the Swedish Tax Reform	8/95
10	Aronsson, Thomas, Magnus Wikström and Runar Brännlund	Wage Determination Under Nonlinear Taxes – Estimation and an Application to Panel Data	8/95
11	Klevmarken, N. Anders jointly with Irene Andersson, Peter Brose, Erik Grönqvist, Paul Olovsson and Marianne Stoltenberg-Hansen	Labor Supply Responses to Swedish Tax-reforms 1985–1992	8/95
12	Ackum Agell, Susanne and Costas Meghir	Male Labour Supply in Sweden: Are Incentives Important?	8/95
13	Björklund, Anders, Mårten Palme and Ingemar Svensson	Assessing the Effects of Swedish Tax and Benefit Reforms on Income Distribution Using Different Income Concepts	8/95
14	von Bahr, Stig	Likformig beskattning av arbete och kapital	8/95

238   *Bibliography*

Number	*Author*	*Title*	*Date*
15	Holmlund, Bertil and Ann-Sofie Kolm	Progressive Taxation, Wage Setting, and Unemployment – Theory and Swedish Evidence	8/95
16	Agell, Jonas, Lennart Berg and Per-Anders Edin	Tax Reform, Consumption and Asset Structure	8/95
17	Modén, Karl-Markus	The Impact of Tax Reform on Foreign Direct Investment	9/95
18	Lundborg, Per and Per Skedinger	Capital Gains Taxation and Residential Mobility in the Swedish Housing Market	11/95
19	Lundborg, Per	Taxes and Job Mobility in the Swedish Labor Market	11/95
20	Englund, Peter, Patric H. Hendershott and Bengt Turner	The Tax Reform and the Housing Market	11/95
21	Bager-Sjögren, Lars and N. Anders Klevmarken	Inequality and Mobility of Wealth in Sweden 1983/84–1992/93	11/95
22	Forsling, Gunnar	Utilization of Tax Allowances: A Survey of Swedish Corporate Firms, 1979–93	10/96
23	Kristoffersson, Anders	Was the Tax Reform Fully Financed?	11/95

Reports in this series can be ordered from

Department of Economics
Uppsala University
Box 513
S-751 20 Uppsala
Sweden

Index

Notes: 1. Page numbers in **bold** type refer to illustrative figures or tables.
2. All entries, unless otherwise indicated, refer to the role and effect of the TR91 tax legislation in the context of the Swedish economy.